# The Constant Two Plan

# The Constant Two Plan

## Reforming the Electoral College to Account for the National Popular Vote

Jay Wendland

LEXINGTON BOOKS

*Lanham • Boulder • New York • London*

Published by Lexington Books
An imprint of The Rowman & Littlefield Publishing Group, Inc.
4501 Forbes Boulevard, Suite 200, Lanham, Maryland 20706
www.rowman.com

86-90 Paul Street, London EC2A 4NE



British Library Cataloguing in Publication Information Available

**Library of Congress Cataloging-in-Publication Data**

Names: Wendland, Jay, 1986- author.
Title: The constant two plan : reforming the Electoral College to account for the national popular vote / Jay Wendland.
Description: Lanham, Maryland : Lexington Books, 2024. | Includes bibliographical references and index. | Summary: "This book explores a novel approach to reform the Electoral College to allocate for two electoral votes from each state to the national popular vote winner, in order to bring the American presidential election process more in line with democratic norms and principles"— Provided by publisher.
Identifiers: LCCN 2024001010 (print) | LCCN 2024001011 (ebook) | ISBN 9781666916249 (cloth) | ISBN 9781666916256 (epub)
Subjects: LCSH: Electoral College—United States. | Presidents—United States—Election. | Election law—United States.
Classification: LCC JK529 .W46 2024 (print) | LCC JK529 (ebook) | DDC 324.6/3—dc23/eng/20240203
LC record available at https://lccn.loc.gov/2024001010
LC ebook record available at https://lccn.loc.gov/2024001011

# Contents

# Acknowledgments

This book began as a paper written for a graduate seminar on federalism. And it initially began as a *defense* of the Electoral College, despite all of its flaws. That graduate seminar paper has clearly evolved a lot since. The circumstances surrounding the 2020 election and the resulting insurrection, coupled with the attempt at using fraudulent electors to elect an illegitimate president, laid bare all of the reasons that the Electoral College, as it currently operates, should no longer be used to elect our president.

I am indebted to a number of friends and colleagues for their continued support and willingness to listen to me talk about Electoral College reform over the past few years. I must start by thanking Eric Lopez and Nikkita Edmond Smith who were part of this research project in that graduate school seminar. This book would have never gotten off the ground without that initial project. I must also thank Barbara Norrander for her continued support and guidance over the past decade.

At Daemen University, I must thank a number of people for their support in helping me see this work to fruition. First, I am extremely grateful to Michael Brogan (executive vice president for academic affairs and provost) for supporting my application for a sabbatical to work on this project. I must also thank the members of Daemen's Faculty Development Committee for their endorsement of my sabbatical application and Penny Messinger for her willingness to extend her term as department chair for a semester so that I could take a sabbatical. Without that uninterrupted research time, this project would not have been possible. Many thanks, as well, to Lisa Parshall for her continued support of my research agenda. Lisa, your proliferative research agenda is enviable—and it spurs me to continue with mine.

I must also thank Lexington Press for agreeing to publish a second book authored by me. Joseph Parry and Sara Noakes were wonderful to work with and graciously extended deadlines when my teaching and service obligations got the better of me. Finally, I must thank Toni Wendland, who once again has learned more than she ever thought she would about the American political system. She also put up with many late nights, my occasional frustrations with this project, and my being constantly distracted. Without her support and understanding, this project would not have been possible.

# Chapter 1

# How We Got This Messed-Up System

The Electoral College is an anti-democratic electoral institution that has been enshrined in the Constitution since its writing. It has been the subject of more than 700 reform proposals in Congress and the cause of frustration for many Americans wondering why the winner of the popular vote in a presidential election is not guaranteed residence in the White House. Instead of allowing the American public to choose their president through the popular vote, the Constitution mandates the use of an antiquated system that places the power of executive selection in the hands of electors—chosen via a process determined by each state's legislature—yet is largely awarded based on the results of each state's popular vote. So, the popular vote of the country is not relied upon, but instead, the popular vote recorded in each state is the determining factor for how a state's electors are asked—or, in most cases, required—to vote.

Of course, the Constitution grants the electors freedom to vote in accordance with their own preferences, but as of this book's publication, 32 states plus the District of Columbia have laws that bind their electors to support the candidate who won the popular vote in the state (Codrington III 2020). More importantly, the Supreme Court upheld the constitutionality of these laws in 2020, with Justice Elena Kagan writing in the majority opinion of the court that laws requiring electors pledge to support the state's popular vote winner, "reflects a longstanding tradition in which electors are not free agents; they are to vote for the candidate whom the State's voters have chosen" (*Chiafalo et al v. Washington* 591 U.S. ___ (2020)). Because electors largely vote for their state's popular vote winner rather than the national popular vote winner, we have several examples of elections in which the national popular vote has been undermined by the Electoral College. The elections of 1876, 1888, 2000, and, most recently, 2016 are examples of what Alexander (2019) calls misfire elections. But just looking at these misfire elections misses other "close call" elections in which the Electoral College and popular vote winners are the same individual, but very nearly resulted in a misfire. Misfires and close calls truly highlight the undemocratic nature of the Electoral College and underscore the need for reform.

My goal in this book is to thoroughly examine a proposal for Electoral College reform that I call the Constant Two Plan. This plan would split each state's electoral vote between the state and national popular votes in an effort to bridge the federal principle (celebrated by Electoral College proponents) with the national will (preferred by Electoral College opponents). Instead of relying solely on the state or national popular vote, each state would award two electoral votes to the candidate who won the national popular vote and award their remaining votes in the manner currently used. This would not require a constitutional amendment, as it technically preserves the Electoral College, but a change in state laws. Given the changing population dynamics across the United States, the Constant Two Plan should be viewed as a compromise between Electoral College supporters and detractors. However, before we delve into the mechanics of this plan, along with its strengths and weaknesses, it is helpful to lay the groundwork for understanding why the Electoral College is so in need of reform. To highlight this need, the 2016 and 2020 presidential elections offer back-to-back examples of closely decided elections that very easily could have resulted in different winners if less than 100,000 voters across a handful of states voted differently, despite not altering the winner chosen by a plurality of voters nationally.

## A TALE OF TWO ELECTIONS

The presidential election of 2016 exemplifies a close election in which the winner of the popular vote lost the electoral vote. Hillary Rodham Clinton was the odds-on favorite to win the presidency in 2016. Nate Silver and his team at the online blog *FiveThirtyEight* had given Clinton an 89.2 percent chance of winning in August 2016 and a 71.4 percent chance of winning on the eve of the November election (Silver 2016). Similarly, prominent UK betting companies gave Clinton an 85 percent chance of winning (Graham 2016), while the U.S. betting markets gave her a slightly lower 80 percent chance (Beckett 2016). Despite a surprisingly challenging primary for Clinton, she was still expected to easily defeat Donald Trump, who was able to wrap up his primary win more quickly than Clinton but still remained deeply unpopular among most voters. On election night, however, as votes were totaled, it became clear that Donald Trump would win the election and become the 45th president of the United States.

In the early morning hours of November 9, 2016, it was announced that Donald Trump had won the presidency. After all votes were tallied, Trump received 304 electoral votes, 34 more than the necessary 270. Yet, despite his decisive Electoral College win, he failed to win more popular votes than Clinton. In fact, Clinton bested Trump by just over 2.8 million votes, or 2 percent of the popular vote. Due to stronger-than-usual support for third-party candidates, we saw neither Trump nor Clinton attain a majority of votes, with Clinton receiving 48.02 percent of the popular vote to Trump's 45.93 percent. However, U.S. elections do not require a president to win a majority of popular votes, just a majority of electoral votes. Despite receiving approximately 46 percent of the popular vote, Trump received 56.5 percent of the electoral vote, while Clinton received only 42 percent.

How did this discrepancy happen? In 2016, Trump won three key states that were expected to fall in Clinton's column: Michigan, Pennsylvania, and Wisconsin. These three states were part of what many pundits referred to as the "blue wall," or states that Clinton was expected to win due to their long history of voting for Democratic presidential candidates (Daniels and Jin 2019; Gilbert et al. 2016; Peralta 2016). Additionally, polling showed Clinton ahead of Trump consistently, albeit by a tightening margin. In 2016, however, all three states voted Republican for the first time since the 1980s (Michigan and Pennsylvania last voted for a Republican presidential candidate in 1988, and Wisconsin did so in 1984). Yet, Trump's victory in these states was quite narrow; he won Michigan by 10,704 votes, Pennsylvania by 44,284 votes, and Wisconsin by 22,748 votes. Thus, Trump became president with the help of these 77,736 voters, or 0.00057 percent of the total number of votes cast nationally. He lost the nationwide popular vote, but because of his narrow victories in these three states, Trump was able to become president.

In contrast to 2016, the 2020 election gives us a similarly close election, but one where the electoral and popular votes align. On November 3, 2020, the citizens of the United States participated in a presidential election in the middle of a pandemic. Many had already voted early or dropped their absentee ballot in the mail or in one of the several dropboxes available to them. Due to Covid-19, many states had adopted rules to make voting easier and more accessible to those who were uncomfortable leaving their homes to stand in line at their polling location. However, these states also included rules about when those early and mail-in ballots could be counted—some were able to be counted on election day while others had to wait. Due to these rules, it was unlikely that the winner of the presidential election would be known that evening. On Saturday, November 7, 2020, four days after the election, Joseph R. Biden was declared the winner when enough votes were tallied in Pennsylvania to add its 20 electoral votes to Biden's total (Detrow and Khalid 2020). After the official certification of the votes, Joseph Biden bested Donald Trump by just over seven million votes and an Electoral College victory of 306 to 232—almost the exact reverse of the Trump-Clinton results just four years prior.

Despite the sizable win by Biden in the end, his victory was in question up until Pennsylvania's electoral votes were awarded to him. In fact, Biden's Electoral College victory came down to slim margins in a handful of states just as Trump's victory over Clinton had. Arizona, Georgia, Pennsylvania, and Wisconsin all handed Biden very narrow victories in the Electoral College. Combined, these states awarded 57 electoral votes (Arizona had 11, Georgia had 16, Pennsylvania had 20, and Wisconsin had 10), among which Biden edged out Trump by 125,084 popular votes (10,457 in Arizona; 11,779 in Georgia; 82,166 in Pennsylvania; and 20,682 in Wisconsin), or 0.0008% of all votes cast in the presidential election. If a majority of these 125,000 votes had swung the other way, Biden would have lost the presidency despite receiving roughly seven million more votes than his opponent. Even more appalling is the fact that had those 125,000 voters chosen Trump over Biden, Biden would still have won more than 50 percent of the popular vote and lost the presidency.

In response to these results, Donald Trump regularly challenged their legitimacy and refused to concede the election. Trump's refusal to accept his electoral loss culminated in the January 6, 2021, insurrection on Capitol Hill, where, after attending a Trump rally near the White House, many of the attendees marched to the Capitol, broke through barricades, and stormed the House chamber in which the electoral votes were being counted (Lonsdorf et al. 2022). At this rally, Trump encouraged Mike Pence to reject the electoral votes as cast and allow him to remain president. In addressing the attendees, Trump said,

> You'll never take back our country with weakness. You have to show strength and you have to be strong. We have come to demand that Congress do the right thing and only count the electors who have been lawfully slated. (Naylor 2021)

As a result, over 2,000 people entered the Capitol building after breaking windows in order to get in, forcing Senators and Representatives to shelter in place in their offices. After the insurrection was quelled by Capitol Police and National Guard troops, Congress was able to return to their work and certify the electoral vote, declaring Joe Biden to be the 46th president of the United States. In the aftermath, we have since learned that the insurrection resulted in millions of dollars worth of damage to the Capitol Building, five deaths, and many injured individuals.

This insurrection led to a second impeachment of Donald Trump (he was acquitted by a vote of 57 guilty to 43 not guilty, with the Senate failing to reach the 67 votes needed to convict), a Select Committee investigation, and a federal indictment of the former president handed down on August 1, 2023. The indictment, handed down by a Washington, D.C., grand jury, consisted of four counts: defrauding the United States, obstructing an official government proceeding, depriving Americans of a civil right, and attempting to obstruct an official proceeding. This indictment also details the other actions the Trump administration took in an attempt to not vacate the presidency. For example, Trump called Georgia's secretary of state, Brad Raffensperger, asking him to find 11,780 votes (just one more vote than he lost Georgia's popular vote by) in an effort to overturn the state's election results and place Georgia in his win column rather than Biden's (Gardner 2021; Gardner and Firozi 2021). When this did not work and all secretaries of state certified the election results as they stood after initial certification, Trump and his administration attempted a fake elector scheme instead.

According to the indictment, the fake elector scheme included soliciting Republican state officials to send fake slates of electoral votes to the Capitol in states that were won by Joe Biden. The states targeted for this scheme included Arizona, Georgia, Michigan, New Mexico, Nevada, and Pennsylvania, but the initial effort was made in Wisconsin. An attorney for Trump, Kenneth Chesebro, wrote in an email that "the plan was to falsely present the fraudulent slates as an alternative to the legitimate slates at Congress's certification proceeding" (Amiri 2023). So, at the president's urging, many Republican officials signed off on fake slates of electoral votes that were sent to Congress to cause confusion among the members of Congress and offer a set of votes for those who wanted to challenge the legitimate votes to support. This plan ultimately failed, as members of Congress ignored the fake slates of electoral votes and confirmed those that were legitimately cast.

So, even with Joe Biden winning both the electoral and popular votes, then-president Donald Trump was still able to orchestrate a scheme by which he would be able to keep the presidency. He undermined the legitimacy of the election, stirred up rally attendees and sent them to break up the counting of the electoral vote, and reached out to state officials to put together fake slates of electors in an attempt to challenge those lawfully cast. All of this was able to be done because Trump's administration was able to target weaknesses surrounding the Electoral College. Granted, these weaknesses have always existed, but the weaknesses, mixed with Trump's willingness to act corruptly, highlight yet another reason the Electoral College is in need of reform: partisan calcification.

Sides, Tausanovich, and Vavreck (2022) argue that the hyper-partisan nature of American politics has led to the calcification of our partisanship. Americans, they argue, are so entrenched in their partisan beliefs that it will take a large shock to the American political system to change voting behavior long term. Small shocks have the potential to have large impacts on the American electoral system; as the American public is so closely divided, small swings in voting blocs can change the partisan make-up of Congress easily. A good example is the closeness of the elections of 2016 and 2020. Both of those elections were decided by fewer than 100,000 voters across a handful of states. Those small groups of voters made large changes to the partisan make-up of Congress and the White House, however these large changes are not likely to last long. This calcification of American partisanship in conjunction with the anti-democratic nature of the Electoral College has led to close, but decisive, victories for Democratic presidential candidates in the national popular vote but losses in the Electoral College. Across all presidential elections since 2000—save 2004—Americans saw Democratic victories in just 2008, 2012, and 2020, just 50 percent of the presidential elections held since then. While we cannot be sure that the same results would hold under different electoral circumstances (e.g., if Gore had become president instead of Bush in 2000, that would have resulted in a very different electoral atmosphere than was actually experienced), there is a chance that a president who consistently wins the support of a plurality of voters would have created more stability in leadership and lessened the calcification found in our political system.

All of this signals that the Electoral College is in need of reform—it has been for some time. Winning the popular vote by seven million (or 4.5 percent of all votes cast) should not leave a candidate's victory in doubt, nor should a candidate's 2.9 million popular vote win lead to a presidential election loss. A candidate should not be able to win more votes than their opponent and lose an election. In fact, under such a scenario, we see a clear violation of democratic norms. Dahl (2000) tells us that all votes must count the same; in other words, we need to treat every voter as politically equal. If one person's vote counts more than another's, then we fail to live up to democratic values. When we see a candidate win more votes than their opponent yet lose elective office, we know that some votes matter more than others. In 2016, it was roughly 78,000 voters spread out over three states that ensured Trump's win over Clinton. In 2020, slim pluralities were won in a handful of states, but these results aligned with the overall popular vote numbers to ensure the popular and electoral vote winner was the same person. If our electoral system's rules cannot guarantee that the candidate with the most votes wins office, it is incumbent that the rules be changed. However, before we begin to unpack the need for reform, we need to better understand how we ended up with the system we currently use. The rest of this chapter discusses how the Founders at the Constitutional Convention arrived at the Electoral College instead of legislative selection or a popular vote. It then concludes by outlining the plan of the book.

## THE CURRENT SYSTEM

The current electoral system used to elect American presidents has voters heading to the polls on the first Tuesday after the first Monday in November. They cast their ballots, which are tallied to determine a popular vote winner in each state. While voters are choosing from the various candidates for president, they are technically voting for that candidate's slate of electors. The number of electors is equal to the sum of the state's number of representatives and senators. Each state's popular vote winner is then awarded that state's electoral votes, except in Nebraska and Maine. These two states use a combination of state and congressional district popular vote results to determine their electoral vote distribution. The winner of the statewide popular vote is awarded two electoral votes, with the remaining electoral votes awarded to the candidate who won the popular vote in each congressional district. Thus, Nebraska and Maine allow for the splitting of their electoral votes. The remaining states award their electoral votes en bloc to the state's popular vote winner.

The winning candidate's slate of electors—either Democratic or Republican—then meet in the state's Capitol on the first Monday after the second Wednesday in December to cast their official ballot for president. After these ballots are cast, they are sent to Washington, D.C., to be counted in the presence of both the House of Representatives and the Senate, with the vice president of the United States presiding over the joint session of Congress, which is held on January 6 unless changed by Congress (Neale 2020). A majority of electoral votes (currently at least 270) is needed in order to win the presidency.

Should a candidate fail to receive a majority of electoral votes, the House of Representatives is tasked with selecting the president from among the top three candidates in the original electoral vote, and the Senate selects the vice president from among the top two finishers. If such contingency elections are required, the voting in the House of Representatives would require *states* to cast votes rather than *individual* Representatives. So, each state's House delegation would meet and poll its members, with the candidate that receives the most votes receiving that state's vote. In order to win the presidency in such a contingent election, a candidate would need to win an absolute majority of states (currently 26, as Washington, D.C., is not granted a vote in a contingent election since it is not a state). Should a candidate not receive a majority of votes, balloting would continue until they do. If the House fails to elect a president, the vice president would become president until the House reaches a decision.

The Senate is responsible for electing the vice president under a contingent election. In the Senate, each Senator is able to vote individually—en bloc voting by state is not required. So, each Senator casts their ballot for vice president, with an absolute majority (currently 51 votes) again required to win the office. This means that should any Senator abstain from voting, that would be counted as a negative vote. So, if the result is a vote of 50–49, a vice president would not be elected. The candidate must receive 51 votes. Similar to the procedure in the House, balloting would continue until a vice president is chosen. If the result is a 50-50 tie, it is unclear whether the current vice president would be able to break a tie. Josephson (2009), for example, argues that because the vice president of the Senate is, according to the Constitution, the president of the Senate, he or she should indeed possess the authority to break the tie. Longley and Peirce (1996), however, argue that because the vice president is not technically a Senator, he or she would be unable to cast a vote in a contingent election. They argue that because the language in the 12th Amendment states "a majority of the whole number shall be necessary to a choice" (U.S. Const. amend. XII), the vice president is not included in the "whole number" of senators—the whole number of senators is 100, or two, from every state (Longley and Peirce 1996).

The delegates to the Constitutional Convention therefore created a system in which the president is selected by a complicated mix of intermediate electors—chosen by a process determined by each state's legislature—casting the official vote for president, with the Congress left to determine the winners should a candidate fail to attain majority support among electors. However, this was not the intention. The Electoral College, rather than being carefully crafted, was designed through a series of compromises and bargaining between the delegates in an effort to finalize their drafting of the Constitution.

## How We Got This System

From mid-May to mid-September 1787, 55 delegates met in Philadelphia, Pennsylvania, to revise the failing Articles of Confederation. All 13 states were invited to send delegates, with all obliging except for Rhode Island, which feared the Convention would give too much power to the national government at the expense of the states. Rhode Island's concerns regarding the revision of the Articles of Confederation were legitimate, as the revision quickly turned into a full overhaul of the U.S. governing system. Yet the chaos from the Articles' creation of a powerless national government necessitated the complete rewriting of the system. In fact, the Articles of Confederation did not create an executive branch, meaning that the decision to create one left the delegates to design both the powers of the executive along with how such an executive should be selected. The delegates ultimately decided upon a complex selection process for the president that takes up more than one-fourth of Article II. The Electoral College was not the first choice among many of the delegates. Instead, several ideas were debated (mainly congressional selection and direct popular vote), with the Electoral College serving as a compromise solution, bringing together many pieces of the various proposals.

### *Congressional Selection*

The method of selecting an executive was first taken up by the delegates on June 1, 1787 (Farrand 1937, vol. I). Considering the absence of an executive under the Articles of Confederation, many decisions were needed: inclusion of a singular or multiple executive, the powers given to the executive, and how the executive should be chosen, to name a few. It was quickly decided that a singular executive would be best as opposed to the main alternative of a triumvirate of executives. James Wilson noted that

> among three equal members, [there would be] uncontrouled [*sic*], continued, and violent animosities; which would not only interrupt the public administration; but diffuse their position thro' the other branches of Govt., thro' the States, and at length thro' the people at large. (Farrand 1937, vol. I, p. 96)

By June 4, the delegates voted in favor of a singular executive, with seven states in favor and three opposed (Farrand 1937, vol. I). This decision was retained with a vote on July 17, with no serious consideration of an alternative thereafter (Peirce and Longley 1981).

The process by which an executive is chosen was not decided upon quite as quickly. Initially, the selection of an executive by the national legislature had the most support. In fact, selection by the legislative branch was included in the Virginia Plan introduced to the Convention on May 29 (Edwards 2004). The Virginia Plan, authored by James Madison, was unveiled by Edmund Randolph of Virginia and called for a bicameral legislature with an independent executive and judiciary. This plan was generally favored by large, more heavily populated states, as both chambers of the legislature were to be based on population size. Smaller, less populated states responded with the New Jersey Plan, calling for a unicameral legislative body with equal representation for each state. Despite the differences regarding the make-up of the national legislative body, both plans incorporated an executive chosen by the legislature.

Roger Sherman, who helped design the Connecticut Compromise that settled the debate regarding the design of the legislative branch, believed that the legislature should be focused on the will of the people, and as such, the executive should be "nothing more than an institution for carrying the will of the Legislature into effect . . . [and] be appointed and accountable to the Legislature only" (Farrand 1937, vol. I, p. 65). George Mason also supported the idea of congressional selection of a chief executive, as he believed that public selection was not practical. Farrand (1937, vol. II, p. 31) notes that Mason liked the idea of the national election of a president but believed that "the extent of the Country renders it impossible that the people can have the requisite capacity to judge the respective pretensions of the Candidates." The delegates to the Convention ended up with 22 days devoted to debate on the selection process and 30 votes on the subject. Of these 30 votes, 6 were in favor of the president being selected by the national legislature (Edwards 2004).

So, it is clear that the delegates generally preferred the idea of involving a more elite group of educated voters in selecting the president rather than selecting a president via direct election. Sinha (2017, 9) compares the Convention delegates' beliefs to those that created Great Britain's "rotten boroughs." Britain's borough system was created to allow the elite to select members of Parliament, with smaller, less populated boroughs able to elect more members to Parliament than larger, more urban centers. Delegates were inclined to prefer a more educated and more attentive political class to select the chief executive officer of the United States. Given the elite nature of the national legislature, a majority of state delegates were initially predisposed to support the idea of the legislature selecting the president. Nonetheless, there was a vocal minority that supported the idea of direct election of the executive by U.S. citizens.

### *Direct Election*

The first vote taken by the Convention for the direct election of the chief executive happened on July 17, and it failed with only 1 state voting in favor of it (Farrand 1937, vol. II). James Wilson was a strong supporter of direct election, arguing that it was the best way to ensure that the executive and legislative branches were independent of each other (Farrand 1937, vol. I, p. 69) and that direct election would inspire more confidence in the executive than would selection by the legislature (Farrand 1937, vol. I, p. 80). While he was not supportive of direct election, Elbridge Gerry was distrustful of selection by the legislature. Gerry feared that

> the Legislature and the candidates would bargain and play into one another's hands, votes would be given by the former under promises or expectations from the latter, of recompensing them by services to members of the Legislature or to their friends. (Farrand 1937, vol. I, p. 80)

The direct election of the executive was also met with support from prominent delegates James Madison, Gouverneur Morris, John Dickinson, Rufus King, Daniel Carroll, and Abraham Baldwin (Farrand 1937, vol. I).

A direct election of the president would help prevent the tyrannical rule from which the newly independent Americans broke from Great Britain. The delegates were also very fearful of collusion and cabal among the elite and wanted to safeguard against them. By creating an executive independent from the legislature, many of the concerns about faction and oppression would have been mollified. Madison tells us that

> a dependence of the Executive on the Legislature, would render it the Executor as well as the maker of laws; and then according to the observation of Montesquieu, tyrannical laws may be made that they may be executed in a tyrannical manner. (Farrand 1937, vol. II, p. 34)

Morris agreed with Madison's concerns about the potential for tyranny when the legislature and executive are not independent of each other—exactly what they had left Great Britain over (Farrand 1937, vol. II, p. 31).

In addition, Gouverneur Morris tried to assuage the concerns raised about the masses being uninformed about the candidates for president and that a group of populous states would band together and elect candidates sympathetic to their concerns rather than those of smaller, less populous states. Morris explained that if states were to conspire on which candidate to elect president, it would be much easier to do so in the Legislature than in each respective state (Farrand 1937, vol. II, p. 30). He pointed to the state of New York, which used a statewide popular vote to elect its governor, as an example of how successful a direct election could be. Regarding the concerns about faction leaders overwhelming the masses, Morris stated, "In particular spots . . . the activity and intrigues of little partizans [*sic*] are successful, but the general voice of the State is never influenced by such artifices" (Farrand 1937, vol. II, p. 31). Further, he argued that while it was likely that a majority of citizens would be unaware of everything that happens in the Capitol, they would be able to meaningfully vote for president because these candidates should have national reputations known to those who pay even the scantest attention. "The multitude . . . will not be uninformed of those great and illustrious characters which have merited their esteem and confidence," Morris argued (Farrand 1937, vol. II, p. 31).

Before the end of the Convention, only one vote was held regarding the direct election of the president, and it failed to gain support from more than one state. While several delegates liked the idea of direct election of the newly created national executive, the concerns about the practicability of the election and the desire of the delegates for a more educated, attentive group of voters won out. However, it was also clear that the delegates were not overwhelmingly in favor of the national legislature choosing the president either. The system eventually adopted by the delegates ensured a more elite group of voters would choose the president, though it seems the intention was that these elites would bring with them knowledge of public sentiment toward the candidates and include the public will in their deliberations.

### *Selection by Electors: The Middle Ground*

Because of the concerns raised regarding the selection of the executive by both direct election and the national legislature, the delegates needed to find a middle ground. Despite voting in the affirmative on several occasions to allow the executive to be chosen by the national legislature, the delegates could not move past this issue due to continued concerns raised regarding this mode of election. Only one vote was held to provide for the direct election of the executive, and that vote received support from only one state's delegation. So it was clear that a middle ground was needed to break the impasse.

James Wilson, a strong proponent of direct election, was the first to propose a compromise solution on June 2. Wilson introduced a proposal that states should be divided into districts and that voters within each district choose electors who would vote for president (Farrand 1937, vol. 1, p. 77). This was thus a clear compromise between the two plans initially considered: direct election would be used to select electors, and these electors would serve as the elite group that would officially select the chief executive. However, when put for a vote shortly after it was introduced by Wilson, the proposal was defeated with only two state delegations voting in support.

However, when the method of election of the executive was once again brought up, Luther Martin (a delegate from Maryland) once again proposed the idea of intermediate electors choosing the president (Farrand 1937, vol. II, p. 32). Elbridge Gerry (a delegate from Massachusetts) supported the idea of electors over direct election and selection by the national legislature, as he believed the public to be largely uninformed and the potential for corruption was too large if the legislature were to choose the executive. Gerry actually advocated for the state executives to be the ones who would select the electors, as he believed this group of elites was best equipped to select the national executive (Farrand 1937, vol. II, p. 57). Martin's proposed plan with intermediate electors selecting the president was adopted by the delegates on July 19 with six states in support, followed by a decision that these electors should be chosen by state legislatures with eight states voting in the affirmative (Farrand 1937, vol. II).

Other than June 2 and July 19, the idea of selection by a group of electors was not brought up by the delegates regularly. Selection by the national legislature or direct election was more likely to be advocated for, as these modes of election were more commonly known to the delegates at the time. On July 25, Oliver Ellsworth (a delegate from Connecticut) endorsed the idea of electors if a president was running for reelection; the initial election should be conducted by the national legislature (Farrand 1937, vol. II, pp. 108–9). By relying on electors for reelection, safeguards would be in place to prevent against cabal and collusion between the executive and legislative branches. Nearer the end of the Convention, on August 24, Gouverneur Morris—originally a strong proponent of direct election—endorsed the selection of an executive via electors chosen by the public because of the many dangers of conspiracy and tyranny he perceived if presidential selection was left up to the national legislature.

Regardless of the lack of discussion of the elector plan, it was included in the Committee of Eleven's series of reports to the Convention in early September. This Committee was convened in an effort to address the outstanding issues left from the Convention's previous business, including the method by which a national executive would be selected. The Committee of Eleven suggested that

> each state shall appoint in such a manner as it's [*sic*] Legislature may direct, a number of Electors equal to the whole number of Senators, and Members of the House of representatives to which the state may be entitled in the legislature. (Farrand 1937, vol. II, pp. 493–94)

This recommendation passed without revision and survives to the present day. While the 12th Amendment altered the voting protocol for electors a bit, the Electoral College system that is still used today was adopted by the delegation after this recommendation from the Committee of Eleven on September 4, 1787.

What the preceding discussion highlights, is that presidential selection was one of the most difficult decisions the delegates to the Constitutional Convention faced. The Convention convened on May 25, 1787, and adjourned on September 17, 1787, and the method of presidential selection was not adopted until September 4—only 13 days prior to adjournment. Wilson stated, "The Convention, Sir, were perplexed with no part of this plan so much as with the mode of choosing the President of the United States" (Farrand 1937, vol. III, p. 166). There was never an overwhelming consensus that one method was preferred to another; in fact, whatever method was debated, significant concerns were raised to accompany that method. Wilson further summarizes the sentiments surrounding the compromised selection process:

> Was the president to be appointed by the legislature? Was he to continue a certain time in office, and afterwards was he to become ineligible? To avoid the inconveniences already enumerated, and many others that might be suggested, the mode before us was adopted. (Farrand 1937, vol. III, p. 167)

So what is clear is that the delegates to the Convention did not carefully and meaningfully devise this method of presidential selection because they thought it was the best possible way to select a president. Instead, this method was chosen because it was the only one the delegates could pass.

It is important to note that the elector plan was not the first choice of many of the delegates; rather, it was the compromise position that they were willing to accept. Many of the delegates liked the idea of a popular election of the president but found the idea impractical. The masses would not be aware enough to make an educated choice for president. Nor did the country have the technological capabilities at the time to pull off an election across such a vast area. Many of these same delegates, after the popular election was defeated, liked the idea of the electors being chosen by the public—the delegates then would have an awareness of what the public will was when choosing a president. Presently, this is largely how the process works. The popular vote determines which slate of electors is chosen to cast the official vote for president. However, with advances in technology, the original concerns regarding the impracticability of direct election are largely moot. Quibbles can still be raised about how aware and/or educated the average voter is, but the opportunity for voter education is much greater now than it was when the delegates gathered in Philadelphia. Additionally, voting technology has advanced significantly to allow for direct popular elections nationwide without difficulty.

## PLAN OF THE BOOK

The Electoral College is thus ripe for reform. It is clear that even when originally adopted, there was no overwhelming support for the Electoral College. Instead, it was a compromise solution between a direct popular vote and legislative selection. The concerns raised about the direct election are largely moot today, and the concerns about legislative selection are still valid, especially considering the increased partisan behavior of Congress. The Constant Two Plan, unveiled here, demonstrates that there is a way to reform the Electoral College to account for the national popular vote while maintaining the structure of the Electoral College so as not to require a constitutional amendment.

Chapter 2 will focus on the strengths of the Electoral College as currently structured. Continuing to rely on Farrand's (1937) records as well as notes from various delegates from the Constitutional Convention and *Federalist No. 68*, it is clear that there are indeed some strengths of this electoral system. These strengths include entrusting the election of the president to a more attentive, educated group of voters, preventing cabal and conspiracy, and creating an executive independent from the legislature. Though, as will be demonstrated, the Electoral College is not the only mechanism that provides these safeguards. Chapter 3 will focus on the weaknesses and problems associated with the Electoral College, again relying on notes from various delegates along with *Antifederalist No. 72*. These weaknesses include the lack of popular input on presidential selection and the lack of accountability of the president to the people.

Chapter 4 will focus on the racial biases entrenched in the Electoral College. These biases include the initial decision of the delegates to count slaves as three-fifths of a person, the small state bias aiding more demographically homogeneous states, and the current struggle with national voter ID laws. Chapter 5 details the main reform plans that have received popular attention, including the district plan, the proportional plan, the automatic plan, the direct vote plan, and the National Popular Vote Interstate Compact. Chapter 6 will outline the Constant Two Plan. The Constant Two Plan calls for the awarding of two electoral votes from each state to the winner of the nationwide popular vote, while awarding the remaining electoral votes according to a state's discretion. The winner of the popular vote nationwide therefore would receive 102 electoral votes (two each for each of the 50 states plus Washington, D.C.), with the remaining 436 electoral votes distributed according to state law. With this allocation of electoral votes, the popular vote winner will also win the electoral vote, and the historical cases of these winners being different candidates would have been remedied. Finally, chapter seven will offer further discussion and justification of the Constant Two Plan. Specifically, I will evaluate the Constant Two Plan using the framework offered by Schumacker (2002, 2010).

Schumacker (2002, 2010) clearly lays out nine criteria with which we can evaluate electoral systems: simplicity, equality, sincerity, neutrality, participation, legitimacy, governance, inclusivity, and feasibility. His argument is that any electoral system adopted should aim to accomplish as many of the nine criteria as possible. The closer a system gets to meeting all nine criteria, the better the system is. Schumacker's (2010) criteria urge us to adopt an electoral system that is simple to understand, treats voters equally, allows voters to vote their sincere preference, demonstrates neutrality when it comes to the candidates, increases participation, produces legitimate results, allows for an easy transition to governance, allows for inclusive ideas and candidates of all backgrounds to run for office, and has a feasible path to implementation. What is clear from looking at other Electoral College reform ideas is that none of them meet all of these criteria. However, some perform better than others. In chapter 7, I will demonstrate that the Constant Two Plan would perform better than the current structure of the Electoral College. It will also be made clear in chapter 5 that many of the already-existing reform plans (such as the District Plan, Proportional Plan, and the Automatic Plan) perform worse than the current Electoral College system.

In his treatise, *Common Sense*, Thomas Paine wrote, "A long habit of not thinking a thing wrong, gives it a superficial appearance of being right, and raises at first a formidable outcry in defense of custom" (Conway 1894, 68). This is the current state of the Electoral College. It, as an institution, has been in place since 1787, when it was agreed upon by the delegates to the Constitutional Convention as a compromise solution to how to select an executive. Since then, 46 presidents have been elected under its current structure, but of those 46 presidents, 5 have failed to win the popular support of the American people. Two of these five elections have happened since the 2000 presidential election. Technological and societal advances now allow for a meaningful and engaged popular vote. It is time to reform the Electoral College to ensure that the candidate with the most popular support wins the presidency. We should not let our habit of inaction on reforming the Electoral College prevent us from further democratizing the presidential election process.

# Chapter 2

# It's Not "Excellent," But It's Not All Bad

Alexander Hamilton, in his defense of the Electoral College, wrote in *Federalist No. 68*, "I venture somewhat further, and hesitate not to affirm, that if the manner of it be not perfect, it is at least excellent" (Hamilton 2008). While Hamilton believed the Electoral College to be excellent, it is clear that this opinion is not held by many voters today. However, while it is not now a well-liked institution, there were several benefits the Founders believed it to possess, leading them to adopt it to begin with. As demonstrated in chapter 1, the Electoral College was not carefully crafted in an effort to create the perfect mode by which to select the country's executive. Instead, it is the result of the delegates trying to ease the impasse they arrived at when trying to decide on how to choose an executive, facilitate a compromise, and finish their business in Philadelphia. The delegates succeeded in forging a path forward via the Electoral College, despite it not being anyone's first choice. While the Electoral College may not be perfect, the delegates believed it to have many benefits, and with its adoption, they were able to combine their desire to have a more elite group of citizens choose the president while also taking into account the will of the people. A summary of the benefits the delegates believed the Electoral College to have can be found in table 2.1. The Convention delegates truly believed that the method of electing the president would accommodate the needs of the fledgling country while preserving the newly created governing system. Alexander Hamilton (2008) writes that the Electoral College "affords a moral certainty, that the office of President will never fall to the lot of any man who is not in an eminent degree endowed with the requisite qualifications." The discussion of Trump's role in the January 6, 2021, insurrection on Capitol Hill in the previous chapter clearly shows how wrong Hamilton was.

**Table 2.1 Benefits of the Electoral College Given by Hamilton in *Federalist No. 68***

| |
|---|
| 1. The public would choose the electors, ensuring the people's will would be included. |
| 2. Selection of the president would be conducted by citizens more aware of, and attentive to, the needs of the country to ensure the candidate chosen would be well equipped for the job. |
| 3. The Electoral College does better than its alternatives at ensuring that the election of the president is as free from "tumult and disorder" as possible. |
| 4. Corruption and cabal are guarded against. |
| 5. It ensures the executive is separated from the legislature and dependent only on the people for reelection. |

*Source*: Table created by the Author.

## INVOLVING THE PUBLIC: LETTING THE PEOPLE PICK THE ELECTORS IS GOOD ENOUGH?

While the delegates opted to not entrust the public with the responsibility of selecting the president, they did not, however, want the public completely left out of the process. Several of the delegates actually liked the idea of allowing the public to choose the president but were unwilling to commit to this method of election due to the vast size of the country. Additionally, they did not want the legislature to be solely in charge of selecting the executive. So, the delegates created a separate group of people selected specifically for the job of picking the country's executive. The intention was for the public to have a say in selecting the members of the Electoral College. Hamilton (2008) writes, "It was desirable that the sense of the people should operate in the choice of the person to who so important a trust was to be confided." Electoral College members were thus supposed to bring with them an understanding of the needs of the public. So, while there may not have been a direct election of the executive, the intent was for the Electoral College to include in its deliberation the public will.

Additionally, by creating the Electoral College, there was a special group of people assembled to elect the president—one that would be re-assembled every four years with the same goal. Importantly, this group of electors was not to be made up of the same individuals every four years. The goal of the Electoral College was to prevent a pre-established body (e.g., the national legislature) from selecting the president. Should the legislature have been tasked with selecting the executive, one of the fears was that the executive would be subservient to the legislature. Gouverneur Morris argued that

> he will be the mere creature of the Legislature if appointed and impeachable by that body . . . If the Legislature elect, it will be the work of intrigue, of cabal, and of faction . . . real merit will rarely be the title to their appointment. (Farrand 1937, 29)

So, to avoid the pitfalls of associating the selection of an executive with the legislative branch, the Electoral College was created. The delegates believed that the structure of the Electoral College would prevent the types of problems associated with cabal and faction because each state's electors would meet in their respective state capitals and not all gather together in the national Capitol. Should one state fall victim to the undue influence of a charismatic individual or group, the influence would be limited to the state's electors rather than all electors. Should the national legislature be tasked with selecting the president, all electors would be exposed to the same influences and would be more prone to problems of cabal and corruption.

Many of these problems should no longer be viewed as such, given the advances of technology since the late eighteenth century. The public is currently involved in national elections—despite the official selection of the president by the Electoral College, there is a popular vote in which citizens from all states vote for their preferred presidential candidate. So, the infrastructure and technology already exist for a meaningful popular vote to take place. Because of this, conducting a nationwide popular vote is now possible despite the vast size of the United States, the reason several delegates declined to support the idea of a direct election of an executive. Additionally, the technological and societal advances over the past centuries have made it possible for the electors, despite the distance between state capitals, to fall victim to the problems of faction and intrigue. Prior to the age of X (formerly Twitter), TikTok, high-speed internet, and cable news, keeping the electors insulated in their respective states could potentially prevent conspiracy and collusion from one state's electors to another. Today's technology, however, would not prevent this type of cabal; instead, it is clear that some electors have no problem publicly discussing their vote intentions.

The time period between Election Day 2016 and the day on which the electors cast their official votes for president (December 19, 2016) presents us with an interesting case study of both the electors going public with their intentions as well as the public's ability to influence the electors. During the run-up to December 19, 2016, Michael Baca, a Democratic elector pledged to Hillary Clinton, organized what he dubbed the "Hamilton Electors movement" (Wegman 2020). Baca reached out to several other electors, asking them to join him in voting for John Kasich—a Republican primary competitor of Donald Trump who continued far into the nomination contest despite only winning his home state of Ohio, in an effort to force a contested convention to prevent Trump from securing the nomination. His actions were not due to a dislike of the Democratic candidate, Hillary Clinton. In an interview with NBC, Baca notes, "It would have been an honor to vote for Clinton, but voting for her would not have prevented a Trump presidency . . . I just felt like I had to do everything I could to prevent that from happening" (Edelman 2020).

Baca relied on the writings of Alexander Hamilton—specifically Hamilton's argument that the Electoral College will guard against a demagogue from winning the presidency, to justify his actions. Baca reached out to many electors in an effort to secure 37 electors that would join him in voting against both Trump and Clinton in an effort to force a contingent election in which the House of Representatives would pick the president and the Senate would pick the vice president. He did not ask any of the Republican electors to vote for Clinton; he simply asked them to vote for anyone but Trump. He selected Kasich because he thought he would be able to more easily entice these "faithless" Republicans to vote for a fellow Republican candidate rather than a Democrat. While he wanted a Democratic president, and so did the state of Colorado, as evidenced by its 2016 popular vote results, he claimed Colorado's strongest preference was to prevent Donald Trump from obtaining the presidency. Baca states,

> I thought this plan would give Colorado a better deal . . . They didn't want Trump. They wanted anybody but Trump. I thought that if it got kicked to the House and they picked a more moderate Republican, it would have been good for Colorado voters (Edelman 2020).

Ultimately, Baca's plan failed. As soon as he cast his vote for Kasich, the Colorado Secretary of State removed him from his post as elector and replaced him with somebody who would vote for Clinton—a vote in-line with the state's popular vote results. This action was taken because Colorado—along with many other states—has a law requiring electors to vote according to the state's popular vote results (i.e., preventing faithless electors). Baca sued the Colorado Department of State and received a favorable ruling in the U.S. Court of Appeals for the 10th Circuit. However, the Supreme Court overturned the Appellate Court's decision, stating that the state is perfectly within its constitutional right to hold an elector to their pledge of supporting the state's voters' choice (*Colorado Department of State v. Baca* 591 U.S. ___ (2020)). Overall, then, Baca's plan to lead a movement of "Hamilton electors" to force the first contingency election for president since 1824 came to a rather uneventful close.

In addition to Baca's quest to form a Hamiltonesque movement among the 2016 presidential electors, it was clear that electors were not insulated from public pressures. After hearing reports of potential Russian interference in the election, there was some coordination between electors in an attempt to secure a briefing from the director of national intelligence, James Clapper. On December 12, 2016, 10 electors (nine Democrats and one Republican) signed a letter to Clapper requesting a briefing on the status of the investigations into potential ties between Donald Trump and the Russian government (Cheney and Debenedetti 2016). Additionally, almost five million people signed a Change.org petition asking all electors to vote for Hillary Clinton over Donald Trump due to her decisive victory in the popular vote (Mihalcik 2016). The petition failed to influence any Republican elector to support Clinton over Trump. Even celebrities participated in the attempt to get Republican electors to support a different candidate than Trump. Martin Sheen, in his best Jed Bartlet reenactment, led a group of Hollywood celebrities in reminding electors that they did not need to vote for Clinton in order to block Trump from becoming president—they could vote for anyone and let the House of Representatives decide the victor (Wegman 2020). Given the makeup of the House in 2016, however, Trump likely would have still become president.

This digression into the behavior of the 2016 electors highlights the fact that the country has long since evolved to the point where electors are now easily able to coordinate with one another whenever they would want to do so. The Founders initially wanted the electors to have some knowledge of how the public felt about presidential candidates and to weigh that knowledge against the needs of the nation. They also believed that making the electors meet in their respective state capitals would prevent them from coordinating with other states' electors. All of this, today, is moot. Technology has advanced to the point where we are now able to get instantaneous news updates on our phones and call, text, or video chat with others at any time. So today, it is no longer good enough to allow for public input into just who the electors are; instead, the public should have a much larger role in presidential selection.

Baca's actions were taken as a result of his beliefs that the Electoral College had made the mistake of electing a corrupt demagogue in Donald Trump—something the Founders believed the Electoral College would prevent. As a result, instead of *preventing* a demagogic executive, the Electoral College actually *elected* one over the winner of the national popular vote. Electors tried to "sound the alarm," but to no avail. Due to the reliance on state laws binding electors to the state's popular vote results, electors that may have voted against their state's wishes were replaced by electors that voted "correctly." Many of these rules have been passed to ensure electors comply with the wishes of the state's voters, even if those wishes come at the expense of the national will. So, the democratic principle of one person, one vote is undermined at the national level in order to uphold state preferences. Because all states are not equal in population size, this type of allocation system places more electoral power in the smaller states than in the larger ones. Since electoral votes are worth more in smaller states (i.e., there are fewer voters associated with each electoral vote), the voters that reside in these states have a stronger voice in the Electoral College than voters that reside in larger states—clearly violating the democratic principle that all votes should be counted equally.

## Presidential Voters Need to Be Aware of National Needs

"The immediate election should be made by men most capable of analyzing the qualities adapted to the station . . . [who] will be most likely to possess the information and discernment requisite to such complicated investigations" (Hamilton 1788). Writing on behalf of the Federalists, Hamilton made it clear that they wanted the president to be chosen by men (and I say men because that is who the Founders wanted voting for president) that were educated on the needs of the entire nation. Many people use this to say that the Founders did not want average voters to participate in presidential selection and that these voters were not educated enough to meaningfully participate in a national election (Beard 1913; Smith 1907). However, that is not at all the case. Based on the Founders' statements at the convention, it is clear that the problem for the Founders was not education or a lack of desire to include the public in the decision of who should be president. Instead, the problem was ignorance—the lack of information available to the public.

At the time of the Constitution's drafting, a vast majority of this country was rural. In fact, only five cities had a population of more than 10,000 residents, and everyone lived without electricity or indoor plumbing (Wegman 2020). Additionally, formal education was sparse, newspapers (if they existed) focused on local news, and travel was incredibly limited—as Wegman (2020, 39) notes, "even by stagecoach, the jetliner of its day, getting from New York to Boston could take almost a week in bad weather." Today, that trip takes one hour by plane or four hours by car. So, given the nature of society in 1787, it is not hard to understand how ignorant average citizens were of governmental activity or national needs. It is therefore understandable that the Founders had concerns about the ability of average citizens to select a president in-line with the country's needs rather than the needs of the state in which they resided.

Despite the Founders' concerns about public ignorance, many of them were still supportive, at least theoretically, of allowing the public to pick the president. James Wilson was probably the most vocal in his opinion that the public should play a role in selecting their representatives—he advocated for popular election of Representatives, Senators, and the president. Wilson believed that the people should speak for the themselves and pointed to both New York and Massachusetts as examples of how successful the popular election of executive officers could be, as both of these states used the popular election to select their governors (Farrand 1937). Unfortunately, Wilson failed in his attempt to convince the other convention delegates to support the popular election of the president; by the end of the convention, only the House of Representatives was chosen by popular election. For president, the delegates settled on the Electoral College.

Given the state of technology today, it would be possible to institute a national election and allow the popular vote to select the president. In fact, we already hold the national election, we just fail to let the results speak for themselves; instead, we focus on the popular vote in each state. Not only is the country now technologically capable of holding a national election, but there are far fewer reasons for voters to remain ignorant of national needs than there were in 1787. There are roughly 1,260 daily newspapers circulated throughout the United States, cable news channels report news 24/7, and major news outlets (e.g., the *New York Times*, the *Washington Post*, *CNN*, and *ABC News*) all provide instantaneous updates online or via their smartphone apps. This, of course, does not necessarily mean that all voters are well versed in what policies are needed across the country, but it does mean that today's ignorance is much more willful than it was in the late eighteenth century.

Despite this willful ignorance, it nonetheless makes a lot of sense to reform the Electoral College to ensure the winner of the presidential election is the candidate who receives the most votes nationwide. The Founders' initial objections to relying on the popular vote are now completely moot, and the Electoral College has demonstrated an ability to undermine the national will and thus democratic principles—largely those calling for equality of votes and allowing the candidate with the most votes to govern. All of this has happened despite the fact that technological advancements have made it even easier for electors to stay apprised of the national mood—the national mood being something the Founders wanted the electors to take into account when electing the president.

## It's Better than the Alternatives

As mentioned at the beginning of this chapter, the members of the Constitutional Convention understood that the proposed Electoral College was not perfect, but they did believe it was better than the alternatives—at least the alternatives available to them at the time. As the Founders were deciding on how best to select a president, a majority of the debate focused on selection by the legislature or by the national popular vote. In his presentation to the Maryland House of Representatives, Luther Martin (as quoted in Farrand 1937, vol. III, p. 158) summarizes the debate nicely,

> Mr. Hamilton of New York wanted the President to be appointed by the Senate, others by both Branches, others by the People at large—others that the States as States ought to have an equal voice—The larger States wanted the appointment

according to numbers—those who were for a one General Government, and no State Governments, were for a choice by the People at Large.

As the Founders were deciding on how best to select a president, a majority of the debate focused on selection by the legislature or by the national popular vote. As discussed earlier, the Founders were largely supportive of the citizenry having a say in their national executive but were afraid of their ignorance of the policy needs of the nation as a whole. So, their debate then focused on how best to select a president that was knowledgeable of national needs. The first inclination was to allow the national legislature to choose, but this violated the idea of separation of powers that many of the Founders agreed was important. The fear was that the legislature would abuse its power and simply revert the fledgling United States into a monarchy—or at least a system that focuses more on the ruling class than the needs of the citizenry.

After ruling out selection by the legislature, those at the convention then debated the possibility of allowing the citizenry to pick the president. The idea of a popular vote was, again, supported by many in attendance at the convention; however, fears persisted. Many were concerned about the ability of the entire citizenry to educate themselves on the needs of the country as a whole and select a worthy candidate to tend to those needs. Gouverneur Morris also highlighted the potential for state partisans to rule the state, fearing that they would be able to manipulate the less-attentive members of the state (Farrand 1937, vol. I, p. 80). James Wilson remained the sole delegate, firmly committed to the popular election of all government officials—both legislative and executive. Therefore, compromise was needed, which is exactly how the Electoral College came to be.

Presently, many other alternatives exist to the Electoral College. In fact, today there are four commonly discussed plans to reform the Electoral College: direct election of the president, the Proportional Plan, the District Plan, and the National Popular Vote Interstate Compact. Direct election, for which the Electoral College would be dismantled and the president would be elected by the national popular vote, is much more feasible today than in the late eighteenth century. This, however, would require a constitutional amendment, which is wholly unlikely to happen. The Proportional Plan calls for the allocation of electoral votes according to the proportion of the popular votes won in each state (i.e., receiving 60 percent of the vote in New York would net the candidate 60 percent of New York's electoral votes). This plan may avoid the necessity of a constitutional amendment (depending on how votes are ultimately divided) and seems to align much better with democratic norms regarding participation. However, as will be demonstrated in chapter 5, this plan regularly fails to select a majority winner, necessitating a contingent election in which the House of Representatives would select the president and the Senate would select the vice president. In many cases, the proportional plan thus devolves into legislative selection

The District Plan, already in use in Nebraska and Maine, would preserve the Electoral College but award electoral votes according to the popular vote results in congressional districts rather than states (though two votes would be awarded to the statewide popular vote winner). This plan also does not require the passage of a constitutional amendment and theoretically brings the selection process closer to the people. However, there are clear problems with gerrymandering associated with this plan, and were it to be adopted, the major parties likely would be even more focused on gerrymandering than they are now. And, as will be demonstrated in chapter 5, this plan does not always align with the popular vote winner either. Finally, the National Popular Vote Interstate Compact calls on each state to sign onto a compact pledging all of their state's electoral votes to the national popular vote winner rather than the state popular vote winner. This would, indeed, ensure that the national popular vote winner becomes president. However, it is not likely that this plan will gain the support of traditionally red states. The Republican Party has benefited from the current structure of the Electoral College more than the Democratic Party, and so far, none of these red states has signed the compact. All of the proposed reform plans will be more thoroughly reviewed in chapter 5, but a brief discussion of these plans here was needed to show that more options are now more feasible than they were when the Electoral College was initially adopted.

## GUARDING AGAINST CABAL AND CORRUPTION

Given the fledgling status of the democratic system created by these delegates, many of them were wary of potential cabal and corruption. Entrusting the governance of the newly formed country to just one executive official made many of the Founders concerned, given what they experienced with Great Britain. Thus, a fierce debate was waged about how best to form the executive office. Some of the delegates believed that the executive powers should be vested in one individual, and others believed the executive should consist of a committee. Still others believed the executive powers should be given to just one person, but that individual should be required to have a committee of advisors with whom they must regularly consult. Additionally, the Founders needed to then decide how to couple the structure of the executive with the selection method in order to avoid the problems associated with factions and how to prevent corruption.

Of the delegates in favor of a singular executive, James Wilson was initially the most vocal. He argued, for example, that it would make accountability easier—if there were just one executive officer, there would be no question about who was in charge and responsible for all executive decision-making (Farrand 1937 vol. I). He went on to argue that a singular executive would be less prone to despotism than a group of executives—citing the fact that the American colonists were largely against Parliament rather than the king (Farrand 1937 vol. I). Wilson, therefore, argued that it would be easier for an office of multiple executives to exploit and abuse their power rather than just one individual, as the corrupt executives would be able to band together to influence the legislature and/or the citizenry at large. A singular executive would have a more difficult time doing so.

Others pushed back slightly on Wilson's argument, agreeing that a singular executive would work, but only if that individual were surrounded by a committee of advisors from whom they could solicit advice on how to respond to national issues. James Madison and Elbridge Gerry were vocal in their support of such an executive system, with Madison arguing that the singular executive would be sure to be well informed by this council. Madison went so far as to say the executive would ignore the council's advice at their own peril, signifying he wanted the executive to have final decision-making authority, though also signaling how important a role he wanted the council to play (Farrand 1937 vol. I). Gerry took the power of the proposed council even further. He wanted the council members to be held accountable for their advice given to the executive, calling for their ability to be impeached should they be found guilty of misconduct in office (Farrand 1937 vol. I). In response to this, however, Hugh Williamson suggests that there is no difference between what Madison and Gerry are arguing for and the multiple executives argued for by Edmund Randalph, Roger Sherman, and George Mason. In fact, he implied that this is more complicated than just adopting a multiple executive, so the decision should really be made between the two rather than this seemingly compromise position supported by Madison and Gerry (Farrand 1937 vol. I).

Edmund Randolph believed that a multiple executive would guard best against monarchy and abuse of power, as it would be more difficult for a three-person executive, for example, to become a tyrant than it would be for just a singular executive (Farrand 1937 vol. I). Roger Sherman was more ambivalent about the actual number affixed to the executive, preferring to allow the legislature to determine how many executive officials were needed. Sherman believed the national legislature should be in charge of selecting the executive officer, as his vision of an executive was to simply ensure that the laws passed by the legislature were properly enacted. Therefore, he believed that the number of executive officers should be determined by the legislature (Farrand 1937 vol. I). George Mason also spoke at length about his preference for a three-person executive, arguing that an executive officer from the north, south, and middle of the United States would best represent the different interests of such a vast country (Rowland 2017, 112–15).

What the preceding discussion highlights is the fact that these convention delegates debated at length how to craft an executive that would not be vulnerable to cabal and corruption. They wanted an executive that was strong enough to manage the executive affairs of the country, enact legislative accomplishments, and take the lead in foreign relations, but not one that would lead the country back to the governing system they left behind in Great Britain. But, after the debate about the structure of the executive, they were left with the debate about how to select that executive. During these convention debates, they ultimately agreed that the Electoral College would be better suited to prevent corruption than either the national popular vote or legislative selection. Given the challenges at the time of the Constitution's drafting of selecting an executive by a nationwide popular vote, the framers were wary that those that would participate in such an election would be those that would be more prone to cabal—at least cabal among the more populous states. They would be the more elite members of society, and that ran the risk of them exploiting those who were not able to participate in an election. Additionally, the prospect of election via the legislature raised the same concerns about cabal: the elite that would be sent to serve in the legislature would coordinate with each other and overrun those that did not agree. Concerns also existed that the more populous states, which would have greater representation in the House, would be able to overpower the less populous states, leading to large state dominance in the executive. Thus, the Electoral College was seen as a compromise on this front—the voters would get a say in who their electors were, and the electors would be tasked with balancing their state interests with the interests of the nation when selecting the executive. And, while forcing the electors to participate in an election in their state Capitol, rather than all of them converging on the national Capitol they believed it would keep the electors from coordinating with one another on their vote.

At present, however, many of the concerns voiced by the Founders that once seemed to be solved by the Electoral College are no longer remedied. Travel is much easier today, technology has advanced to the point of allowing anyone in the world to talk with anyone else in a matter of seconds, and the United States has grown significantly in size. This all makes cabal and corruption much easier to coordinate. Thus, reform of this institution is much needed. The Electoral College no longer serves as a bulwark against cabal and corruption—in fact, as demonstrated in the aftermath of the 2020 election, without legislators standing up for democratic principles, efforts made to completely overturn legitimate election results were done within the confines of the Electoral College. Importantly, legislators were not unified on that front. Still today, several claim that Donald Trump was the legitimate winner of the 2020 election despite losing the popular vote by seven million votes.

## Separation of Powers and Public Accountability

Finally, the Founders believed that the Electoral College was the best way to ensure that the separation of powers between the executive and legislative branches remained intact while also providing for public accountability. The Electoral College prevents both the legislature and the public from directly selecting the president. The electors were purposefully designed to be different from legislators and were to be chosen by the public—thereby coupling public opinion with more elite members of society being chosen for their knowledge of national concerns rather than just local or state concerns. They were fearful of legislative selection because of the potential for corruption and cabal among these elected leaders, and they were fearful of popular election because of the impracticality of a national election coupled with the citizens' inability to fully inform themselves on issues of national importance.

It is important to remember that not only would these electors be separate from the legislature, they would also be charged with executing their own best judgment on who should be named president. They were not to be bound to vote for any particular candidate, because, as Hamilton writes in *Federalist No. 68*, the electors would be "most likely to possess the information and discernment requisite to such complicated investigations" (Hamilton 2008). It was thus the electors job to ensure that the president was qualified for the position—in fact, the hope of the Founders was that electors would be men that were of a more privileged position in their state so that they would be knowledgeable of both state and national needs (Korzi 2016). These electors, then, would be eminently qualified for such decision-making—at least that was the hope of the Founders.

However, the contingent election put in place for when a candidate fails to receive a majority of support among electors fully vests the selection of both the president and vice president in the hands of the legislature. Should the Electoral College fail to select a president with a majority vote, the House of Representatives (the chamber closest to the people) would be charged with selecting the president, and the Senate would be charged with selecting the vice president, giving the legislature the full authority to select the executive leaders. However, should a contingent election be needed, each member of the House would not get to cast a ballot for president, instead voting would be conducted by the state. So, state delegations would need to meet to decide which candidate they would support as a state, not as individual representatives. This was done in an effort to assuage concerns that large states would dominate small states should the House need to decide on the president.

Despite the contingent election, the Founders believed that by allowing the House of Representatives to select the president rather than the Senate, the will of the people would be voiced more, as the House was the only piece of the federal government directly elected by the public. Thus, the overall hope of the Founders was that some aspect of public accountability would still be preserved. If the public was unhappy with the choice made by the House, theoretically they would be able to vote out the problematic members within two years. Overall, the Founders believed that they had devised a method of presidential selection that allowed for both public accountability and the preservation of the separation of powers. What they failed to anticipate was the rise in prominence and power of political parties, or, to borrow Hamilton's concern in *Federalist No. 10*, factions—a concern that will be more thoroughly discussed in the following chapter. And with the failure to anticipate the power of parties in American politics, they could not have foreseen the problems associated with the calcification of our partisanship as seen today (Sides, Tausanovitch, and Vavreck 2022). This calcification coupled with the continuous undermining of democratic principles has created an atmosphere that is in desperate need of electoral reform.

## MORE MODERN APPEALS FOR PRESERVING THE ELECTORAL COLLEGE

I'd like to conclude this chapter by moving beyond the benefits the Founders believed the Electoral College possessed and focus a bit on more modern justifications for its preservation. These reasons include the preservation of American federalism, encouraging more national campaigns, preserving more deliberative decision-making, and creating clear and decisive outcomes. All of these justifications, of course, hold some merit, but none so much as to rule out reform, if not full abolition of the Electoral College. In fact, I will demonstrate that these justifications are largely no longer applicable to the discussion of Electoral College reform today (table 2.2).

First, let's examine the issue of federalism. Federalism requires the sharing or separation of powers vertically—there is a central (or federal) government as well as regional (in this case, state) governments, each with their own separate and concurrent powers. The Electoral College clearly acknowledges this federal system of government, as electoral votes are based upon each state's popular vote totals. And should a contingency election be necessary, the votes for president are to be cast by the state rather than by individual

**Table 2.2 Modern Justifications for Keeping the Electoral College**

- Preserves the federalist ideal
- Forces candidates to compete nationwide rather than just in the populous areas
- Maintains a more deliberate decision-making process
- Ensures a clear, decisive, and majoritarian winner
- Preserves the two-party system

*Source*: Table created by the Author.

representatives. Several defenses of the Electoral College cite the federal principle as a main reason to preserve such an institution—specifically, its ability to force candidates to put together a broad coalition of support. In other words, the United States is a large and diverse landmass, and in order to win the presidency, the candidates must appeal to a diverse set of interests.

Judith Best (1996) argues that victorious candidates are the ones who are able to put together the broadest coalitions of interests across the various states. Ross (2017, 33–34) agrees with Best in her assessment, writing that under the current system, "the federalist (state-by-state) nature of the presidential election requires candidates to broaden their base of appeal. The alternative, a direct national election, would most likely produce a president who represented narrower special-interest groups, such as those based on region, state, or ideology." While both are correct in their assessment that a successful presidential candidate is one who is able to piece together broad appeals to form a winning coalition, they are wrong that this is a function of the federalist principle inherent in the Constitution. Regardless of how a presidential election is structured, a candidate must put together a campaign in which he or she makes appeals across the United States. Under the current structure of the Electoral College, candidates have a clear understanding of which states are safely located in their column and which ones are firmly in support of their opponent. This means that candidates for president focus mainly on battleground states—those in which polling shows that either candidate could win. This has been demonstrated repeatedly by those who study campaign strategy—both in terms of candidate visits or rallies (Arceneaux 2007; Devine 2018; Devine 2019; Shaw 2000) and in terms of advertising (Devine 2013; Patterson 1980; West 2017). To say that the Electoral College necessitates the candidates campaigning in a variety of states and paying attention to a broad set of states' concerns is absolutely incorrect. If anything, the Electoral College forces candidates to focus on approximately ten battleground states every four years, meaning 40 are left with little-to-no attention beyond what they may normally receive.

Naysayers may argue that candidates running for president in a system in which the Electoral College does not exist would ignore almost all of the states in favor of the most populous. That may be true, but the most populous states are where actual voters live. Wyoming, Montana, and Alaska may indeed be much larger in size than states like New York, Massachusetts, and Pennsylvania, but the combined population of the former three states is roughly 2.4 million people, while the latter three account for roughly 39 million voters. As Earl Warren wrote in his decision for the 1964 Supreme Court case, *Reynolds v. Sims*, "Legislators represent people, not trees or acres. Legislators are elected by voters, not farms or cities or economic interests" (*Reynolds v. Sims* 377 U.S. 533 (1964)). Were the Electoral College to be reformed or eliminated, candidates would still need to put together a broad coalition of voters in order to win—it will not help a Democrat to simply focus on New York and California nor a Republican to focus solely on Texas and Florida. There are not enough partisans who live in any of these states to clinch an election for a candidate. More importantly, this undermines democratic principles because presidents are not elected to represent the land, but the people. Any electoral mechanism that does not account for the fact that more people live in California, Florida, or New York than Wyoming is a mechanism that undercuts the sentiments expressed by Warren in the 1964 *Reynolds* decision.

In order to put together a winning coalition, candidates will need to focus on voter interests, which may necessitate their focus being placed on more populated states because that is where the voters are. However, Electoral College reform may help some of the liberal voters in red states and some of the conservative voters in blue states feel like their voice is being heard, along with the majority of partisans that live in those states. Currently, the unit rule (pledging all of a state's electoral votes to the statewide popular vote winner) is in use in 48 states, meaning that any candidate receiving a plurality of votes receives all of a state's electoral votes, leaving the voters who did not vote for that plurality winner feeling disenfranchised.

After the 2000 election debacle, in which George W. Bush defeated Al Gore in the electoral, but not popular, vote, historian Jack Rakove (2000) noted in the *New York Times*:

> States have no interest, as states, in the election of the president; only citizens do . . . The winner-take-all rule might make sense if states really embodied coherent, unified interests and communities, but of course they do not. What does Chicago share with Galena, except that they both are in Illinois.

Chicago tends to vote quite heavily Democratic, while Galena tends to vote in favor of Republican candidates. The unit rule, again, is going to leave the voters of one of these cities feeling as though their voices are not heard in a presidential election (and given Illinois's history of supporting Democratic candidates, it is likely to be the residents of Galena). The same rationale can be applied to New York. The New York City area tends to vote overwhelmingly for Democratic candidates; the rest of the state, however, looks quite red. This is not to say, of course, that Galena, IL, or upstate New York should dictate the entire state's presidential vote. It does, however, highlight the problem with the unit rule. Requiring all electors of a state to vote for the same candidate makes voters in the minority political party feel disenfranchised in presidential elections.

Next, some argue that the structure and rules of the Electoral College ensure a more deliberative decision-making process surrounding presidential selection. This definitely seems in-line with what the Founders had hoped, as Madison wrote in *Federalist 68* that

> the immediate election should be made by men most capable of analyzing the qualities adapted to the station, and acting under circumstances favorable to deliberation, and to a judicious combination of all the reasons and inducements which were proper to govern their choice. (Yale Law School 2008)

However, the Electoral College, as currently structured, is no longer needed to ensure a deliberative decision-making process occurs. Nor does the Electoral College ensure that a deliberate process takes place. The Founders were wary of public passions having too much power to sway an election and wanted to ensure that those who were in charge of selecting the president were focused on the needs of the nation (Bennett 2010). In fact, the Founders believed that,

> popularity, may alone suffice to elevate a man to the first honors in a single State, but it will require other talents, and a different kind of merit, to establish him in the esteem and confidence of the whole Union, or of so considerable a portion of it as would be necessary to make him a successful candidate for the distinguished office of President of the United States. (Yale Law School 2008)

However, this "benefit" of the Electoral College can hardly be considered a benefit today. Electors are no longer chosen to debate the pros and cons of potential presidential candidates—in fact, they are not chosen to select candidates at all. Our election process has changed greatly since the late eighteenth century, with primaries and caucuses used to nominate presidential candidates and electors' names no longer appearing on the ballot in most states. That means that when people vote for president, they are voting for the candidate they would like to be president rather than voting for the electors they would like to send to their state Capitol to select a president on their behalf. Many voters do not even know who their electors are, they just know which candidate they would like to see become president (Ross 2004). Further, many of the electors are chosen due to their party loyalty rather than their neutral, deliberative nature. In fact, many of the electors are more partisan than those who voted in the election. Alexander (2019, 141) confirms that electors are at least more politically active than their counterparts, writing, "Nearly all electors work for a party or a candidate, attend political meetings, try to influence others how to vote, and contact public officials. Few members of the electorate report engaging in these same activities." He goes on to point out that many of them have actually even held elective office in the past—with an even greater number reporting having held an elected position within their party (Alexander 2019).

In terms of how the electors are actually selected, there are a few ways that happen, all of which are party-centric. Alexander (2019) explains that 25 states select their slates of electors at their state party conventions, 14 states do not use a set, uniform method of selecting electors (e.g., an ad hoc committee may be formed, state party leaders may get to choose), ten states use a state party committee to choose slates of electors, California allows each candidate for the U.S. House of Representatives and the U.S. Senate to select an elector, and Pennsylvania allows the party's nominee to select their own slate of electors. Regardless of how an elector is selected, he or she is still very much entangled with the state party organization. While parties are likely very happy with this arrangement, and it does largely reflect the will of a plurality of state voters, it is a far cry from the deliberative body designed by the Founders. Going even further, with 32 states and Washington, D.C., having laws on the books binding electors to the popular vote in that state (or district), the deliberative nature of the Electoral College is completely removed. Overall, then, it seems clear that the "benefit" of the deliberative nature of the Electoral College is no longer applicable as a defense of the Electoral College. There is no debate or deliberation; there is just a rubber stamping of the state's popular vote.

Some defenders of the Electoral College also point to its ability to bring an election to a clear and decisive end as one of its greatest strengths (Goidel 2014; Ross 2017). This much is true: the president is guaranteed a majority victory in the Electoral College, or else a majority victory in the House of Representatives—something that has not happened since 1824. The Electoral College was indeed designed to give the president a majority of support—to demonstrate the support of their constituents while governing. And it has, indeed, lived up to this expectation. Table 2.3 lists all of the presidential elections from 1824 through 2020, along with their popular and electoral votes and margins of victory. With the exception of 1824 (the only election in which a contingent election was needed), the Electoral College provided the president with a majority of support—at least in the electoral vote. However, what this table also shows is the tendency for the Electoral College to exacerbate the winning candidate's margin of victory.

Take, for example, Joe Biden's win in 2020. He won the popular vote nationwide by a fairly comfortable margin of 4.5 percent, but when we look

**Table 2.3 Margin of Victory Exacerbated by Electoral College**

| *Election Year* | *Candidate* | *Popular Vote (%)* | *Margin of Victory (%)* | *Electoral Vote (%)* | *Margin of Victory (%)* |
|---|---|---|---|---|---|
| 2020 | Joseph Biden | 51.26 | 4.5 | 56.9 | 13.8 |
| | Donald Trump | 46.8 | | 43.1 | |
| 2016 | Donald Trump | 45.93 | −2.09 | 56.5 | 14.3 |
| | Hillary Clinton | 48.02 | | 42.2 | |
| 2012 | Barack Obama | 51.01 | 3.86 | 61.7 | 23.4 |
| | Mitt Romney | 47.15 | | 38.3 | |
| 2008 | Barack Obama | 52.86 | 7.26 | 67.8 | 35.6 |
| | John McCain | 45.60 | | 32.2 | |
| 2004 | George W. Bush | 50.73 | 2.47 | 53.2 | 6.5 |
| | John Kerry | 48.26 | | 46.7 | |
| 2000 | George W. Bush | 47.87 | −0.51 | 50.4 | 1.0 |
| | Al Gore | 48.38 | | 49.4 | |
| 1996 | Bill Clinton | 49.23 | 8.51 | 70.4 | 40.8 |
| | Robert Dole | 40.72 | | 29.6 | |
| 1992 | Bill Clinton | 43.01 | 5.56 | 68.8 | 37.6 |
| | George H. W. Bush | 37.45 | | 31.2 | |
| 1988 | George H. W. Bush | 53.37 | 7.72 | 79.2 | 58.6 |
| | Michael Dukakis | 45.65 | | 20.6 | |
| 1984 | Ronald Reagan | 58.77 | 18.21 | 97.6 | 95.2 |
| | Walter Mondale | 40.56 | | 2.4 | |
| 1980 | Ronald Reagan | 50.75 | 9.74 | 90.9 | 81.8 |
| | Jimmy Carter | 41.01 | | 9.1 | |
| 1976 | Jimmy Carter | 50.08 | 2.07 | 55.2 | 10.6 |
| | Gerald Ford | 48.01 | | 44.6 | |
| 1972 | Richard Nixon | 60.67 | 23.15 | 96.7 | 93.5 |
| | George McGovern | 37.52 | | 3.2 | |
| 1968 | Richard Nixon | 43.42 | 0.70 | 55.9 | 20.4 |
| | Hubert Humphrey | 42.72 | | 35.5 | |
| | George Wallace | 13.53 | | 8.6 | |
| 1964 | Lyndon Johnson | 61.05 | 22.58 | 90.3 | 80.6 |
| | Barry Goldwater | 38.47 | | 9.7 | |
| 1960 | John Kennedy | 49.72 | 0.17 | 56.4 | 15.6 |
| | Richard Nixon | 49.55 | | 40.8 | |
| 1956 | Dwight Eisenhower | 57.37 | 15.4 | 86.1 | 72.4 |
| | Adlai Stevenson | 41.97 | | 13.7 | |
| 1952 | Dwight Eisenhower | 55.14 | 6.76 | 83.2 | 66.4 |
| | Adlai Stevenson | 44.38 | | 16.8 | |
| 1948 | Harry Truman | 49.55 | 4.48 | 57.1 | 21.5 |
| | Thomas Dewey | 45.07 | | 35.6 | |

**Table 2.3 Continued**

| Election Year | Candidate | Popular Vote (%) | Margin of Victory (%) | Electoral Vote (%) | Margin of Victory (%) |
|---|---|---|---|---|---|
| 1944 | Franklin Roosevelt | 53.39 | 7.5 | 81.4 | 65.5 |
| | Thomas Dewey | 45.89 | | 18.6 | |
| 1940 | Franklin Roosevelt | 54.72 | 9.95 | 84.6 | 69.2 |
| | Wendell Willkie | 44.77 | | 15.4 | |
| 1936 | Franklin Roosevelt | 60.80 | 24.26 | 98.5 | 97.0 |
| | Alfred Landon | 36.54 | | 1.5 | |
| 1932 | Franklin Roosevelt | 57.41 | 17.76 | 88.9 | 77.8 |
| | Herbert Hoover | 39.65 | | 11.1 | |
| 1928 | Herbert Hoover | 58.22 | 17.43 | 83.6 | 67.2 |
| | Alfred Smith | 40.79 | | 16.4 | |
| 1924 | Calvin Coolidge | 54.03 | 25.21 | 71.9 | 46.3 |
| | John Davis | 28.82 | | 25.6 | |
| 1920 | Warren Harding | 60.35 | 26.23 | 76.1 | 52.2 |
| | James Cox | 34.12 | | 23.9 | |
| 1916 | Woodrow Wilson | 49.25 | 3.14 | 52.2 | 4.4 |
| | Charles Hughes | 46.11 | | 47.8 | |
| 1912 | Woodrow Wilson | 41.83 | 14.44 | 81.9 | 65.3 |
| | Theodore Roosevelt | 27.39 | | 16.6 | |
| | William Taft | 23.18 | | 1.5 | |
| 1908 | William Taft | 51.57 | 8.53 | 66.5 | 33.0 |
| | William Byan | 43.04 | | 33.5 | |
| 1904 | Theodore Roosevelt | 56.42 | 18.83 | 70.6 | 41.2 |
| | Alton Parker | 37.59 | | 29.4 | |
| 1900 | William McKinley | 51.66 | 6.15 | 65.3 | 30.6 |
| | William Bryan | 45.51 | | 34.7 | |
| 1896 | William McKinley | 51.02 | 4.31 | 60.6 | 21.2 |
| | William Bryan | 46.71 | | 39.4 | |
| 1892 | Grover Cleveland | 46.02 | 3.01 | 62.4 | 29.7 |
| | Benjamin Harrison | 43.01 | | 32.7 | |
| 1888 | Benjamin Harrison | 47.80 | –0.83 | 58.1 | 16.2 |
| | Grover Cleveland | 48.63 | | 41.9 | |
| 1884 | Grover Cleveland | 48.85 | 0.57 | 54.6 | 9.2 |
| | James Blaine | 48.28 | | 45.4 | |
| 1880 | James Garfield | 48.31 | 0.09 | 58.0 | 16.0 |

(Continued)

**Table 2.3 Continued**

| *Election Year* | *Candidate* | *Popular Vote (%)* | *Margin of Victory (%)* | *Electoral Vote (%)* | *Margin of Victory (%)* |
|---|---|---|---|---|---|
| | Winfield Hancock | 48.22 | | 42.0 | |
| 1876 | Rutherford Hayes | 47.92 | −3.00 | 50.1 | 0.2 |
| | Samuel Tilden | 50.92 | | 49.9 | |
| 1872 | Ulysses Grant | 55.58 | 11.80 | 81.3 | 62.5 |
| | Horace Greeley | 43.78 | | 18.8 | |
| 1868 | Ulysses Grant | 52.66 | 5.32 | 72.8 | 45.6 |
| | Horatio Seymour | 47.34 | | 27.2 | |
| 1864 | Abraham Lincoln | 55.03 | 10.08 | 91.0 | 82.0 |
| | George McClellan | 44.95 | | 9.0 | |
| 1860 | Abraham Lincoln | 39.65 | 21.45 | 59.4 | 35.6 |
| | John Breckenridge | 18.20 | | 23.8 | |
| 1856 | James Buchanan | 45.29 | 12.2 | 58.8 | 20.3 |
| | John Fremont | 33.09 | | 38.5 | |
| 1852 | Franklin Pierce | 50.83 | 6.95 | 85.8 | 71.6 |
| | Winfield Scott | 43.88 | | 14.2 | |
| 1848 | Zachary Taylor | 47.28 | 4.79 | 56.2 | 12.4 |
| | Lewis Cass | 42.49 | | 43.8 | |
| 1844 | James Polk | 49.54 | 1.45 | 61.8 | 23.6 |
| | Henry Clay | 48.09 | | 38.2 | |
| 1840 | William Harison | 52.87 | 6.05 | 79.6 | 59.2 |
| | Martin Van Buren | 46.82 | | 20.4 | |
| 1836 | Martin Van Buren | 50.79 | 14.2 | 57.8 | 33.0 |
| | William Harrison | 36.59 | | 24.8 | |
| 1832 | Andrew Jackson | 54.74 | 17.81 | 76.0 | 59.0 |
| | Henry Clay | 36.93 | | 17.0 | |
| 1828 | Andrew Jackson | 55.93 | 12.25 | 68.2 | 36.4 |
| | John Quincy Adams | 43.68 | | 31.8 | |
| 1824 | John Quincy Adams | 30.92 | −10.44 | 32.2 | -5.7 |
| | Andrew Jackson | 41.36 | | 37.9 | |
| | William Crawford | 11.21 | | 15.7 | |
| | Henry Clay | 12.99 | | 14.2 | |

*Source*: Popular vote and electoral vote percentages from Dave Leip's Atlas of U.S. Presidential Elections.

at the Electoral College margin of victory, we see he won by almost 14 percent. In 1980, Ronald Reagan won the popular vote nationwide by a margin of just under 10 percent but won the Electoral College by a whopping 82 percent. In 1968, Richard Nixon won the popular vote by just 0.7 percent of the popular vote but won the electoral vote by 20 percent. These discrepancies largely inflate a president's popularity and their claims surrounding their mandate for governing. So, while the Electoral College does indeed provide a president with a majority of support among electors, this majority does not translate to a majority in the popular vote, nor does it accurately reflect the amount of support a president may have for implementing their platform. This relationship between a president's mandate and their ability to govern is explored by Julia Azari in her 2014 book *Delivering the People's Message*. In it, Azari (2014) argues that when a president's popularity is waning and there are legitimacy concerns, the president will lean into mandate rhetoric more often than when their popularity is high. The exacerbated margin of victory provided by the Electoral College may therefore help a president already suffering from legitimacy issues due to a loss in the popular vote claim a mandate when one does not actually exist—a further undercutting of democratic principles. We should then anticipate presidents who lose the popular vote but win the Electoral College to lean into mandate rhetoric early on to help establish legitimacy. The Electoral College makes this easy for presidents because it over-inflates a president's margin of victory.

Included in the more modern defenses of the Electoral College is its ability to contain accusations of fraud, problematic vote counting, and other election improprieties to a particular state or states rather than the entire country. For example, while the entire country waited for a result in the 2000 election, all eyes were on Florida. Only Florida was subject to such an extensive recount, with ballots being carefully examined for missing and hanging chads (the small, circular piece of paper that is "punched" out of a ballot in the punch card voting machines). The "problem" was contained to one state rather than calling into question the validity and certainty that the vote count was correct throughout the rest of the country. However, what this does not capture is that regardless of the recount outcome, Al Gore still defeated George W. Bush in the national popular vote. Despite losing Florida's popular, and thus electoral, vote by 537 votes, Gore still won more votes nationally than did Bush.

Until the aftermath of the 2020 election, there were also doubts that accusations of fraud, illegal voting, and corruption would be lobbed by serious politicians and presidential candidates. The United States has had a long history of peaceful transitions of power—the citizenry votes, the electors cast their ballots accordingly, the losing candidate concedes, and the winning candidate becomes president. Even after the 2000 election, while Americans were largely unhappy with George W. Bush becoming president and the Supreme Court stepping in to halt the Florida recount, the country largely accepted the result, and Al Gore conceded the presidency to Bush. After the 2020 election, President Donald Trump lobbed wild and ultimately incorrect accusations of voter fraud and corruption, declaring his victory despite losing both the popular vote as well as the electoral vote. In fact, Trump called the secretary of state of Georgia and said, "So look. All I want to do is this. I just want to find 11,780 votes, which is one more than we have. Because we won the state" (Gardner 2021). The state of Georgia officially certified Joe Biden's victory over Trump by 11,779 votes on November 19, 2020.

So, while the Electoral College "contains" problems of voter fraud or human error, it also allows, as Trump demonstrated, a presidential candidate to point to states that they narrowly lost and shout accusations of fraud without any evidence to back up their claims. This problem was not prevented by the Electoral College—nor will it be prevented by any reform, as this was not actually a problem with electoral rules. Instead, this was a problem of corruption within the Trump White House and his allies in the Republican Party. All of this is to say that accusations of corruption and fraud can be levied even with the Electoral College in place. And even if the Electoral College were to be reformed, many states have laws on the books that call for automatic recounts when the margin of victory is small and allow state officials and, even in some cases, candidates running for office to call for further recounts if they suspect problems. The 2020 presidential election clearly demonstrated that the Electoral College does little to contain accusations of fraud and corruption, despite its purposeful construction to ensure a clear and decisive majoritarian winner. In the re-telling of the 2020 election results and their aftermath in the previous chapter, the fake elector scheme advocated for by the Trump administration after the election was called for Joe Biden was discussed. This scheme highlights exactly how fraudulent action is not necessarily contained by the Electoral College. When the fraudulent activity is being coordinated from within the White House, it is difficult to see how the Electoral College, as an institution per se, helps contain it.

Finally, some point to the preservation of the two-party system as a major strength of the Electoral College. In fact, the American Political Science Association commissioned a committee that issued a report about 70 years ago calling for a strengthened two-party system because of the perceived weaknesses in the system at the time. The committee argued that a strong two-party system benefits voters, candidates, and the party organization alike. Voters are more easily educated with more simplified position-taking on issues. Voters are also able to hold candidates accountable more easily, as it is clearer which party has been in control, because there is no need for coalition-building like in a multiparty system. Candidates are more easily recruited, and elections more easily run. And the party organization is more easily organized in the legislature to make public policymaking easier. The two-party system that has dominated the American political landscape since the Federalists and Antifederalists fought over constitutional ratification is historically familiar to American voters and viewed as largely stable in comparison to multiparty systems that rely on coalitional governments. V. O. Key Jr. (1964) famously notes that while the issues may change over time, the two major parties have found ways to adapt to these changes and maintain their relevance—including the duality between them. The Electoral College has gone a long way toward supporting the two-party system in the United States.

Preserving the two-party system also requires fewer changes to our electoral system at large, along with the rules surrounding it. Duverger (1954) clearly links single-member districts coupled with winner-take-all systems with two-party dominance. The plurality-winner-take-all system used in the United States leads to a two-party system. All a candidate needs to do is get at least one more vote than all their competitors in order to win elective office. And with single-member rather than multi-member legislative districts, there is no representation for the minority party in any legislative district. With the unit rule used in 48 states and Washington, D.C., the Electoral College also supports a two-party system. In order to win a single electoral vote, a presidential candidate must win the popular vote in a state, something very unlikely to happen to a third-party candidate. Or, a faithless elector must cast a vote for a non-major party candidate. Even if this scenario were to happen, that candidate would be very unlikely to win the presidency. H. Ross Perot managed to win almost 20 percent of the national popular vote in 1992 and did not win a single electoral vote. Historically, the best-performing third-party candidate in the Electoral College was Teddy Roosevelt, who managed to win 88 electoral votes (about 17 percent of the electoral vote total) after he created the Bull Moose Party in an attempt to reclaim the presidency from fellow Republican William Howard Taft, with whom Roosevelt was disappointed after his single term in the White House. Then, in 1968, George Wallace was able to win 46 electoral votes in the South, running as a member of the American Independent Party on a segregationist platform. He was the last third-party candidate to win electoral votes by winning the popular vote in a state, demonstrating the difficulty for anyone to compete for the presidency outside the two major parties—especially in today's hyper-partisan climate.

Of course, the two-party system has its critics. Lee Drutman (2020), in his reform-centered book *Breaking the Two-Party Doom Loop: The Case for Multiparty Democracy in America*, argues that for decades, the United States *was* a four-party system masquerading as a two-party system in which liberal Democrats, conservative Democrats, liberal Republicans, and conservative Republicans all coalesced into two separate Democratic and Republican parties. These four different parties were able to build more unique bipartisan coalitions that responded more broadly to pressing issues of the day rather than being constrained by the Republican or Democratic label attached to them. Instead, liberal Democrats were able to forge coalitions with liberal

Republicans and conservative Democrats with conservative Republicans. Drutman (2020) argues this is largely due to the rise of culture war politics, a more unified messaging strategy from the parties, and a more top-down approach to committee and subcommittee work.

In addition to this recognition that American party history may have had a feel of a multiparty system while still remaining an outwardly two-party system, other critiques of the two-party system abound. Multiparty democracy diversifies representation and increases voter turnout. Drutman (2020, 209) writes,

> In a diverse country, just two parties can't possibly come anywhere close to representing that diversity. More parties can better represent a meaningful range of political views. And when voters are better represented, they are happier and more engaged.

When we examine the elected leaders of the United States, we can see a severe lack of diversity. In fact, of the 45 different presidents we have had, all of them have been male, and only one has been non-white. There is ample evidence that multiparty systems (which tend to rely on proportional representation) do a better job at electing minorities to public office (Bowler, Farrell, and Pettitt 2005; Canon 1999). Further, studies of proportional representation systems find that multiparty systems, when compared with two-party systems, do indeed lead to increased voter turnout (Eggers 2015; Karp and Banducci 1999; Selb 2009). And when we look at turnout rates in the United States, it is hard to argue that they are impressive (DeSilver 2018). Finally, there is evidence that two-party systems have more negative and less policy-focused campaigns. Negative campaigning likely cannot be eliminated altogether, though many Americans complain about the negativity in electoral campaigns (see Jamieson 2000). While there is evidence that voters can learn from *some* of this negativity (Mattes and Redlawsk 2015), it is a difficult balancing act for candidates, as negative campaigning can also turn voters off and create a toxic campaign environment (Ansolabehere and Iyengar 1995; Ansolabehere et al. 1994; Lau, Sigelman, and Rovner 2007). Minimizing the negativity of campaigns seems like an important goal and one that multiparty systems tend to do better at than two-party systems due to the necessary coalition-building that comes with it (Elmelend-Praestekaer 2008). Instead of attacking one another, candidates in multiparty systems tend to focus more on their policy differences to differentiate themselves for the voters (Drutman 2020). While the purpose here is not to advocate for a multiparty system over the current two-party structure, it suffices to say that while preserving the two-party system may be seen as a benefit of the Electoral College by some, it is clearly not seen that way by all.

## CONCLUSIONS

At the time of the Constitutional Convention, it was clear that the Founders truly did believe, as Madison wrote, that the Electoral College was indeed "excellent." They debated presidential selection over the course of the entire Convention, held over 30 votes on the matter, and forged a compromise selection method that they thought would properly balance the popular will with the knowledge of national needs among the more politically attentive and active citizens of the day. The Founders believed that the Electoral College would take into account the public's will since the public was able to choose the electors. Additionally, they believed that these electors would be more aware of, and attentive to, the needs of the nation as a whole, ensuring the president chosen would truly be up to the job. The Founders also believed that the Electoral College was better than the alternatives (selection by the legislature or by popular vote) in preventing "tumult and disorder" in the presidential selection process; they also thought it was best at guarding against corruption and cabal. Finally, they believed that the Electoral College was the best way to ensure the separation of powers between the executive and legislative branches.

Over time, the defenses of the Electoral College have evolved to include other matters. Of these more modern defenses, the biggest is the preservation of the federalist ideal: making sure small, less populated states are not overpowered by larger, more populous states. Modern Electoral College defenders also argue that it forces candidates to compete nationwide and build broad winning coalitions, whereas its elimination would free up candidates to simply compete in the most heavily populated areas. Some also argue that the Electoral College helps maintain a more deliberative decision-making process while also ensuring that any sort of problem or accusation of fraud is contained to a state (or just a few states) rather than turning into a countrywide problem. The Electoral College also ensures that the winner receives a majority of support (at least in electoral votes), signaling a clear and decisive winner. Finally, defenders point to the preservation of the two-party system as a strength of the Electoral College.

Given the technological advances since the late eighteenth century, many of the benefits pointed to by the Founders cease to be benefits of this particular setup. Reading through the discussions and debates that were had at the Convention, it is clear that many in attendance would have supported the president being selected by popular vote if it were practical at the time.

However, that was not the case. The Founders were likely correct in their assumption that most people would have been focused not on issues of national importance but on issues of state importance at the time. Today, however, it is clear that if a voter is ignorant of the news of the day, it is not by happenstance but by choice. Technology allows us to get instantaneous news updates on our cellphones that hardly ever leave our hands—something unthinkable in the late 1780s. Capturing the public's opinion on presidential candidates is much more practical today than it has ever been. And in terms of the Founders' concerns about cabal, corruption, tumult, and disorder, the 2016 and 2020 elections clearly point out that all of these things can happen even with the Electoral College in place.

As for the more modern justifications of the Electoral College, these are largely indefensible as well. The Founders did not count federalism among the great strengths of the Electoral College. Sure, they wanted to ensure that small states were not overpowered by large states, but they were more focused on how to balance the national needs with the public will while also preserving the separation of powers, rather than state interests—at least in terms of how to best select a president. Additionally, democratic principles dictate that every vote counts the same; in other words, nobody's vote should be worth more because of which state they live in. The current structure of the Electoral College privileges the votes of residents of less populous states, making them worth more than votes from those who reside in more populous states—a clear violation of democratic norms. The Supreme Court has even stepped in to verify that elected officials are selected to represent people, not land, underscoring even more the anti-democratic nature of the Electoral College. While federalism is indeed an important component of the structure of American government, it was not part of the original justification for the Electoral College. It is, indeed, a rewriting of history to make such an assertion.

Presidential elections will also always be fought on battlegrounds. Under the Electoral College, those battlegrounds are states, and should the Electoral College be reformed, those battlegrounds may move to cities rather than states. But, regardless of where those battlegrounds are, there will still be many areas that receive less attention than these battlegrounds. The Electoral College is also no longer the deliberative body it was once designed to be. The unit rule binds electors to the state's popular vote (at least in 32 states and the District of Columbia), precluding them from even entertaining the thought of meaningful debate over each candidate's pros and cons. While these electors regularly hand the president a majority of support, that majority of support does not always align with the majority of actual voters. There have now been two elections within the past 22 years in which the Electoral College handed the presidency to a candidate who did not win even a plurality of voters nationwide. So while that may be seen by some as a clear and decisive victory, it is a victory that seems to violate the democratic norms and principles that U.S. citizens have come to appreciate. Finally, preserving the two-party system is not seen as a benefit to all voters. Some voters would prefer a multiparty system. And many voters view voting for a third party as a waste of a vote, despite actually agreeing more with that third party than with the candidate they actually voted for.

So, while each of these benefits has some merit to it, it is clear that none of them should prevent discussion of Electoral College reform. They should also not stand in the way of taking action toward reforming this archaic institution. I'll conclude by quoting those appointed to the American Political Science Association's committee on political parties:

> Support for needed change comes from understanding of the change needed. If the case for change is conclusive, it makes no sense to ignore it stubbornly. To magnify the risk of change out of proportion is to urge equally or more risky inertia. Doing nothing is no help when something ought to be done. (APSA 1950)

In order to understand the change needed in the Electoral College, it is important to acknowledge the benefits pointed to by its defenders. However, to point to these benefits and throw up our hands and ask what can be done to fix the problems in spite of these benefits is wrong. The problems with the Electoral College vastly outweigh the benefits pointed to by its proponents. It is these problems that will be the focus of the next chapter.

# *Chapter 3*

# 700 Attempts at Reform

## *Examining the Drawbacks of the Electoral College*

Over 700 proposals to reform the Electoral College have been introduced in Congress since the adoption of the Constitution. While the Founders believed their creation to be "excellent," it is clear that many legislators over the course of American history did not agree, else 700 proposals would not have been needed to try to reform the Electoral College. Not all of these proposals were researched, given a full hearing, or a vote, but based on the sheer number of proposals for reform, it is clear that over the past 250 years, many national legislators found the Electoral College problematic enough to offer ideas for reform. While the 2000 and 2016 presidential elections renewed calls for reform, these reforms are hardly new. In fact, one of the very first—and I'd argue one of the most unique—proposals for reforming the presidential selection process came in 1808 from Senator James Hillhouse of Connecticut. Hillhouse was a Federalist and concerned, as many of the Founders were, about the dangers of political parties. His solution was to not just revise the presidential selection process but the term length of senators as well. He proposed that senators would be appointed to three-year terms, with one-third of the Senate retiring annually. Of the retiring senators, each would draw a ball out of a box, all of which but one would be white. The Senator that drew the colored ball would be named president for one year, at which point the process would be repeated (Peirce 1968). Needless to say, this reform plan was not enacted.

To say that all possible revisions to the presidential selection process have been discussed seems an understatement. Hillhouse's proposal that we essentially pick the president by random draw out of a hat was never actually discussed as a legitimate proposal. However, several proposals for reform have been put forward, from completely abolishing the Electoral College and instituting a direct popular vote to keeping the Electoral College but changing the rules about how electoral votes are allocated. These reform plans have been offered because of the many problems associated with the Electoral College. First, I will discuss some of the problems highlighted by the Antifederalists at the time of constitutional ratification and then turn to more modern concerns about the Electoral College. Most of the concerns raised by Antifederalists revolve around the idea that the public should have a voice in presidential selection. To place this process in the hands of those who could violate the public will was thought unwise by these Founders. More modern concerns about the Electoral College revolve around the same concerns, though today we have plenty of evidence to demonstrate that the country is better prepared for a national election than it may have been in 1787. Today, we also have several examples of elections in which the public will was undermined by the Electoral College—something the Antifederalists did not have. We also have evidence, in the wake of the 2020 election, of the corruption and abuse of power that could be used by the president to obscure the validity of the electoral vote. Finally, I will conclude this chapter by discussing some of the attempts by Congress to reform the Electoral College along with a timeline of those attempts. This timeline perspective really underscores the ongoing debate surrounding the Electoral College and the persistent push to reform this archaic institution into something more in line with democratic norms and values.

## ANTIFEDERALIST ARGUMENTS AGAINST THE ELECTORAL COLLEGE

Most of the concerns the Antifederalists raised in objection to the Electoral College centered on the fact that the president is not popularly elected. This lack of public input on who the president should be led to concerns about unknown statesmen voting on the public's behalf as well as the potential for corruption and abuse of power. These concerns were outlined in *Antifederalist No. 72*, appearing in *The Kentucky Gazette* on March 1, 1788—approximately two weeks prior to the publication of *Federalist No. 68*, the Federalist defense of the Electoral College discussed in the previous chapter. A summary of these arguments can be found in table 3.1, though a discussion of the arguments is what we now turn to.

### The Trouble with Unknown Proxy Voters

The Antifederalists did not refer to electors as proxy voters per se but raised several objections to the idea that the president would be elected by an electoral middleman rather than the citizenry itself. Republicus (1788), the pseudonym used by the author of *Antifederalist No. 72*, writes,

**Table 3.1 Antifederalist Objections to the Electoral College from *Antifederalist No. 72***

- Citizens need to relinquish their right to vote to others on their behalf
- No guarantee that citizens will know who the electors are
- Contingent election procedure removes all citizen input and places executive selection in the hands of the legislature
- President can easily use their power to make presidency hereditary and follow personal ambitions due to lack of public accountability
- Without public accountability or term limits, the president is apt to absorb legislative power with help of oligarchical Senate and give us "law at the bayonet's point"

*Source*: Table created by the author.

> Is it then become necessary, that a free people should first resign their right of suffrage into other hands besides their own, and then, secondly, that they to whom they resign it should be compelled to choose men, whose persons, characters, manners, or principles they know nothing of?

The concern raised here by Republicus is thus twofold: (1) citizens must give up their right to vote while entrusting electors with the duty of presidential selection, and (2) there is a good chance that the citizens are not going to know who the electors are.

While the president is not the only federal official, the presidency was designed to be the sole nationally accountable office of the United States. The House of Representatives was to be made up of individuals who represented their respective district concerns; they were to be directly elected by the citizens of those districts and accountable to them. The House was also the chamber that would be closest to the people and thus the most responsive to public opinion. The Senate, on the other hand, was designed to represent the concerns of the state; senators were originally appointed to their positions by state legislatures and thus not necessarily accountable or responsive to public opinion. James Madison argued that the Senate should explicitly guard against the "fickleness and passion" that may consume the House, stating, "A necessary fence against this danger would be to select a portion of enlightened citizens, whose limited number, and firmness may seasonably interpose against impetuous counsels" (Farrand 1937, vol. 1, p. 422). The president, however, was supposed to be a national leader, an individual who carried out policies that were best for the nation as a whole. To that end, many Founders argued the president should be accountable to the entire nation (Farrand 1937, vol. 1). Some, like Roger Sherman, argued the president should be accountable and chosen by the legislature, since he believed the president's sole responsibility should be carrying out the policies enacted by the legislative body. This argument, however, failed to gain traction among many of the convention attendees.

Upon deciding that the president should mainly be focused on issues of national importance, it would make sense to choose an election mechanism that guarantees the president is chosen by the nation. The Electoral College, as demonstrated by Republicus, fails to do this. Sure, an argument can be made that the individual states combined make up the entirety of the nation. However, the initial design of the Electoral College fails to do so. The Antifederalists are correct here: the Electoral College forces the citizenry at large to forfeit their voting rights to intermediary electors. Under the Electoral College system today, in which a popular vote is conducted, yes, the citizenry of a state determines how those states' electoral votes are allocated, but that still does not mean that the public will determine the winner, as we have now seen five elections in which the popular vote winner did not become president.

The big question in response to this, of course, is whether or not this is actually problematic. I, and several other researchers, argue that it is (Alexander 2019; Edwards 2004; Wegman 2020). It is problematic that a plurality of American citizens can vote for candidate A, but candidate B becomes president. As discussed in chapter 2, there is nothing that prevents the United States from conducting a national election today—the technology is available. Citizens have the capability to become educated on the issues and candidates if they desire. A review of the notes from the Constitutional Convention clearly conveys that many of the Founders actually supported the popular election of the president, except that they found it impractical. That is no longer the case; a national popular vote is possible—in fact, it is conducted every four years, we just use a different metric to determine the winner of the presidency.

Robert Dahl (1998, 37–38), one of the foremost thinkers on democracy, outlines five criteria by which we should evaluate the democratic process: effective participation, voting equality, enlightened understanding, agenda control, and inclusion of adults. According to Dahl's criteria, we should all be able to make our opinions known on policy; everyone's vote should count the same; we should be able to understand the issue(s) up for debate (including relevant alternatives) and their likely consequences; we (as a society) should have control over what policy items are placed on the agenda; and all adult residents should have the ability to participate. For Dahl, the importance of democracy revolves around political equality: everyone in society must be equal politically; violating any of the five criteria he lays out infringes on political equality (Dahl 1998). These five criteria are thus necessary conditions for democracy, implying that violating just one of them prohibits democratic rule.

Keeping these in mind when thinking about the structure of the Electoral College, it is easy to see that the Electoral College is prohibitive of democracy for the very reasons mentioned in *Antifederalist No. 72*, specifically that citizens forfeit the right to select the president in favor of unknown electors. When voting for president, many voters walk into the voting booth and select one candidate over the others, not thinking at all that after their ballot is counted with all the others from their respective state, a slate of electors will be sent to the state Capitol in mid-December to cast their official vote for president, all the while making that individual's single ballot largely meaningless. The ballots cast within a state determine that state's popular vote winner and thus which slate of electors gets sent to the state Capitol, but that is it. Thus, we do not have truly effective participation, as popular votes are only valued in their particular state, not nationally. Further, because not all states have the same population, we do not have voting equality. As will be more fully discussed in chapter 5, not all states' electoral votes are equal. Each of Wyoming's electoral votes represents roughly 194,000 residents, while each of California's electoral votes represents approximately 715,500 residents. This can hardly be considered voting equality. Finally, not all adults are included in the presidential election process. As I will discuss in much more detail in the following chapter, it is much more difficult for some U.S. citizens to cast a ballot than others. So, upon examination of the first concern of the Antifederalists, we are indeed made to forfeit our voting rights to electors. And this forfeiture of voting rights easily violates three of Dahl's five conditions for democracy, meaning that the Electoral College is incongruous with democratic principles.

Republicus also raised the problem of voters not knowing who the electors are. This is as true today as it has ever been. In fact, it might be truer today than it was when the Constitution was drafted. The Founders wanted the electors to be prominent statesmen, citizens who were aware, known, and attentive to political issues. Hamilton says as much in *Federalist No. 68* when he writes,

> The immediate election should be made by men most capable of analyzing the qualities adapted to the state, and acting under circumstances favorable to deliberation, and to a judicious combination of all the reasons and inducements which were proper to govern their choice. (Yale Law School 2008)

The appointment of electors varies by state, as the Founders delegated to the state legislatures the ability to determine how electors would be appointed. The Founders did not list any explicit qualifications for electors but wanted them to be among the most educated and politically aware citizens of a state. That is partially the case today. Robert Alexander (2012) conducted a survey of presidential electors and found that they were more likely to hold high school and college degrees and were much more politically active than the average American. The main difference between the electors of the eighteenth century and today is that today's electors are much more partisan. Alexander (2019) finds that 75 percent of electors had previously held an elective party position. Table 3.2 highlights why this may be the case. If we look at how electors are chosen, it is not difficult to discern why they have gotten more partisan over time: a majority of states allow the parties to pick their electors, either through the party's state convention or central committee. Party service and loyalty are thus rather important factors in elector selection. Additionally, only seven states actually include the names of electors on the ballot, so the voters of 43 states and Washington, D.C., do not actually know the names of the electors for which they are technically voting. Ultimately, all of this highlights the fact that the Antifederalists were correct: a system in which citizens surrender their right to vote to a group of unknown proxy voters does not align well with democratic norms and values.

## Contingent Election Blurs Separation of Powers

Next on the list of concerns among Antifederalists was the contingent election process decided upon by those at the Constitutional Convention. Should a candidate not receive a majority vote in the Electoral College, the House of Representatives will choose the president and the Senate will choose the vice president. The House will require each state delegation to cast a vote rather than each individual Representative; each Representative will get to cast a ballot, but the plurality winner within each state's delegation will receive that state's vote. In the Senate, each senator will get to vote individually for vice president, not as part of a state delegation. Regardless, in order to win the presidency or vice presidency, a candidate must win a majority, so in a contingency scenario, a presidential candidate must receive 26 votes and a vice presidential candidate must receive 51 votes in order to win office.

So, what is wrong with the contingent election procedure? "To entrust Congress with the final decision at last? Is it necessary, is it rational, that the sacred rights of mankind should thus dwindle down to Electors of electors, and those again electors of other electors" (Republicus 1788)? Basically, the problem with the contingent election is that it is even worse than the Electoral College, especially in light of Dahl's (1998) criteria for democracy. Relying on Congress to select the leader of the executive branch requires a complete forfeiture of the citizenry's voting rights along with thevoting rights of the electors. Importantly, we have one example of an election in which a contingency election was needed: the presidential election of 1824. The popular vote plurality was won by Andrew Jackson, as was the electoral vote plurality. Yet neither Jackson nor any of the four major contenders for the presidency were able to secure a majority of support, thus, a contingent election was needed. John C. Calhoun was able to secure a majority vote in his

**Table 3.2 How States Choose Electors and Whether Electors' Names Appear on Ballot**

| *State* | *How Choose Electors* | *Electors on Ballot?* |
|---|---|---|
| Alabama | Political Party Organization | Unnamed (at large) |
| Alaska | Political Party Organization | Unnamed (at large) |
| Arizona | Political Party Primary Election | Named (at large) |
| Arkansas | Political Party State Convention | Unnamed (at large) |
| California | Political Party | Unnamed (at large) |
| Colorado | Political Party State Convention | Unnamed (at large) |
| Connecticut | Political Party State Convention | Unnamed (at large) |
| District of Columbia | Political Party Central Committee | Unnamed (at large) |
| Delaware | Political Party State Convention | Unnamed (at large) |
| Florida | Political Party Central Committee | Unnamed (at large) |
| Georgia | Political Party Organization | Unnamed (at large) |
| Hawaii | Political Party State Convention | Unnamed (at large) |
| Idaho | Political Party State Convention | Named (at large) |
| Illinois | Political Party State Convention | Unnamed (at large) |
| Indiana | Political Party State Convention | Unnamed (at large) |
| Iowa | Political Party Central Committee | Unnamed (at large) |
| Kansas | Political Party Central Committee | Unnamed (at large) |
| Kentucky | Political Party State Convention | Unnamed (at large) |
| Louisiana | Political Party Organization | Named (at large) |
| Maine | Political Party State Convention | Unnamed (1 per congressional district and 2 at large) |
| Maryland | Political Party Organization | Unnamed (at large) |
| Massachusetts | Political Party Central Committee | Unnamed (at large) |
| Michigan | Political Party State Convention | Unnamed (at large) |
| Minnesota | Political Party State Convention | Unnamed (at large) |
| Mississippi | Political Party State Convention (nomination) Primary Election (choice) | Unnamed (at large) |
| Missouri | Political Party Central Committee | Unnamed (at large) |
| Montana | Political Party Organization | Unnamed (at large) |

(*Continued*)

**Table 3.2 Continued**

| *State* | *How Choose Electors* | *Electors on Ballot?* |
|---|---|---|
| Nebraska | Political Party State Convention | Unnamed (1 per congressional district and 2 at large) |
| Nevada | Political Party State Convention | Unnamed (at large) |
| New Hampshire | Political Party State Convention | Unnamed (at large) |
| New Jersey | Political Party State Convention (or central committee) | Unnamed (at large) |
| New Mexico | Political Party State Convention | Unnamed (at large) |
| New York | Political Party Central Committee | Unnamed (at large) |
| North Carolina | Political Party State Convention | Unnamed (at large) |
| North Dakota | Political Party State Convention | Named (at large) |
| Ohio | Political Party State Convention | Unnamed (at large) |
| Oklahoma | Political Party State Convention | Named (at large) |
| Oregon | Political Party Organization | Unnamed (at large) |
| Pennsylvania | Political Party Presidential Nominee | Unnamed (at large) |
| Rhode Island | Political Party State Convention | Named (at large) |
| South Carolina | Political Party Central Committee | Unnamed (at large) |
| South Dakota | Political Party State Convention | Named (at large) |
| Tennessee | Political Party Organization | Named Individually (at large) |
| Texas | Political Party Organization | Unnamed (at large) |
| Utah | Political Party Organization | Unnamed (at large) |
| Vermont | Political Party State Convention | Unnamed (at large) |
| Virginia | Political Party State Convention | Unnamed (at large) |
| Washington | Political Party Organization | Unnamed (at large) |
| West Virginia | Political Party State Convention | Unnamed (at large) |
| Wisconsin | Political Party (state legislative candidates and state officers) | Unnamed (at large) |
| Wyoming | Political Party State Convention | Unnamed (at large) |

*Source*: The National Archives.

quest for the vice presidency, so a contingent election in the Senate was not needed. So, the House had to choose among Andrew Jackson, John Quincy Adams, and William Crawford—Henry Clay was eliminated from contention as he finished fourth in the electoral vote, and the 12th Amendment limits the House to choosing among the top three finishers. However, Clay disliked Jackson and had significant policy differences with Crawford, so he used his power and influence as Speaker of the House to push Representatives toward Adams over Jackson and Crawford. Ultimately, Adams emerged victorious, receiving 13 votes compared with Jackson's seven and Crawford's four (13 were needed to secure a majority, as there were 24 states at the time). Thus, the constitutional process was followed, but neither the popular nor electoral vote plurality winner became president, highlighting even more so the fact that this process requires the forfeiture of voting rights among the citizenry.

The main problem with the contingent election process is that it clearly violates the separation of powers between the legislative and executive branches. As discussed in chapter 2, several delegates to the Constitutional Convention were supportive of allowing the legislature to select the president. Roger Sherman was one of the most vocal supporters of placing executive selection in the hands of the national legislature–he argued that should the choice be left to the people, they

> will never be sufficiently informed of characters, and besides will never give a majority of votes to any one man. They will generally vote for some man in their own State, and the largest State will have the best chance for the appointment (Farrand 1937, vol. II, p. 29)

So for Sherman, executive selection by the legislature would prevent the large states from monopolizing the executive. However, Sherman and some of his allies were also of the belief that the executive should be completely subservient to the legislature. The president, they argued, existed simply to rightly execute the laws passed by the legislature. This view of the executive, however, clearly did not win out at the Convention, with the executive given several explicit powers.

In contrast to Sherman, many Convention delegates were wary of legislative selection of the president as it not only blurs, but completely erases, the separation of power between the two branches—something a majority of delegates felt was important. Gouverneur Morris, for one, argued that

> If the Legislature elect, it will be the work of intrigue, of cabal, and of faction; it will be like the election of a pope by a conclave of cardinals; real merit will rarely be the title to the appointment. (Farrand 1937, vol II, p. 29)

George Mason was in agreement with these concerns, especially for presidents wanting to be reelected, arguing that in order to secure reelection, presidents would largely perform however the legislature wanted them to. Ironically, even Alexander Hamilton, author of *Federalist No. 68*, which defends the Electoral College, writes in that very paper that allowing the national legislature to select the president is problematic. He states,

> They have not made the appointment of the President to depend on any pre-existing bodies of men, who might be tampered with beforehand to prostitute their votes . . . And they have excluded from eligibility to this trust, all those who from situation might be suspected of too great devotion to the President in office. No senator, representative, or other person holding a place of trust or profit under the United States, can be of the number of electors. (Hamilton 1788)

So, based on Hamilton's writing, it is clear that the Founders had deep concerns about the potential for cabal and corruption should the legislature pick the president. Yet, the contingent election places the choice of president and vice president directly in the hands of the legislature. The defense offered of this is that the Electoral College would winnow the candidates Congress could choose from. So this would allow Congress to select both the president and vice president, but it would not give members of Congress free reign over which candidates to consider. Overall, allowing the legislature to select the president still keeps voters from participating in the election of the president, despite the president being a nationally accountable official. Additionally, today's hyper-partisan behavior in Congress makes it all the more likely that Congress will vote strictly along party lines, without serious debate over which candidate is best suited for office. Importantly, it also raises concerns about gerrymandering, which will be discussed in more detail in chapters 4 and 5.

## Presidency Could Become a Hereditary Monarchy

Abuse of power was also high on the list of concerns among Antifederalists. Specifically, abuse of power by a president that was not chosen by the citizenry at large, but rather by a group of statesmen that had no real check on that power.

> Is it not probable, at least possible, that the president who is to be vested with all this demiomnipotence [*sic*]—who is not chosen by the community; and who consequently, as to them, is irresponsible and independent—that he, I say, by a few artful and dependent emissaries in Congress, may not only perpetuate his own personal administration, but also make it hereditary? (Republicus 1788).

The concerns raised here signal the possibility that the presidency (originally established without term limits) could be turned into an hereditary position with the help of a few congressional allies of the president. While Hamilton and the Federalists believed this would be prevented, as Congress would not have a role in presidential selection, except for the possibility of a contingent election, the Antifederalists pointed to the fact that should the president be able to build alliances with members of Congress, they could ensure passage of legislation, the appointment of particular officials and military officers, and exert extensive military control that would preserve presidential power and, more importantly, allow the president to preserve his seat of power. By preventing the citizenry at large from having a role in presidential selection, they argued that this becomes very difficult to check. And while this seems like a far-fetched idea, the 2020 presidential election highlights all too clearly the possibility of such actions.

On January 6, 2021, the United States watched in real time while the president encouraged armed protesters to break up Congress' Constitutional duty to certify the count of electoral votes. Electors, according to protocol, had met in their respective state capitals on December 14, 2020, to cast their official ballots for president. By the end of the day, it was reported that Joseph Biden had defeated Donald Trump by an electoral vote of 306 to 232 (Sherman 2020). Given the Electoral College protocol today, the vote is no longer a surprise—there is no real debate or discussion, just a perfunctory vote in each state Capitol by the slate of electors chosen by the state's popular vote on election day. Again, following the proper protocol, these votes were then sent to Congress, where they were to be counted by Vice President Mike Pence while he presided over a joint session of Congress on January 6, 2021. All the while, Trump had been using the presidency to message to the American public that he was the rightful winner of the 2020 presidential election and that the only reason Biden had won was due to massive voter fraud across the country. None of this, of course, was supported by actual evidence.

While Congress was preparing for the joint session, then-President Donald Trump was once more urging Vice President Mike Pence to reject the electoral votes of states with close margins of victory for then-president-elect Joe Biden. Pence, with Trump's encouragement for several weeks, had considered doing so in the run-up to the January 6 count but ultimately decided against it, as the Constitution does not give him this authority. Trump also pressured members of Congress to challenge/reject the electoral votes of these same states (namely Arizona, Georgia, Nevada, Michigan, and Pennsylvania), with enough Republican Congress members (in both chambers) banding together and challenging Arizona and Pennsylvania's votes later in the day (Sprunt 2021). That same day Trump hosted what he called the

"Stop the Steal Rally" just outside the White House, where he encouraged his supporters in attendance to march to the Capitol to stop the count of the electoral votes. Trump said, "I said something is wrong here, something is really wrong, can't have happened, and we fight. We fight like hell, and if you don't fight like hell you're not going to have a country anymore" (Trump quoted in Phillips 2022). With that, many of the rally attendees began their march to the Capitol. Once they arrived, they blew past the barricades and forced their way into the Capitol building, armed with various weaponry. Members of Congress were forced to barricade themselves in their chambers before being rushed to safety prior to these rally-goers breaking into the congressional chambers.

While this was happening, Trump did nothing but watch Fox News and tweet out encouragements to those disrupting the electoral vote count (Phillips 2022). Based on congressional investigations, hearings, and testimony, Trump was even quoted as saying, "Maybe our supporters have the right idea" in response to learning that chants of "Hang Mike Pence!" had broken out among those who broke into the Capitol building that day (Phillips 2022). After roughly three hours of insurrection in the Capitol (187 minutes to be exact), Trump released a 60-second video telling the protesters to go home, though not as forcefully as many had hoped. Trump signed off with, "Go home, we love you. You're very special" (quoted in Phillips 2020). Finally, about two hours after this video was released, the National Guard was called to the Capitol to secure the building so Congress could return to its business of certifying the electoral vote. Importantly, the National Guard was called in by Vice President Pence, not Trump. Finally, just after 3:00 am, Congress finished certifying Joseph Biden as the president-elect with 306 electoral votes, compared to Trump's 232 (exactly the numbers that had been reported on December 14, when the electors met to cast their official ballots).

I don't include this timeline of events from the January 6, 2021, electoral vote for any reason but to highlight the fact that the Antifederalists (in 1788!) were right. Presidents, with the help of a few key allies in Congress, could indeed abuse their power in an attempt to remain in power. In fact, the events of January 6, 2021, provide an exact blueprint for how to accomplish this. If the president and members of Congress were able to get a few more sympathetic state secretaries or election officials to endorse their objections, we may have seen a completely different result. For instance, if, hypothetically, the secretary of state of Georgia were in agreement with these individuals, could he have reported a different slate of electors than the one he originally did? It seems as though the answer to that question is in the affirmative. However, a majority of Congress would need to approve of the electoral votes submitted, making this situation rather uncertain. Regardless of the level of certainty we feel about the "right winner" being confirmed by Congress, the events of

January 6, 2021, highlight all too well the dangers of the current system—to say nothing about the potential of Congress to pick the executive leaders should a contingent election have been necessary.

## "Law at the Bayonet's Point"

The final objection raised by the Antifederalists in their protest of the Electoral College also concerns the potential for a president to abuse their power to solidify their position in the executive office. Republicus (1788) writes:

> He [the president] may, I say, under all these advantages and almost irresistible temptations, on some pretended pique, haughtily and contemptuously, turn our poor lower house (our only shadow of liberty we shall have left) out of doors, and give us law at the bayonet's point. Or, may not the senate . . . erect themselves into an oligarchy . . . ? To one of which channels, or rather to a confluence of both, we seem to be fast gliding away; and the moment we arrive at it—farewell liberty.

The Antifederalists, again, raised concern about a president abusing their power in order to remain in office, but more importantly, they talked about more than just the president remaining in office, but completely ignoring the House and the Senate deciding to work in conjunction with the president. In that scenario, the public would be able to do nothing in response, as neither the Senate nor the president were elected by the people. The president—elected by the Electoral College—and the Senate—appointed by the various state legislatures—originally had no public accountability. So, if the public were upset with the behavior of either of these bodies, there was little public recourse that could be taken.

This seems like a bit of a far-fetched concern today given the 22nd Amendment limiting the president to two terms in office; however, we once again have an example from the Trump administration. Over the course of his four years in office, Donald Trump was no stranger to outrageous statements uttered with little or no planning. Several times, he mentioned deserving a third term as president. At a rally in Oshkosh, WI, Trump stated, "We are going to win four more years. And then after that, we'll go for another four years because they spied on my campaign. We should get a redo of four years" (Cillizza 2020). Obviously, Trump cannot unilaterally change the Constitution and stay in office past his two terms. Nor is there any "redo" option in the 22nd Amendment. However, there would have been very little that could have been done if Congress were willing to pass an amendment repealing the 22nd Amendment, sending it to the states to be ratified. Trump clearly would have signed the bill, leaving the potential for a repeal of the 22nd Amendment in the hands of the states. Admittedly, this is an unlikely scenario, as this hypothetical amendment would not have the requisite two-thirds majority support in Congress, nor would it have the support of three-fourths of the states. But it is a pathway that likely would have been pursued by Trump had he been able to stay in office past his first term.

More importantly, in-line with the concerns raised by the Antifederalists, staying in power would have been much easier prior to the adoption of term limits. In fact, many early Americans were surprised to learn of George Washington's decision to step down after only two terms—there's even an entire song dedicated to Alexander Hamilton's surprise in Lin-Manuel Miranda's musical *Hamilton*. Washington was an incredibly popular military general, credited with helping America win its independence, so if he wanted to remain president for as long as he liked, he likely could have. This, obviously, is a hypothetical. But, looking at the presidency of Franklin D. Roosevelt, he was easily able to get elected to four terms (I say easily because his lowest margin of victory was 7.5 percent). Roosevelt was nationally popular, was able to successfully pass legislation through Congress, and led the country through World War II and the Great Depression. Franklin D. Roosevelt is our only example of a president holding office for more than two terms, and after he died shortly into his fourth term, Congress passed (and the states ratified) the 22nd Amendment, ensuring he was the only president to do so. It is easy to see how easy it could have been for a president to amass a following that would have allowed them to remain in office for as long as they wanted. Trump was never as popular or accomplished as FDR, but he was able to put together a loyal core group of supporters, both among voters and Republican members of Congress, that would have supported him no matter what. So, prior to the passage of the 22nd Amendment, it is easy to understand the Antifederalists' concerns about a president amassing power, abusing that power, and giving us law "at the bayonet's point."

## CONTEMPORARY CONCERNS WITH THE ELECTORAL COLLEGE

While the Antifederalists raised several rightful concerns about the Electoral College, some of which are less concerning today than when they were initially raised, unsurprisingly, more concerns have been raised since the Constitution was ratified. Importantly, an adjustment was made in response to the election of 1800, in which Thomas Jefferson and Aaron Burr tied in the electoral vote. The Democratic-Republicans had intended to select Jefferson as president and Burr as vice president, but failed to give Jefferson one more vote than Burr. As a result, the House was tasked with selecting which man would be awarded the presidency: Jefferson or Burr. After 36 rounds of

**Table 3.3 Summary of Contemporary Criticism of the Electoral College**

- Faithless Electors Defying the Will of their State
- Contingent Election Still Blurs Separation of Powers
- National Campaign is Nonexistent
- Winner of the Popular Vote Still Loses Sometimes
- Encourages Political Inequality Through Small State Bias and Winner-Take-All Vote Allocation

*Source*: Table compiled by the author.

balloting, the House finally selected Jefferson to be president, who quickly urged Congress to take up an amendment that would clarify separate votes for president and vice president. In response, the 12th Amendment was passed and ratified, making it clear that each elector would cast two separate ballots: one for president and one for vice president. This was all completed prior to the 1804 election so as to avoid the confusion associated with the 1800 election. It was also the last time an amendment was passed clarifying any problems with the Electoral College. Unsurprisingly, then, concerns and criticisms persist. These more contemporary criticisms can be found in table 3.3.

## Faithless Electors

Faithless electors are those who do not vote in line with their state's popular vote; instead, they vote for a candidate whom they, personally, believe would make the best president. We currently have no examples of a faithless elector or group of faithless electors derailing the expected result of an election. However, as Gaines (2016) points out, this is not a possibility we can rule out. Given the state of technology today, it would be easy for an elector to reach out to other electors should they have concerns about a presidential candidate. As discussed in chapter 2, there was a "Hamilton electors" movement in 2016 where a Democratic elector tried to rally other electors to support John Kasich over Hillary Clinton and Donald Trump. While Michael Baca was not opposed to Clinton (he was, after all, a pledged Clinton elector), he believed that it would fall on Democratic electors to agree to support a "moderate" Republican over Donald Trump in the electoral vote. Baca believed that Trump would make a dangerous president and was the very epitome of the dangers the Founders warned about when they wrote about potential corruption, cabal, and abuse of power (Wegman 2020). Additionally, he believed that Democratic electors would need to join with Republican electors in solidarity to defeat Trump and select Kasich as president, as Republicans were unlikely to support Clinton—a well-known, mostly reviled (among Republican voters) member of the Democratic establishment. So, if the goal was to stop a Trump presidency, Democratic and Republican electors would need to band together in opposition and cast faithless ballots in favor of John Kasich.

Baca's efforts to select Kasich over Trump and Clinton ultimately failed, and Donald Trump became the 45th president of the United States. However, this brief scenario highlights how a bit of coordination among electors could ultimately derail a presidential election and select a candidate for whom no one actually voted. It is this very scenario that has caused centuries of concern and consternation over the potential for faithless electors. Attempts have been made to prevent faithless electors: amendments have been debated (more on these later in the chapter), state laws have been passed to bind electors to state popular vote totals, and the Supreme Court has even weighed in on the potential for faithless electors. Currently, 32 states plus the District of Columbia have laws requiring electors to vote in-line with their state's popular vote results, thus removing the free will of the electors in each of these states—in clear violation of the intention of the Founders. Indeed, as Edwards (2004, 25–26) points out, these laws that bind electors raise serious constitutional questions, as the Constitution seems to say that these electors are "free agents." The idea that these electors should be able to act as free agents is confirmed by both the *Federalist Papers* along with the records kept at the Constitutional Convention (see Farrand 1937).

The Supreme Court, however, weighed in on the issue of faithless electors in 1952. Edmund Blair was a Democratic elector from Alabama who refused to sign a pledge to support the Democratic nominee for president and vice president should his slate of electors be chosen via popular vote in the upcoming election. So, if Alabama voted for Adlai Stevenson and John Sparkman for president and vice president, respectively, the pledge would have required Blair to vote for that ticket. Upon his refusal to sign the pledge, Ben Ray refused to certify Blair as a Democratic elector, part of his job duties as Chairman of the Alabama Executive Committee of the Democratic Party. Upset by this, Blair took legal action against Ray, ultimately resulting in a Supreme Court ruling in favor of Ray. In the majority opinion for *Ray v. Blair*, the Supreme Court ruled that parties are free to require pledges of electors as a way to ensure that general election candidates are in-line with the philosophy and leadership of the party (*Ray v. Blair* 343 U.S. 214 (1952)). However, what the court did not mention is what, if anything, could happen should an elector violate that pledge. So, parties are able to require their electors to sign a pledge supporting their nominee, but it is unclear whether or not the state or the party would have any recourse if an elector violated such a pledge. In his dissent, Justice Robert Jackson wrote,

> No one faithful to our history can deny that the plan originally contemplated what is implicit in its text–that electors would be free agents, to exercise an

> independent and nonpartisan judgment as to the men best qualified for the Nation's highest office. (*Ray v. Blair,* 343 U.S. 214 (1952))

However, in 2020, the Supreme Court once again weighed in, asserting that the Constitution, as written, gives state legislatures the power to determine the manner in which electors are chosen. Simultaneously, the court underscored the fact that this power also allows states the authority, then, to require a pledge to support the statewide popular vote winner if the state so chooses (*Chiafalo v. Washington* 591 U.S. ___(2020)).

Ultimately, what we have now is a system in which people are unhappy when an elector exercises their own free will when deciding who to vote for—something electors were originally designed to do. History gives us multiple examples of faithless electors voting for candidates that were not supported by their state's popular vote. Notably, in 2000, an elector from Washington, D.C., abstained from voting for Al Gore (after Gore won the popular vote but lost the Electoral College) in an effort to draw attention to the desire for Washington, D.C., statehood. In 2016, we also saw a number of faithless electors—though none in-line with Michael Baca's quest to make John Kasich president over Donald Trump. Instead, five electors pledged to Hillary Clinton defected, with one supporting Bernie Sanders, three supporting Colin Powell, and one supporting Faith Spotted Eagle. Additionally, two electors who pledged to support Trump defected to John Kasich and Ron Paul. Three additional Clinton electors attempted to defect (including Michael Baca), but were replaced in accordance with their state's laws. The 2016 election presented us with the most faithless electors ever in a single presidential election, signaling the rarity of such actions. Again, many electors are chosen due to their loyalty and service to their party, so it is not surprising that faithless electors are few and far between. Regardless, while many see this behavior as concerning (as it does indeed violate the public will in many instances), it seems in line with how the Founders intended these electors to behave.

## Contingent Election Still a Possibility

The concerns about the contingent election process in which the House of Representatives elects the president and the Senate selects the vice president have been discussed at length previously in this chapter. These concerns do not bear repeating, but what should be highlighted is the fact that these concerns were raised before the Constitution was ratified and they still persist today. Today, the problem of gerrymandering makes the contingent election process even more concerning. The purposeful redrawing of congressional district lines to preserve and/or bolster a party's chances of retaining their seat in Congress and thus their political power is not a new phenomenon, but it has becom more of a problem in past decades.

Take, for example, Project REDMAP. Prior to the redrawing of district lines in 2010, the Republicans spent approximately $30 million—mostly in battleground and Democratic—leaning states like Pennsylvania, Wisconsin, Michigan, and Ohio—to target state-level races that would give them the majority in state legislatures. With that majority, they would be able to more effectively gerrymander legislative districts (both state and national) in their favor, thus bolstering, or at least preserving, their political power (see Daley 2017 for a full discussion of REDMAP and its effects). For example, in 2012, the Republicans were able to pick up 33 House seats, giving them the majority, despite losing the overall popular vote by roughly 1 million votes. Fast forward six years to the 2018 midterms, and we saw the Democrats pick up roughly 40 seats in the House and reclaim the majority, all of which mirrored the overall popular vote. So, gerrymandering may or may not always play a role in congressional election outcomes, as each election brings with it its own idiosyncrasies. However, should a contingent election ever be needed in today's more highly polarized climate, the impact of gerrymandering on a state's congressional delegation should not be overlooked.

## The Electoral College Makes National Campaigning Nonexistent

Yet another criticism of the Electoral College is that it requires candidates to focus on battleground states rather than running a nationalized campaign. Again, the president is the sole national official. The president is really the only elected official that is elected on a national scale, focuses on national issues, and is accountable to the entire country. However, the race for the presidency—because of the Electoral College—is run at the state level. More importantly, it is run in the battleground states while a majority of the country is ignored by the candidates running for office. Campaigns are run on limited resources, and candidates need to make strategic decisions about how and when to campaign in order to maximize both turnout as well as their vote share. So, a Republican candidate is not likely to spend a lot of time campaigning in a solidly red state, and a Democratic candidate is unlikely to spend a lot of time campaigning in a solidly blue state, as these states are already in their "win" column. Democrats are also not going to spend a lot of time trying to flip a solidly red state, and Republicans are not going to spend much time trying to flip a solidly blue state. All of the focus of both the Democratic and Republican presidential candidates is going to be on the purple battleground states (Stonecash 2016).

Edwards (2004) confirms this to be the case. He pulls together data on candidate visits and advertisements from the 2000 election, as these are two major tools candidates have with which to appeal to voters. Campaign visits are an important component to the candidate's strategy. In fact, they can serve as a way to level the playing field, as the cost of visits is not very high. Candidates with large warchests and candidates that are struggling to raise funds to continue their campaigns are both able to afford to conduct visits to appeal to voters (see Wendland 2017 for a larger discussion of campaign visit strategy). Campaign ads, on the other hand, can price out many candidates. Candidates need to purchase ad space in a variety of formats (e.g., print, television, digital) and in a variety of media markets. Additionally, the price of ad space differs by medium, by media market, and, in the case of television ads, by the date and time the ad airs. So, when we examine the data on visits and ads from the 2000 election, we get a pretty clear picture of where candidates are competing and that the campaign is not evenly spread across the entire country.

Looking specifically at the pattern of campaign visits from 2000 as presented in Edwards (2004), Delaware was the only one of the seven small states (i.e., those with just three electoral votes) to receive a visit from either major party candidate. If Washington, D.C., is counted as well since it also receives three electoral votes, it did receive five visits from Al Gore, but this was also his place of residence, so these visits were likely not as impactful or important for promoting his candidacy. The District of Columbia is also the most reliable Democratic Electoral College constituency, having voted in support of the Democratic candidate since receiving electoral votes in 1961, so it is unlikely these voters needed convincing to vote for Gore. Overall, 18 states received zero visits from either presidential candidate, and of those states, 12 failed to receive a visit from a vice presidential candidate either (Edwards 2004). Of the 30 states plus Washington, D.C. that have fewer than ten electoral votes, only one state (Iowa) received double digit visits. Iowa was a battleground state in 2000, with Gore besting Bush by roughly 0.5 percent of the popular vote there. Additional battleground states in 2000 included Tennessee, Missouri, Wisconsin, Ohio, Pennsylvania, Michigan, and Florida, all of which received more than ten visits each (some well into the twenties and thirties) (Edwards 2004). Ultimately, this highlights that candidates focus their visits on battleground states because they need to be strategic with their time and money. They are not running a national campaign, but a campaign focused on the battlegrounds of that particular election year. To ensure this was not just a fluke election year, Edwards (2004) also compiled data on visits conducted during the 1976 election (the most competitive prior to 2000) and found very similar results.

Lastly, Edwards (2004) pulls together data on advertising in the 2000 election. Advertising is regularly the largest component of campaign expenditures and is normally seen as the most important way by which candidates can reach voters. And again, looking at where the spending happened during the 2000 election, Edwards (2004) shows that the highest spending occurred in the large, battleground states of Florida, Michigan, Pennsylvania, and

Ohio. More importantly, he shows that both presidential candidates failed to run any advertisements in 35 of the 75 media markets during the entirety of the campaign (Edwards 2004). That means almost half of the country received no ads throughout the general election campaign. In sum, it seems clear that the Electoral College does not necessitate a national campaign. Instead, candidates need to be strategic with their limited time and money, so they focus that time and money on where it is most likely to have an impact: battleground states, especially those with large hauls of electoral votes. If national campaigning is the goal of presidential elections, the Electoral College system encouraging state-by-state campaigning needs to be reformed.

## The Popular Vote Winner Loses Sometimes

The most obvious criticism of the Electoral College is that the candidate who receives the most votes from the public can actually lose the election. The United States has seen 59 presidential elections, and five of them have resulted in a presidential candidate who won the popular vote but lost the Electoral College. So, almost 10 percent of our presidential elections have been won by candidates with fewer popular votes than their opponents. The election of 1824 resulted in the only contingent election that was needed, as no candidate received a majority of electoral votes. So, this is not necessarily a cut-and-dried example of a "wrong winner," but Andrew Jackson won a plurality of both popular and electoral votes but ended up not winning the contingent House election (as discussed earlier in this chapter). A clearer example of a "wrong winner" is the election of 1876, in which Rutherford B. Hayes defeated Samuel Tilden despite losing the popular vote by three percent. This election saw a dispute over electoral votes in three southern states, all of which ended up being awarded to Hayes. In 1888, the popular vote favored Grover Cleveland by roughly one percent, but Benjamin Harrison ended up winning the electoral vote. After several reputable reports of fraud, it is difficult to determine who the rightful winner should have been. The 2000 election saw Al Gore win the popular vote by roughly half a million votes but lose the Electoral College to George Bush 266–271. This was an extremely close election and one in which the Supreme Court ended up stepping in to end a Florida recount more than a month after the election was held. Finally, in 2016, Hillary Clinton bested Donald Trump by approximately three million votes but lost the electoral vote 227–304. Each of these elections will be discussed in more detail in chapter 5, but overall, in each election, we see a clear winner among the nationwide popular vote that ends up losing the electoral vote.

Now, technically, this is how the Electoral College is supposed to work. It is not a bug in the system, but a feature. The Founders wanted the electors to have discretion over who to vote for and did not want them to simply rubber stamp the popular vote results. In fact, as was discussed in the first two chapters, they did not include a popular vote in the process at all; they wanted the electors to weigh the public's will while they debated, but the Founders gave the electors full discretion over who to select as president. However, the Founder's version of the Electoral College was short-lived. The Founders left it up to each state legislature to determine how the state would select electors. Because the Founders were largely supportive of including some measure of the public will in the presidential selection process, it is unsurprising that some states very early on opted to choose electors via popular vote. Peirce (1968) tells us that even in the first four elections, two or three states used statewide popular votes to select electors. By 1836, 25 states used the statewide popular vote to choose electors, with only South Carolina holding out on allowing the public to vote on who their electors should be (Peirce 1968). Today, all states hold a popular vote by which electors are chosen. And most importantly, many of these states require their electors to pledge to vote for their state's popular vote winner, giving them no discretion whatsoever in who they will support for president. As Korzi (2016, 47) writes, "There are really two Electoral Colleges: the one that the framers' envisioned and the one that evolved basically by the middle of the nineteenth century and which we still live with today."

Ultimately, we are left with a choice. We have watched the Electoral College evolve slightly over time. It has not evolved much, but it has evolved: separate votes for president and vice president, slates of electors chosen by state popular vote, electors bound by their state's popular vote, and individual electors chosen through a variety of means, usually in reward for party loyalty or service. So, change is not impossible, but it is difficult and does not happen very often. Regardless, we should work to find a way to ensure that the popular and electoral votes align in every election. Now that the country is better equipped to conduct nationwide elections and regularly inform its citizens of political happenings, there is little reason to undermine the national popular vote. We can be relatively certain that American elections are conducted fairly on a regular basis and that American citizens have several options through which to get their political information. So, to prevent the nationwide popular vote winner from taking office because their voters are not properly distributed throughout the country violates the values of democracy on which our country was founded (Dahl 2003, 89).

## The Electoral College Breeds Political Inequality

Finally, the Electoral College brings with it a number of political inequalities. It contains within it the small state bias, the winner-take-all system does little to support feelings of political efficacy, and it has racist origins. The small state bias and winner-take-all system will be discussed in much more detail in chapter 5, and the racial problems and history of the Electoral College will be the focus of the following chapter, so I will just briefly introduce these ideas now. The small state bias is due to the fact that small states (those with three or four electoral votes) are overrepresented in the Electoral College while those more heavily populated states (e.g., California, Texas) are underrepresented. Take, for example, Alaska and Texas. Alaska has three electoral votes and a population of roughly 737,000 people, while Texas has 38 electoral votes and a population of 28.64 million people. That means each of Alaska's electoral votes represents approximately 246,000 people, while each of Texas' votes represents approximately 754,000 people. This is clearly problematic.

The winner-take-all allocation of electoral votes leaves voters who supported the losing candidate feeling as though their votes do not matter, decreasing their feelings of political efficacy. Democratic voters in reliably red states and Republican voters in reliably blue states regularly feel disenfranchised from the electorate. Feeling disconnected from the political system lowers turnout, which can lead to elected leaders appearing out of touch with American voters and unaware of what these voters actually care about. Depressed turnout also raises concerns for democracy, as democracy depends on citizen participation to work. The Electoral College also magnifies the margin of victory for the winning candidate, making the voters who supported the losing candidate feel even more dejected than they may have felt as a result of the popular vote. This was really highlighted in 2016, when Hillary Clinton won 48 percent of the popular vote compared to Donald Trump's 46 percent. Yet when we look at the Electoral College results, Donald Trump won 57 percent of the electoral vote compared with Clinton's 42 percent. The winner-take-all allocation of electoral votes makes Clinton voters feel even more wronged by the Electoral College, considering Clinton's three million-vote victory in the popular vote.

This electoral inequality is exacerbated by the growing partisan polarization across the country. David Hopkins highlights this exact phenomenon in his book, *Red Fighting Blue*. Hopkins (2017) argues that with the nationalization of the American political party system over the past several decades, the parties have simultaneously become more constrained in terms of their geographic appeal. The American political party system has clear national messaging and appeal; across the vastness of the United States, the Democrats and Republicans have national reputations that are difficult, if not impossible, for local- or state-level political actors to ignore. And while the liberalness or conservativeness of a party may still vary by state (e.g., New York Republicans may be a bit more liberal than Alabama Republicans), there is still a consistent national party narrative that unites these party members. Because of that, we are generally watching blue states and red states remain solidly blue or red rather than shifting in a more purple direction. In fact, Hopkins (2017) tells us that we should expect these patterns to further entrench themselves, as the national trends are starting to be mirrored by state and local elections as well. The calcification of American polarization, as described by Sides, Tausanovitch, and Vavreck (2022), is the direct result of the further entrenchment of polarized geographic trends. What this means for the Electoral College is that the inequality currently found in how electoral votes are distributed is not likely to be changed any time soon. If American partisanship is calcified and geographic changes are not likely on the horizon, we should anticipate similarly close presidential elections (à la 2016 and 2020) for the foreseeable future. And, if small states continue to favor the Republican candidate as they currently do, we can expect this inequality in the Electoral College, coupled with the closeness of the popular vote, to continue to create an environment in which the popular vote winner does not win the presidency, further eroding democratic principles that should be foundational to American elections.

Finally, just like many of the institutions created at the founding of the United States, the Electoral College has a problematic racial history. The racist three-fifths compromise written into the Constitution counted slaves as three-fifths of a person. The North advocated for not counting slaves in the population size as they were not given citizenship rights and were treated as property. The South advocated for counting them as full persons in order to increase their population size. This inflated population size led to increased delegations sent to the House of Representatives, which led to an increase in the number of electoral votes each southern state received. Ultimately, many Southern states received more electoral votes than they should have because they were able to partially count slaves as citizens despite not providing them with any of the rights or privileges of citizenship. Today, things have changed drastically on the citizenship front. However, we now face several other problems related to race, namely voter ID laws. As will be discussed in much more detail in the following chapter, voter ID laws disproportionately impact minority voters, reducing turnout in elections as a result.

Ultimately, the Electoral College has been plagued by problems and criticized widely since its inception. Some of these criticisms have been addressed, while others persist to the present day. In addition, new problems have emerged that were not as evident in the late 18th Century. It should not be surprising, then, to learn that several attempts have been made to reform this archaic system. In fact, more than 700 pieces of legislation have been introduced in Congress to reform the Electoral College. A timeline of these efforts to reform the Electoral College along with brief descriptions can be found in table 3.4. While I will not discuss all 700 attempts, a brief rundown of the various proposals is warranted.

**Table 3.4 Timeline of Electoral College Reform Efforts**

District Plan Attempts:

1800—Representative John Nicholas of Virginia proposed the division of states into districts that equal the number of Representatives and Senators the state sends to Congress.

- The plan is introduced in Congress 30 times between 1800 and 1826
- Passed the Senate in 1813, but the House refused to act

1817—Senator Mahlon Dickerson of New Jersey proposed one elector per district and two more (corresponding to the number of Senators) determined by a statewide popular vote.

- Dickerson keeps introducing this plan through 1826
- Passed the Senate in 1819, but the House refused to act

1823—Senator Thomas Benton of Missouri proposed a district system based on popular vote, eliminating intermediate electors.

- Kept introducing this plan through 1844, but it never got a vote
- President Andrew Jackson offered support
- Martin Van Buren (the Senator from New York) effectively kills the idea with his discussion of how it dilutes large state power

1870—Senator Oliver Morton of Indiana proposed a district system with two votes determined by a statewide popular vote and rest (based on number of the representatives) determined by a district-wide popular vote.

- Eliminated electors
- Debated in 1875 in both the House and Senate, but no votes were taken
- Brought back after the 1876 debacle, but Morton died and no one was willing to lead the charge

1949—Representative Frederic Coudert, Jr., of New York, proposed a replica of Morton's plan, but with electors.

- Also kept a contingency election, but proposed allowing both House and Senate to vote for president and giving each individual their own vote, not vote by state
- Voted on it in 1956, but failed to get the two-thirds majority vote needed for the constitutional amendment

Proportional Plan Attempts:

1848—Representative William Lawrence of New York proposed dividing the electoral vote based on the proportion of statewide popular vote won and eliminating electors, but no action was taken.21 years later, Representative James Ashley of Ohio proposes same plan but with electors, which also spurred no action in either chamber of Congress.

1875–1889—20 proposals for proportional division of electoral votes were introduced.

- In 1877, Representative Jordan Cravens of Arkansas becomes first to advocate for rounding the electoral vote to the nearest one-thousandth instead of whole numbers (adopted by almost every future attempt)
- In 1878 and 1880, The House Select Committee reported favorably on a proportional plan but failed to be brought to debate because of states' rights arguments

1928–1933—Representative Clarence Lea of California regularly introduced the proportional plan.

- In 1933, House committees reported on it favorably, but never brought it to a vote.

**Table 3.4 Continued**

1934—Senator George Norris of Nebraska proposed the adoption of a proportional plan.
- Debated by the Senate Judiciary Committee, which reports out a bill that just abolishes the office of elector but leaves the original design of the Electoral College in place.

1948–1956—Lodge-Gossett takes center stage.
- Senator Henry Cabot Lodge of Massachusetts and Representative Ed Gossett of Texas teamed up to introduce the proportional plan in both chambers
- In 1948, received favorable reports from Judiciary Committees, but no further action
- In 1950, the proposal once again received favorable reports from Judiciary Committees
  - The Senate votes 64–27 in favor (three votes over the two-thirds majority requirement)
  - Stalls in House Rules Committee for 5 months, after which it fails 134-210
- In 1956, Senators Estes Kefauver of Tennessee and Price Daniel of Texas introduce it again, but it fails to get two-thirds majority support in the Senate, and no action is taken in the House

Automatic Plan Attempts:

1826—Representative Charles Haynes of Georgia proposes eliminating electors and writing the winner-take-all rule into the Constitution.
- There is no appetite for this in either chamber of Congress, so no is action taken.

1932—Senator George Norris of Nebraska proposed the proportional plan but Judiciary Committee switched it to the automatic plan, which he accepted.
- In 1934, it was reintroduced and received debate, but failed to get a two-thirds majority vote.

1950—Senator Homer Ferguson of Missouri offered the automatic plan as an alternative to Lodge-Gossett, but it failed with a 20–71 vote

1956—Senator John F. Kennedy of Massachusetts offered support for the automatic plan, but never introduced it in the Senate

1965–1966—President Lyndon B. Johnson offered support for the automatic plan, but Congress had no appetite for it and never brought it up

Direct Popular Vote Attempts:

1816—Senator Abner Lacock of Pennsylvania is the first to introduce direct election of president.
- Met with states' rights and federalism arguments
- Voted down 12–21

1826–1830—Representative William McManus of New York proposed the direct vote nine times, but it failed each time.

1865–1880—25 resolutions for direct election were put forward but each one failed.
- 12 proposed a runoff election should no candidate get a majority
- Four proposed to keep the Congress-centric contingent election
- Remainder eliminated all contingency elections and accepted plurality as the winner

1947—Proposal for a direct election and a national primary election—failed 14–66

1950—Proposal for a direct election and a national primary election—failed 31–60
- Stripped national primary from proposal but still failed 28–63.

*(Continued)*

**Table 3.4 Continued**

1956—Proposal for a direct election debated and failed 13–69
- Senator John F. Kennedy of Massachusetts was the main opponent, claiming it was a breakdown of the American federal system

1961—12 amendments advocating for direct election proposal—all failed.
1963–1964—Four amendments proposed—all failed.
1966—Four major events spurred excitement over the potential for direct election of the president.
- The Chamber of Commerce of the United States endorse direct election of the president
- The first Gallup poll conducted on electoral reform—63 percent of respondents favored the direct election
- The American Bar Association established a Blue Ribbon Commission on direct election and endorsed it in a final report published in 1967
- Senator Quentin Burdick of North Dakota polled the 50 state legislatures and found majority support for direct election (most assumed the opposite until this point)

1969—Representative Emanuel Cellar of New York and Senator Birch Bayh of Indiana introduced an amendment calling for the direct election of a president with a runoff if no candidate received at least 40 percent of the vote.
- April 29—the House Judiciary Committee approved amendment 28–6
- August 14—The Senate Judiciary Committee approved amendment 11–6
- September 18—The House of Representatives approved the amendment 339–70
- September 30—President Nixon gives his approval and encourages the Senate to pass
- Filibustered in the Senate with two attempts at cloture, both of which failed 54–36 and 53–34

1977—Jimmy Carter advocated abolishing the Electoral College in favor of direct election.
- House never took it up
- The Senate failed to pass it with a two-thirds majority vote

2000s—Several attempts, but all failed.
- 2005 and 2009—proposals by Representative Gene Green of Texas
- 2009—proposal by Representative Jesse Jackson, Jr. of Illinois
- 2016—proposed by Senator Barbara Boxer of California
- 2017—proposed by Representative Steven Cohen of Tennessee
- All of these proposals died in committee

*Source*: Timeline compiled from Peirce (1968), table created by the author.

## PREVIOUS ATTEMPTS AT REFORM

Just 12 years after the Constitution was ratified, the first plan to reform the Electoral College was introduced in Congress. Representative John Nicholas of Virginia introduced what is now largely referred to as the District Plan (Peirce 1968). The district plan states that the Electoral College should be structured a bit differently; instead of allocating votes at the state level, votes should instead be awarded at both the state and congressional district levels. Each state should allocate two votes to the statewide popular vote winner, and the remaining electoral votes should be allocated to the candidate(s) that won each congressional district. A state, then, could split its electoral votes among the candidates running for office. Currently, both Nebraska and Maine allocate their electoral votes in accordance with the District Plan. Other reform plans introduced regularly include the Proportional Plan, the Automatic Plan, and the Direct Vote Plan. The Proportional Plan calls for electoral votes to be allocated in accordance with the proportion of popular votes won in each state. So, if a candidate wins 55 percent of a state's popular vote, they would receive approximately 55 percent of the state's electoral votes. This plan would arguably better align with the state's residents' preferences, as it would assign some votes to more than just the winning candidate. The Automatic Plan eliminates physical electors and automatically assigns the state's electoral votes according to the current set of rules (i.e., win a plurality of a state's votes, win all of their electoral votes). This would change very little of the current Electoral College. And finally, the Direct Vote Plan would abolish the Electoral College and award the presidency to the winner of the nationwide popular vote. This is the plan with the biggest changes involved with it, as it calls for the total elimination of the Electoral College. Each of these plans' pros and cons will be evaluated in much more detail in chapter 5.

The earliest reform debates were mostly focused on the District Plan, which was introduced dozens of times throughout the 1800s and a few more times in the mid-1900s. The District Plan actually passed the Senate in 1813 and 1819, but the House refused to act on it (Peirce 1968). It was last voted on in Congress in 1956 but failed to garner the two-thirds support needed for a constitutional amendment in either chamber. The Automatic Plan was introduced the fewest times, received endorsements from both Presidents Kennedy and Johnson, but never made it through either chamber in Congress with the necessary two-thirds support. Congress never really seemed to have an appetite for the Automatic Plan, as this plan required an amendment to be enacted but actually accomplished very little—it kept the Electoral College, just eliminated the electors. The Proportional Plan was introduced dozens of times and actually received multiple votes in Congress. Its most recent champion was Senator Henry Cabot Lodge Jr. from Massachusetts in the mid-1900s. Lodge was able to get it through the Senate with a two-thirds vote, but it stalled for five months in the House. During those five months, many Representatives worked to kill the reform movement, pointing to the dangers of electoral reform. These efforts were ultimately successful, as the House eventually killed the bill with a 134–210 vote.

Finally, the Direct Popular Vote plan was also introduced many times but came very close to passing in 1969. Senator Birch Bayh, who is credited with drafting and steering both the 25th and 26th Amendments through Congress, began to champion reform of the Electoral College in the form of support for the Automatic Plan (Wegman 2019). However, he was quickly won over by the Direct Vote Plan and abandoned his support for the Automatic Plan. With Bayh on board, many assumed that the amendment would eventually get passed, given his track record as a "one-man constitutional reform machine" (Wegman 2019). He partnered with Representative Emanuel Celler of New York, and the Direct Vote Plan was favorably reported out of both the House and Senate Judiciary Committees in the spring and summer of 1969, respectively. Then, in September of the same year, the House of Representatives passed the bill 339–70, easily clearing the two-thirds majority needed to pass an amendment. Just 12 days later, President Richard Nixon came out in favor of the amendment, encouraging the Senate to pass the bill. However, the amendment was met with a filibuster in the Senate. Senator Strom Thurmond of South Carolina led the charge, as senators realized that moving away from the Electoral College system toward a direct popular vote would drastically change who was likely to vote; in other words, those who largely felt disenfranchised by the Electoral College (political and racial minorities alike) would see their votes matter under a system in which the national popular vote decided election outcomes (Wegman 2019). Thurmond and his allies were successful in their bid to derail this effort, as the two efforts to invoke cloture failed by votes of 54–36 and 53–34. This was as close as Congress has ever come to enacting Electoral College reform. And this final failure was due to purely political reasons, as Republicans realized that a direct popular vote was more likely to benefit their Democratic opponents. Any attempt at reforming the Electoral College since this effort in 1969 has failed to pass either chamber of Congress with the necessary two-thirds majority support.

## CONCLUSION

Given the above discussion, maybe it would be best to return to Senator Hillhouse's suggestion from 1808 and just select our president from a random draw out of a box of retiring senators. In all seriousness, reforming the Electoral College is difficult work. It has been attempted more than 700 times, and each time it has failed, save for what eventually became the 12th Amendment. However, what these 700 attempts at reform clearly signal is that there are problems with the Electoral College that need to be addressed. Some of these problems were pointed out by Antifederalists even before the Constitution was ratified. For one, citizens had to relinquish their voting rights to electors to vote on their behalf, which is largely problematic due to their second concern: there was no guarantee the voters knew who these electors were. These concerns are exacerbated by the contingent election process, in which the citizenry is completely removed from the election process and Congress is put in charge of selecting the president and vice president if the Electoral College fails to reach a majority consensus among candidates. Lastly, the Antifederalists pointed to the problems that accompany a lack of public accountability: the president could abuse their power, follow their personal ambitions, turn the presidency into a hereditary monarchy, or—in alliance with an oligarchical Senate—govern with only their interests in mind.

More modern concerns include faithless electors defying the will of the people, continued concerns with the contingent election process, campaigns focused on a subset of states rather than the entire country, political inequalities inherent in the system, and the fact that the candidate that wins the most votes from the citizenry does not always get to become president. All of these concerns are largely focused on democratic norms and values. Americans claim to value democracy, and democracy demands political equality. The Electoral College clearly does not align with the idea of political equality, yet it has continued to persist—even in spite of the more than 700 attempts to reform it (and, in some cases, completely abolish it). The following chapter takes a close look at one of the biggest inequalities associated with the Electoral College: racial inequality.

# *Chapter 4*

# The Inherent Racism of the Electoral College

## *The Three-Fifths Compromise, Voter ID Laws, and Racial Inequality*

In 1969, Senator James Allen of Alabama wrote, "The Electoral College is one of the South's few remaining safeguards. Let's keep it" (quoted in Keyssar 2020). Senator Allen, in defending the Electoral College in the face of a push for electoral reform, inadvertently makes a strong argument in favor of its reform. The method by which we select a president should not be seen as favoring a particular state, region, or individual over another. Democratic principles dictate that all votes should be counted equally. Edwards (2004, 157) writes, "In an election for a national officeholder, each voter has a right to expect that he or she will stand in the same relation to the national official as every other voter." However, that is not the case under the Electoral College. The Electoral College actually creates political inequality, giving more electoral power to states with lower populations. While the South may not contain any "small states" (those with just three electoral votes), throughout its history and to this day, the South has been home to many policies that have inflated its population size, giving it more power in the Electoral College that it likely deserved. This chapter explores the relationship between political inequality and the South's history of racist policies that have allowed it to inflate its population size, thereby making it even more unequal.

Since the creation of the Electoral College at the Constitutional Convention, the South has benefited greatly from it. The South gained a large benefit with the passage of the three-fifths compromise, with which the country decided to count slaves living in the United States as three-fifths of a person. Since slavery was not practiced in the North, it was the South that benefited from this compromise. After the Civil War—and the passage of the 13th, 14th, and 15th Amendments—the South benefited even more: slaves were counted as full citizens, meaning their populations grew by two-fifths, giving them an even larger role in the Electoral College. While many agreed that it was good for all Black Americans to be given citizenship status and counted as full persons, many others believed it would have been much better if the South had awarded these citizens all of the rights and privileges of citizenship to accompany the title. Instead, the South passed a number of laws and adopted several norms that disenfranchised Black voters. Since the Constitution was adopted, the South has had the ability to count Black people as part of their population in some capacity in order to increase their presence in the House as well as their electoral power in the Electoral College. Importantly, all of this was done while keeping these same Black Southerners from actually participating in elections.

Presently, many would ask why any of this still matters. The three-fifths Compromise was undone with the 13th Amendment, and the discriminatory practices of the Jim Crow era were largely undone by the passage of the Civil Rights Act, the Voting Rights Act, and the 24th Amendment. Yet, today, discriminatory practices still exist: polling locations are inexplicably closed in minority neighborhoods, minority voters are purged from the voting rolls without a meaningful explanation, and voter ID laws have been put in place to suppress minority votes under the guise of preventing election fraud. Ultimately, the inherent racism of the Electoral College has been a problem since its creation and persists to this day. While the racial underpinnings of the Electoral College may not be obvious to all, they exist and should be acknowledged as one of the biggest problems associated with this outdated institution.

Throughout the rest of this chapter, I will trace the chronology of how many Southern states actively worked to disenfranchise Black voters in an effort to underscore how these states were able to increase their power in the Electoral College while ignoring a large part of their state's population. Specifically, I would like to shed light on the impact of voter identification laws that have been passed throughout the 2000s on the results of the Electoral College. It is no secret that these voter ID laws improve the electoral chances of the Republican candidate vis-à-vis the Democrat (Hajnal et al. 2016). However, examining the use of voter ID laws in light of a state's racial composition and voting patterns provides useful information on how the discriminatory effects of the Electoral College still persist today.

## ADOPTION OF THE THREE-FIFTHS COMPROMISE

The Convention delegates decided that the membership of the House of Representatives would be dependent on the population size of a state, while the Senate would ensure equal representation for each state (i.e., each state receives two senators). So, for representation in the Senate, the population size and makeup did not matter; each state's legislature would select two Senators to send to the Capitol to represent state concerns. For the House of Representatives, population size would be incredibly important—the more people living in a state, the more representatives they would get to send to the Capitol. So, of course, debate ensued about how to tally up a state's population. This seems like a fairly straightforward procedure (and for Northern states, it was): count the number of citizens residing in a state. Yet, for Southern states, the debate centered around slavery. If states were treated as property and not citizens, should they be counted as citizens?

Delegates from non-slave states argued that slaves should not be counted as members of a state's citizenry. James Wilson, a Pennsylvania delegate, demonstrated that there is little justification for a fractional counting of Black inhabitants. He argued that if they were to be treated as property, they should not be counted as part of the population, and if they were to be treated as full-fledged citizens (and not property), they should be counted as a full person (Farrand 1937, vol. 1, p. 587). Gouverneur Morris, another Pennsylvania delegate, was of a similar opinion, stating he was "reduced to the dilemma of doing injustice to the Southern states or to human nature, and he must therefore do it to the former" (Farrand 1937, vol. 1, p. 588). Morris believed that if the Southern states were allowed to count their slaves as part of their population, they would never be willing to discuss the eradication of the slave trade (Farrand 1937, vol. 1, p. 588).

In contrast, slave states wanted to count slaves as full persons for the purposes of representation. Pierce Butler and Charles Pinckney, both of South Carolina, advocated for counting slaves as residents of their respective states because they are indeed inhabitants of these states (Farrand 1937, vol. 1, p. 580). Butler goes on to justify his belief in counting slaves as full citizens for the sake of representation by arguing that their labor value and production capacity were the same as a "freeperson on Massachusetts" and that wealth is the appropriate way to justify equal representation (Farrand 1937, vol. 1, p. 580). Some of the Northern State delegates were also supportive of counting slaves as full persons, given their beliefs that representation should be driven by population. Dr. William Samuel Johnson argued that because of this, slaves needed to be counted as full citizens because they did, indeed, live in those states (Farrand 1937, vol. 1, p. 593). Some delegates, however, took a more forceful approach to counting slaves as full citizens. William Davie went as far as to say that if the Convention were not to agree to count slaves as at least three-fifths of a person, North Carolina (the state he represented) would refuse to ratify the Constitution (Farrand 1937, vol. 1, p. 593).

Responding to this debate, Gouverneur Morris argued that because the Constitution was to be voluntarily agreed upon by the various states, it would be good to compromise between not counting slaves at all and counting them as full citizens—specifically pointing out that Southern states should not expect a state like Pennsylvania to agree to count slaves as full citizens while Pennsylvania should not expect Southern states to leave out slaves from enumeration. So, the delegates agreed to compromise and count slaves as three-fifths of a person (or, more precisely, that they would count every five slaves as a total of three people). George Mason, a delegate from Virginia (a slave state), was unwilling to count slaves as full citizens because "he could never . . . regard them as equal to freemen and could not vote for them as such" (Farrand 1937, vol. 1, p. 581). Nathaniel Gorham, of Massachusetts, was convinced that three-fifths was the right proportion to use to enumerate slaves because Southern states argued they should be counted as full people while Northern states argued they should not be counted at all—though importantly, Congress had counted them at the three-fifths rate for taxation purposes (Farrand 1937, vol. 1, p. 580).

So the three-fifths compromise passed, and the delegates codified in the Constitution that slaves would be counted as three-fifths of a U.S. citizen. However, it was still the case that slave owners were not in any way expected to treat these slaves as citizens or provide them with any sort of citizenship rights or privileges. According to Humes et al. (2002), the three-fifths compromise led to a 6 percent advantage for Southern states in the Electoral College through 1860. Southern states were thus able to continue to treat slaves as non-citizens while also receiving an increase in electoral power in both the House of Representatives and the Electoral College.

In addition to the three-fifths compromise, the delegates also agreed to prohibit Congress from ending the importation of slaves until 1808. At the urging of Thomas Jefferson (then-president), Congress did prohibit the importation of slaves through legislation passed in 1800, which went into effect in 1808. But, notably, this legislation did not touch the domestic slave trade, allowing slavery to continue to exist throughout the Southern United States (Finkelman 2014). Because slavery was allowed to continue throughout the United States, the Southern states had a vested interest in preserving it, something they were very successful in doing. One of the reasons the South was so successful in this endeavor was because of their strategy of ensuring the presence of a southerner on all winning presidential tickets—a successful strategy up until 1860, when Abraham Lincoln and Hannibal Hamlin (both from the North) were elected (Blake 2019). In fact, four out of the first five presidents were slave owners from Virginia (Hartmann 2020). That means that for the first 18 presidential elections, a Southerner was either president or vice president, providing the South a prominent position within the executive branch to ensure that slavery was preserved.

## POST–CIVIL WAR RACIAL POLITICS SURROUNDING THE ELECTORAL COLLEGE

With the Lincoln-Hamlin presidential ticket winning the 1860 election, the South no longer had a grip on the executive branch, and secession from the Union among several Southern states started, signaling the beginnings of the U.S. Civil War. After the war and the resulting Reconstruction era came to an end, slaves were freed, and three important amendments were passed to officially put an end to state-sponsored slavery. The 13th Amendment officially ended slavery throughout the entirety of the United States; the 14th Amendment, often referred to as the citizenship amendment, prohibited states from making or enforcing laws that infringe on citizenship rights, required due process if anyone was to be denied life, liberty, or property, and required states to provide equal protection under their laws to anyone within their jurisdiction; and the 15th Amendment provided the right to vote to all men regardless of race.

Regardless of these amendments, which were supposed to help protect the rights of former slaves, there were many efforts taken to keep African Americans from participating in politics. The South, of course, implemented many state laws that instituted requirements to vote that prohibited Black people from casting a ballot. Grandfather Clauses required Black people to demonstrate that their grandfathers could vote in order for them to vote, which was impossible because of their grandfathers' slave status. Poll taxes were set at a rate to keep Black people from being able to afford them, while literacy tests were often required of Black people under the guise of ensuring they were literate enough to read the ballot. These literacy tests, however, were nothing more than constitutional knowledge quizzes, difficult for the average citizen, and nearly impossible to pass if you were prohibited from seeking formal education for years, like almost all Black U.S. citizens. Additionally, there were white primaries used extensively throughout the South, which only allowed white voters to participate in primary elections. South Carolina instituted them first in 1896 (Walton Jr. et al. 2012), followed by Florida (Farris 1954), Mississippi, and Alabama in 1902 (Perman 2001), Texas in 1905 (Perman 2001), Louisiana (Walton Jr. et al. 2012), and Arkansas (Gordon 2007) in 1906, and Georgia (Bartley 1990) in 1900. The Democratic Party had such a strong hold on the South that the meaningful choice voters got to make in elections was made at the primary stage rather than the general election stage, so by preventing Black people from participating in primary elections, these states were depriving Black people of any sort of meaningful choice in their elections.

Sharecropping was another means by which Black people were exploited and kept from voting after the abolition of slavery. This was a phenomenon where Black people would work on white-owned farms and were kept continuously in debt by the farmers who owned the land. Campbell (2010, 74) writes that the debt was so bad that "in the 1950s Martin Luther King Jr. met Southerners who had never seen the US currency." Sharecropping thus kept Black citizens in poverty, preventing their ability to move west, as Republicans were encouraging voters to do during this time period. The 1862 Homestead Act made land available practically for free if the inhabitants of the land were willing to cultivate it. It was the hope of Republicans that they could increase the number of inhabitants of land out west and admit states to the Union strategically in order to bolster the number of Republican Senators, Representatives, and electors (Blake 2019). Specifically, their hope was that Black citizens would move out west in pursuit of this land and, in doing so, fill these sparsely populated areas with more Republican voters, thus increasing their electoral power in the House and Electoral College. However, the land was largely non-arable, so it remained largely unattractive to many Americans, but the Congress was able to admit Wyoming, Washington, and break the Dakota territory into two separate states in order to increase the power of the Republican Party (Blake 2019). In addition to the problem of non-arable land, Black farmers struggled to amass the funds to free themselves from their sharecropping responsibilities on white farms, so they were unable to move west to claim any of this land (Berlin 2010). So, while Black people would have likely benefited more from Republican-sponsored legislation, many were unable to help populate Western states, as sharecropping kept them largely immobile.

This is clearly not an exhaustive list of the struggles faced by Black American citizens—and it is not meant to be. It is a discussion of the major policies, laws, and practices that prohibited Black people from meaningfully participating in American elections. The practice of discrimination throughout the United States (regardless of the state's ties to slavery) has been long noted and thoroughly documented (Fredrickson 1997; Mendelberg 2001). My goal here was not to ignore any of this important research or in any way downplay its impact on the participation rate of Black people in elections, but simply to bring together that which is most pertinent to Electoral College reform.

## PRESENT-DAY RACIALIZED POLICIES THAT IMPACT THE ELECTORAL COLLEGE

The aforementioned discriminatory policies were largely outlawed during the Civil Rights era. The Civil Rights Act and Voting Rights Act ended literacy tests along with many other discriminatory practices in the South, the 24th Amendment outlawed poll taxes, and in 1944 the Supreme Court ruled that it was unconstitutional to prevent Black people from participating in primary elections in the case *Smith v. Allwright* (Klarman 2001; Weeks 1948). The Supreme Court also invalidated Grandfather Clauses in the 1915 case *Guinn v. United States* (238 U.S. 347), arguing that they violated the 15th Amendment. So, by the end of the Civil Rights era, all of the racialized policies discussed in the previous section were undone and outlawed. However, this does not mean that racial discrimination no longer had an impact on the Electoral College. Instead, many of the policies shifted from being explicitly racist to being implicitly racist, mirroring the shift in racial appeals made by candidates seeking public office, as noted by Mendelberg (2001).

These implicitly racist policies include misinformation campaigns, deregistering voters, and the expansion of voter ID laws. In order to deregister, or purge, a voter from the rolls, a voter must meet one of four criteria: they had to have been convicted of a felony for which they were disenfranchised, they had to have been found to be mentally incapacitated, they had to have died, or changed their residence (National Voter Registration Act 1993). Additionally, voters can request to be removed at any time for any reason, and the state and/or party can purge a voter from the rolls if they were registered when they were ineligible to do so (e.g., under the age of 18). According to a report published by the Brennan Center for Justice, comparing purge rates from 2006–2008 with those from 2014–2016, the number of counties that purged more than 15 percent of their voter rolls increased from 97 to 205 (Brater et al. 2018).

While increased purge rates are not inherently a bad thing, concerns should be heightened in this case because purge rates increased at a higher rate in counties that were once subject to preclearance. Under the Voting Rights Act of 1965, preclearance required certain jurisdictions (i.e., those with a history of election discrimination) to obtain federal permission to make any election changes (including voter purges). The purpose of preclearance was to ensure that none of the proposed election changes would harm minority voters or were done with the intent to discriminate. The Supreme Court threw out this requirement in its 2013 ruling in *Shelby County v. Holder*, arguing that Congress inappropriately determined which jurisdictions would require preclearance. So, when comparing purge rates before and after the *Shelby* decision in jurisdictions that were subject to preclearance and those who were not, concerning patterns emerge. The purge rate of jurisdictions not subject to preclearance from 2012–2014 and the rate from 2014–2016 were the same, while the rate in jurisdictions previously subject to preclearance was 20 percent higher after the *Shelby* decision (Brater et al. 2018). Put another way, "67 percent of residents in previously covered jurisdictions lived in areas where the removal increased, compared to just 46 percent of residents in non-covered jurisdictions" (Brater et al. 2018, 4). Further, Brater et al. (2018) admit that this does not demonstrate these purges were done maliciously, but they did find a positive, statistically significant relationship between increased purge rates and an increase in voters showing up to vote and being unable to do so. So, all of this signals that voter purges are likely harming minority voters, adding the additional hurdle of re-registering to vote in order to cast a ballot.

In addition to voter purges, misinformation campaigns have been raising concerns for several election cycles, reaching a fever pitch in 2020 when Donald Trump refused to accept the results of the presidential election, instigated an insurrection at the Capitol on the day when electoral votes were counted, and insisted that he was the rightful winner of the 2020 election despite a complete lack of evidence. In fact, this has become so commonplace that it is referred to colloquially as "the big lie" (the lie, among Trump and his supporters, being that Joe Biden lost and Trump was the rightful winner of the 2020 presidential election). The fact that voters are neither fully informed nor politically attentive on a regular basis is not a new finding (Delli Carpini and Keeter 1996). Yet, when public opinion results are aggregated, public opinion appears rational, calming many concerns about the public's involvement in politics (Page and Shapiro 1992). Regardless, there are still reasons for concern.

Sanchez et al. (2022) demonstrate that concerns about misinformation are legitimate, with over 50 percent of white respondents to the Collaborative Multi-Racial Political Study believing that there was at least some level of voter fraud in the 2020 election, along with over 30 percent of Latinos and Black voters believing the same. They also point to a Howard University-sponsored poll that found over 50 percent of respondents believed that Black Americans were the focus of fake news efforts (Sanchez et al. 2022). In their exploration of misinformation surrounding the Covid-19 pandemic, Druckman et al. (2021, 652) find that "African-Americans hold significantly more misperceptions and fewer correct beliefs relative to Whites." Even more telling, according to a report to Congress compiled by A.I. software company Yonder, extra efforts were taken to target the Black community over and above the efforts taken to target all other racial communities (Yonder 2018). Overall, misinformation presents a clear threat to American democracy, but it seems to be a particularly acute threat to the Black community. This is a concern for electoral politics, as increased misinformation campaigns lead to an increased number of disillusioned voters who no longer want to participate in elections. With Black voters receiving a disproportionate focus among misinformation campaigns, it stands to reason that these Black voters will be more apt to sit out the election and therefore not influence the election result.

## THE GROWING THREAT OF VOTER ID LAWS

Despite the evidence and threats posed by voter purges and misinformation campaigns, voter ID laws likely pose an even bigger threat to Black voters. Many Republican officials have said publicly that the goal of voter ID laws is to keep Democratic voters from participating in elections. Glenn Grothman, a Wisconsin Republican Congressmember said, "I think Hillary Clinton is about the weakest candidate the Democrats have ever put up. And now we have photo ID, and I think photo ID is going to make a bit of a difference as well" (Wright and Scott 2016). Jim DeMint, a former Republican Senator and president of the Heritage Foundation, said that voter ID laws are "something we're working on all over the country, because in the states where they do have voter ID laws you've seen, actually, elections begin to change towards more conservative candidates" (Brennan Center for Justice 2016). And finally, Pennsylvania state representative Mike Turzai said that "voter ID [would] allow Mitt Romney to win the state of Pennsylvania" (Brennan Center for Justice 2016).

While these politicians have made it clear that voter ID laws tend to benefit the Republican Party over the Democratic Party, they do not confirm the racialized aspect of voter ID. Yet that, too, is something a few politicians have let slip over the past decade or two. In testimony during a legal challenge to Wisconsin's voter ID law, Todd Allbaugh (who, at the time, worked for a state Senator) stated, "She [a state senator] got out of her chair and hit her finger on the table and said, 'Hey, we've got to think about what this would mean for the neighborhoods around Milwaukee and the college campuses'" (Marley 2016). He further testified that Glenn Grothman (who was then a state senator) said, "What I'm concerned about is winning, and that's what really matters here. . . . We better get this done quickly while we have the opportunity" (Marley 2016). It is important to note that while neither of these state senators stated anything about race, Milwaukee is 34 percent White (non-Hispanic) according to the 2020 census, making it a minority-majority city. Grothman was concerned with the ability to pass a voter ID law before more state legislators would be elected who would oppose such a law. The female state senator referenced above was trying to underscore what she believed to be the dangers posed to the whiter Milwaukee-area suburbs without voter ID laws in place. Bouie (2013) highlights an analysis by the Associated Press that demonstrates South Carolina's proposed voter ID law would hit Black communities the hardest. He goes on to say the same holds for Alabama (Bouie 2013). Additionally, he responds to the most common defense of these voter ID laws—that the state provides IDs free of charge—by pointing to the fact that they are still difficult to receive. He writes that in Mississippi, where one-in-five residents live below the poverty line, you must produce a birth certificate (which costs $15), a marriage certificate if you are a married woman whose birth certificate shows her maiden name (which can cost up to $20), and a photo ID (Bouie 2013). That's right. In order to obtain a birth certificate to secure a free photo ID which will allow you to cast your ballot in Mississippi, you must pay $15 and show a photo ID to prove your identity (Gaskins and Iyer 2012).

An additional challenge to obtaining a photo ID with which to vote is getting to a government office that issues the ID. According to a Brennan Center report by Gaskins and Iyer (2012, 1), of the 11 percent of voters who are eligible to vote but lack the appropriate ID:

- Roughly half a million voters live more than ten miles from an ID-issuing office and lack access to a vehicle to get them there.
- Over ten million voters live more than ten miles from an ID-issuing office that is open more than two days per week.
    - Of these ten million voters, 1.2 million are Black and half a million are Hispanic.
- Many ID-issuing offices keep inconsistent business hours (e.g., not open every day, not open the same hours every day), and many of them are in rural areas.

All of this, taken together, signals that minorities and poor people are going to have a tougher time voting than their White, wealthier counterparts. Several studies have demonstrated that it is indeed the case that minorities, low-income, and low-education voters are most affected by these laws (Barreto et al. 2009; Hood and Bullock 2008). So, with voter ID laws being passed under the guise of election security, they are actually depressing turnout—among already underrepresented populations.

Importantly, voter ID laws are on the rise, heightening concerns about the depressive effect these laws can have on turnout. There are five different categories of voter ID laws that a state might adopt: (1) no identification is required; (2) non-strict, non-photo; (3) non-strict, photo; (4) strict, non-photo; (5) strict, photo. Non-strict, non-photo identification states request voters to provide some form of identification (with or without the individual's photo) when voting, and if one is not provided, the voter may vote on a regular ballot provided they sign an affidavit affirming that they are who they say they are or the state verifies their identity via predetermined means. Non-strict, photo identification states request that voters provide a photo identification when voting, and if one cannot be provided, the voter may sign an affidavit affirming their identity, or the state may require additional steps after the election to verify their identity (e.g., provide ID within a specified number of days, verify the voter's identity by mail, etc.). Strict, non-photo identification states require voters to provide identification (with or without a photo) in order to have their ballot counted. If they do not provide ID at the polling location, they may cast a provisional ballot and provide ID within a pre-specified number of days in order to have their ballot counted. Strict photo identification states require voters to present a valid photo identification in order to cast a ballot. If one is not presented on election day, the voter must provide one in order to have their provisional ballot counted. Some states, like Missouri, require voters to return to the polling location the same day in order to have their ballot counted.

With these election laws on the rise, it is important to examine how many electoral votes are determined by states with voter ID laws in place. There are a total of 318 electoral votes that are available in states with some form of voter ID on the books, or roughly 60 percent of the Electoral College. Of these 318 votes, 60 come from states with strict photo requirements, 38 from states with strict non-photo requirements, 124 from states with non-strict photo requirements, and 96 from states with non-strict non-photo requirements. Studies have shown that states with voter ID requirements are disenfranchising about 10 percent of their voters (Gaskins and Iyer 2012). Even worse, according to the Brennan Center for Justice (2006), is that 25 percent of Black voters do not have a government-issued photo ID, compared with 8 percent of white voters and 16 percent of Hispanic voters. In addition to this racial breakdown, we also see that 18 percent of voters 65 or older and 15 percent of voters earning less than $35,000 per year do not have a photo identification. So, in these states that employ some form of voter ID law, states that make up a majority of votes in the Electoral College, state officials are needlessly disenfranchising voters.

Figure 4.1 shows that there has been a steady increase in voter ID laws over time. Starting in 2000, when these laws started to pop up, we saw only 13 states require some sort of voter identification—and all 13 of these states had non-strict ID laws. That guaranteed that all of these voters would be able to cast a ballot on election day and would not necessarily need to present an ID in order to cast a ballot. By 2004, the number of states requesting an ID at the polls increased to 19, though all of these states remained non-strict. The 2008 presidential election saw the first examples of strict voter ID laws enacted. There were 24 total states that had voter ID laws on the books, 20 of which were non-strict, while Arizona and Ohio adopted strict, non-photo laws, and Indiana and Georgia adopted strict photo laws. By the 2012 presidential election, 29 states had adopted some form of voter ID law, seven of which were strict (Arizona, Georgia, Indiana, Kansas, Ohio, Tennessee, and Virginia). For the 2016 presidential election, 33 states had adopted a voter ID law, ten of which were strict (Mississippi, Texas, and Wisconsin joined the others from

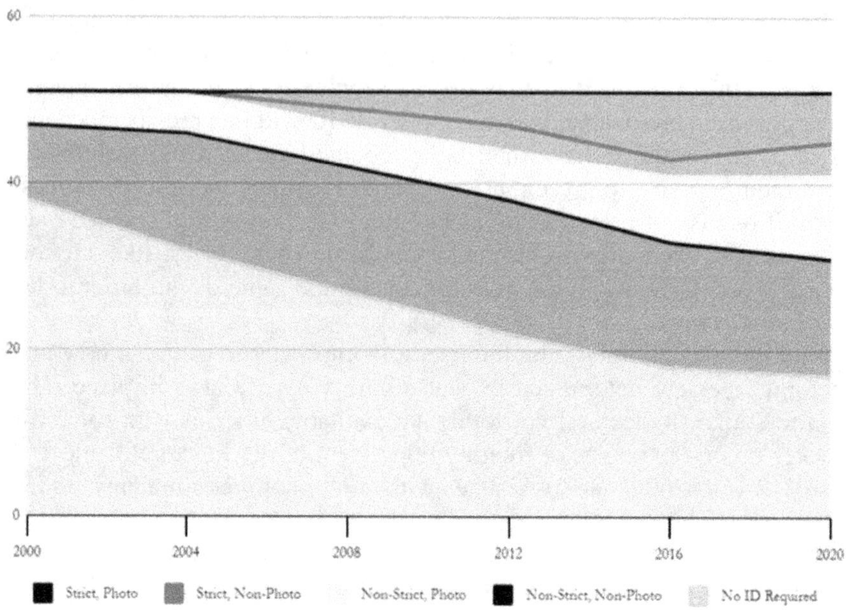


**Figure 4.1 Timeline of Voter ID Implementation.** *Source*: National Conference of State Legislatures.

2012, with Virginia moving from strict non-photo to strict photo). Finally, for the 2020 presidential election, there were a total of 34 states that had voter ID laws on the books, 10 of which were strict—the full breakdown of voter ID laws by state for the 2020 election can be found in figure 4.2. Virginia actually reverted from a strict photo requirement to a non-strict, non-photo requirement, while Arkansas and North Dakota went from non-strict, non-photo to strict, non-photo. Overall, what this highlights is the fact that in just 20 years, we have seen almost a complete flip in the number of states requiring some form of identification in order to vote. In 2000, 38 states did not require any identification in order to vote, and by the 2020 election, 34 states required some form of identification in order to cast a ballot, with Wyoming passing a strict, non-photo requirement after the 2020 election.

One of the problems highlighted here is the fact that these laws are fluid. There is no guarantee that the identification requirements are going to be consistent across election cycles. So, in order to meaningfully participate in elections in these states, voters must learn about the candidates as well as what form of identification they need to bring with them—or if they need to bring one with them at all. Virginia is a good example of this fluidity. For the 2000, 2004, and 2008 presidential elections, Virginia had a non-strict, non-photo identification requirement, a strict, non-photo requirement for the

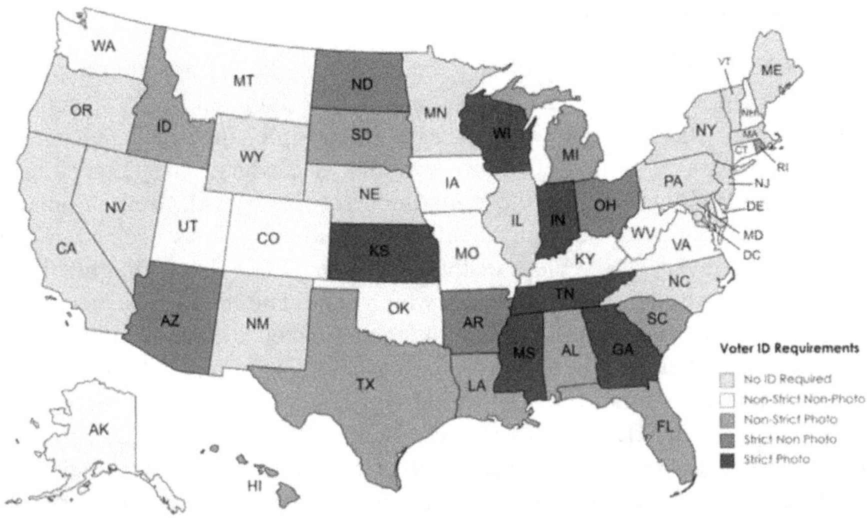


**Figure 4.2 Voter ID Laws by State as of the 2020 Presidential Election.** *Source*: National Conference of State Legislatures.

2012 elections, a strict photo requirement for the 2016 elections, and then reverted back to the non-strict, non-photo requirement for the 2020 elections. So, for three consecutive presidential election cycles, the voter ID requirements were different. This is largely due to the partisan makeup of the state legislature and the partisanship of the governor. It was a Republican governor who signed the strict, non-photo requirement into effect for the 2012 election, and the same governor increased the requirement to strict photo requirements for the 2016 election. Through the 2012 and 2013 state legislative sessions, Republicans controlled both chambers of the state legislature as well as the Governor's office. It was this Republican trifecta that passed increases in identification requirements for both the 2012 and 2016 presidential elections. Then, when Democrats took control of the state legislative chambers and governorship in 2020, laws were passed quickly to lessen the identification requirements for voters. Virginia highlights well the fluidity with which voter ID requirements can change in a state depending on the partisan make-up of the state's legislative chambers and governorship—adding one more hurdle for voters to overcome in order to cast a ballot. More importantly, those who have to work harder at overcoming these hurdles are likely to not participate in the election, either because they were unable to secure an ID, were ignorant of the ID requirement, or simply became frustrated with the process. These voters tend to be minorities, less wealthy, and less educated than those who do participate (Barreto et al. 2009; Hajnal et al. 2016; Hood and Bullock 2008).

## Voter ID and Southern States

To get a better understanding of how these laws might be impacting minority voters, let's now look at voter ID specifically in the southern states—defined here as those that fell below the Mason–Dixon line, including the border states of Missouri, Kentucky, West Virginia, and Maryland. These states, highlighted in figure 4.3, are those in which slavery was allowed and many of which continued to rely on racially discriminatory laws even after the abolition of slavery at the close of the Civil War. Table 4.1 highlights these states along with their racial makeup, which candidate they supported in the past three electoral cycles (for which the racial makeup, taken from the 2010 Census, applies), and the type of voter ID laws they have on the books. These 15 states contain a total of 193 electoral votes, and all but one of them have some form of voter ID law in place. Maryland is the only state that does not require voters to provide an ID in order to vote, and while it was indeed a slave state, it is presently a reliably Democratic state, so the lack of voter ID law is not overly surprising. Most of the other states are reliably Republican states—in fact, only two of the states in this table, Maryland and Virginia, have voted for the Democratic candidate in the three elections examined here. Florida voted for the Democratic candidate in 2012 and Georgia went blue in 2020, but with those few exceptions, all of the other states have voted continuously for the Republican candidate. In fact, Republicans benefit greatly from these states in the Electoral College: in 2012, Mitt Romney won 141

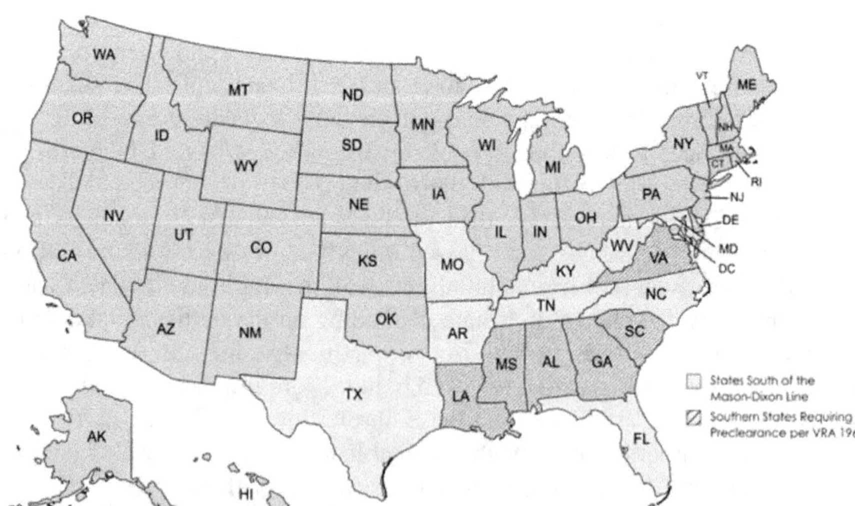


**Figure 4.3 Southern States and Preclearance Requirements per Voting Rights Act of 1965.** *Source*: U.S. Department of Justice.

**Table 4.1 Racial Makeup, Electoral History, and Voter ID Laws of Southern States**

| *State* | *Population* | *Electoral Votes* | *White (%)* | *Hispanic (%)* | *Black (%)* | *Asian (%)* | *Mixed (%)* | *Other (%)* | *2012* | *2016* | *2020* | *Voter ID* |
|---|---|---|---|---|---|---|---|---|---|---|---|---|
| Alabama | 4,841,164 | 9 | 66.2 | 3.9 | 26.5 | 1.3 | 1.6 | 0.6 | R | R | R | 2 → 3 ('14) |
| Arkansas | 2,968,472 | 6 | 73.4 | 6.9 | 15.5 | 1.4 | 2 | 0.9 | R | R | R | 2 |
| Florida | 19,934,451 | 29 | 55.6 | 23.4 | 16.4 | 2.6 | 1.7 | 0.5 | D | R | R | 3 |
| Georgia | 10,099,320 | 16 | 54.1 | 8.7 | 31.2 | 3.7 | 1.8 | 0.5 | R | R | D | 5 |
| Kentucky | 4,411,989 | 8 | 85.4 | 3.2 | 7.9 | 1.3 | 1.8 | 0.3 | R | R | R | 2 |
| Louisiana | 4,645,670 | 8 | 59.3 | 4.6 | 32.2 | 1.7 | 1.6 | 0.7 | R | R | R | 3 |
| Maryland | 5,959,902 | 10 | 52.5 | 8.7 | 29.6 | 6.1 | 2.6 | 0.5 | D | D | D | 1 |
| Mississippi | 2,989,192 | 6 | 57.2 | 2.8 | 37.5 | 1 | 1 | 0.5 | R | R | R | 1 → 5 ('14) |
| Missouri | 6,059,651 | 10 | 80 | 3.8 | 11.6 | 1.8 | 2.2 | 0.6 | R | R | R | 2 |
| N. Carolina | 9,940,828 | 15 | 64 | 8.6 | 21.5 | 2.6 | 2 | 1.4 | R | R | R | 2 → 1 ('20) |
| S. Carolina | 4,834,605 | 9 | 63.9 | 5.1 | 27.4 | 1.4 | 1.8 | 0.5 | R | R | R | 2 → 3 ('20) |
| Tennessee | 6,548,009 | 11 | 74.5 | 4.9 | 16.8 | 1.6 | 1.8 | 0.4 | R | R | R | 5 |
| Texas | 26,956,435 | 38 | 43.4 | 38.3 | 11.9 | 4.4 | 1.6 | 0.4 | R | R | R | 2 → 5 → 3 ('16, '20) |
| Virginia | 8,310,301 | 13 | 63.1 | 8.3 | 19.2 | 6.1 | 2.8 | 0.5 | D | D | D | 4 → 5 → 2 ('16, '20) |
| W. Virginia | 1,846,092 | 5 | 92.4 | 1.4 | 3.4 | 0.8 | 1.7 | 0.3 | R | R | R | 2 |

*Source*: U.S. Census and National Conference of State Legislatures.

**Note*: Southern states defined as those 11 that originally seceded from the United States and 4 border states. Coding for voter ID Laws: 1 = No ID required, 2 = non-strict, non-photo, 3 = non-strict, photo, 4 = strict, non-photo, 5 = strict, photo.

electoral votes from these states compared with Barack Obama's 52; in 2016, Donald Trump won 170 electoral votes compared with Hillary Clinton's 23; and in 2020, Trump won 154 of these electoral votes to Joe Biden's 39. These southern states therefore seem to provide an electoral stronghold for Republican candidates.

Many of these states have also seen changes to their state's voter ID laws. Eight out of the 15 states have remained stagnant with their laws of the past three presidential election cycles; the other seven states, however, have changed their laws at least once—Texas and Virginia have changed twice. Most of the changes have been in the stricter direction (i.e., moving from a non-strict to a strict requirement). Alabama changed from a non-strict, non-photo requirement to a non-strict, photo requirement in 2014; South Carolina did the same in 2020. Georgia moved to a strict photo requirement in 2008 from a non-strict, non-photo requirement previously. Mississippi moved to a strict photo requirement in 2014 after requiring nothing prior to this law's adoption. The state of Texas also moved to a strict photo requirement from a non-strict, non-photo requirement in 2016, but reverted to a non-strict photo requirement for the 2020 election due to legal challenges. Virginia also saw changes in their identification law over each of the three election cycles cited, with those changes—largely driven by partisanship—discussed previously. North Carolina is the only state among these Southern states to move in a less restrictive direction. It moved from a non-strict, non-photo requirement to not requiring an ID in order to cast a ballot. However, this was not done by choice. The state lawmakers have attempted to strengthen the identification requirements throughout the state since 2008 (i.e., make the law even stricter), but have been met with significant legal challenges that the state has failed to win. So, with federal judges tossing out North Carolina's attempts at strengthening their voter ID laws, we have seen the state actually loosen their requirements—the only state South of the Mason–Dixon line that has seen a reduction in identification requirements—though not for lack of trying.

When we look at these states' racial makeup, they are noticeably more diverse than the average state at this time. Based on the 2010 U.S. census, the average state is roughly 69 percent white. Ten of these 15 Southern states' white population is less than the national average, signaling a significant number of minority voters. Three of the five states that have white populations higher than the national average (Kentucky, Missouri, and West Virginia) were actually border states. Nonetheless, this higher-than-average minority population in these southern states highlights the potential for electoral malfeasance when it comes to suppressing the voice of these minority voters. Many of these minority voters are expected to vote for the Democratic candidate. According to a Pew Research Center (2016) report on party identification that looked at trends through 2016, 87 percent of Black Americans identify as Democrats or lean Democrats, with 63 percent of Hispanics and 66 percent of Asian Americans doing the same. For reference, among white voters, only 39 percent identify with, or lean toward, the Democratic Party. Based on these numbers, we should expect that as the minority population of a state increases, the more likely those states' votes will go to the Democratic candidate. Yet, again, many of these states continuously vote Republican. I should note that I have not presented any data to support any sort of causal mechanism between the racial make-up of these states, the likelihood of these states having a strict voter ID law, and that law impacting turnout; yet, there does appear to be some anecdotal evidence that there is a connection between these three variables.

Now I would like to take a closer look at the states that were originally required to seek permission from the federal justice system in order to make any changes to their electoral system (i.e., they were required to seek preclearance under the Voting Rights Act of 1965). These states include Alabama, Georgia, Louisiana, Mississippi, South Carolina, and Virginia—all of which are included in table 4.1 and highlighted in figure 4.3. There were additional states eventually included in that list, but these were the six states included in the original 1965 Voting Rights Act. Because of these states' histories of racial discrimination, they were required to submit any planned election-related changes to the federal justice system in order to ensure nothing was being done that would in any way infringe on the voting rights of minorities. However, in 2013, the Supreme Court, in their decision in *Shelby County v. Holder*, removed the preclearance requirement saying that the criteria for it were outdated and placed a disproportionate burden on Southern States. Justice Clarence Thomas argued even further that the discriminatory behavior noted back in the 1960s no longer exists, undermining the need for preclearance to occur (*Shelby County v. Holder* 570 U.S. 520 (2013)).

Looking at these states' voter ID laws over the past three presidential election cycles, it is clear that with the removal of the preclearance requirement, many of these states moved to tighten their identification requirements. Alabama has had some version of voter ID laws on the books since 2008. Starting in 2008, Alabama had a non-strict, non-photo requirement, and in 2014, the state strengthened the requirement to a non-strict, photo requirement. South Carolina had a similar trajectory, starting with a non-strict, non-photo requirement in 2000 and then transitioning to a non-strict, photo requirement in 2020. Georgia started with a non-strict, non-photo identification requirement in 2000 but increased their requirement to a strict photo identification in 2008, remaining there ever since. Louisiana has maintained a non-strict photo requirement since 2000. So, while voters are asked to provide a photo ID when voting, that requirement has remained steady for the past 20 years. Mississippi actually did not require identification from voters until 2014, when the state adopted strict photo requirements. Finally, Virginia had non-strict, non-photo requirements from 2000–2008; then in 2012 they adopted a strict, non-photo requirement only to increase it to a strict photo requirement in 2016, and then reverted back to the non-strict, non-photo requirement in 2020.

Within these six states that were subject to preclearance until 2013, five of them have had some version of voter ID law on the books since at least the 2000 presidential election. Only Mississippi had done so without an identification requirement, but that changed in 2014 when the state drastically changed to a strict photo requirement. During the 2016 election cycle, half of these states had a strict photo requirement, and by 2016, one-third of them did (just a slight decrease), though this number would have remained steady if Virginia had not changed from unified Republican control to unified Democratic control of the state legislature and governorship. This demonstrates that all of these states are supportive of some form of identification requirement in order for people to cast a ballot. That means that some voters will be disenfranchised due to this requirement. Research demonstrates that the voters likely to be disenfranchised are minorities, less wealthy, and less educated (Barreto et al. 2009; Hajnal et al. 2017; Hood and Bullock 2008). In terms of the Electoral College, many of these states are safe Republican states, so the impact of voter ID may not appear to be severe. However, over time, we have seen Virginia become a battleground state, shifting now to a state that leans Democratic in presidential elections. In 2020, Georgia supported a Democratic candidate for the first time since the 1992 election, though the margin of victory for Joe Biden over Donald Trump was only 11,779 votes. So, the disenfranchisement of minority voters (more likely than not Democratic voters) may continue to have a strong impact on the outcome of presidential elections going forward if the margins of victory continue to remain this tight.

## Voter ID and Battleground States

To further explore the role of voter identification laws in the Electoral College, let's take a look at the battleground states over the past few presidential elections. These states can be found in figure 4.4. First, it is notable that many of these battleground states have been battlegrounds through all three electoral cycles under consideration here. Colorado and Virginia have moved from being considered battleground states in 2012 and 2016 to likely Democratic states in the 2020 (and likely future) presidential election cycles. In 2020, Georgia, Minnesota, and Texas were added to the list of battleground states—Georgia and Texas, given their growing population of non-white voters, have them trending from safe Republican states to battleground states, and Minnesota is potentially trending from a safe Democratic

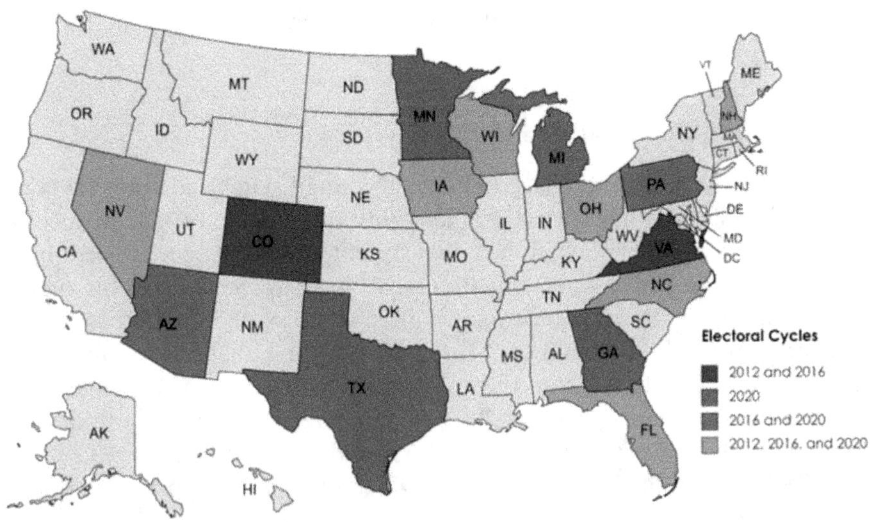


**Figure 4.4 Battleground States by Electoral Cycles 2012–2020.** *Source*: Created by the author using data from the *New York Times*.

state to a battleground state due to a growing rural-urban divide throughout the state (Biegon 2020). Arizona, Michigan, and Pennsylvania have been considered battleground states in 2016 and 2020, largely due to Arizona's growing population of Hispanic voters, Michigan's population of blue-collar white voters, for whom Trump's economic message resonated, and Pennsylvania's rural-urban divide. In addition to these states, seven states have remained battleground states over the past three presidential election cycles: Florida, Iowa, Nevada, New Hampshire, North Carolina, Ohio, and Wisconsin.

Now, how do these battleground states compare with the voter ID requirements presented in figure 4.2? Of the 15 battleground states presented in figure 4.4, only four states did not have any identification requirement for voters—though North Carolina did have a non-strict, non-photo requirement during the 2016 presidential election. Four of these 15 battleground states had strict requirements, while three had non-strict photo requirements, and four had non-strict, non-photo requirements. Of these battleground states, Texas and North Carolina have voted solidly Republican over these three presidential election years and Nevada, Colorado, Virginia, New Hampshire, and Minnesota have consistently voted for the Democratic candidate. Obama was able to win Florida, Ohio, and Iowa in 2012, but they have gone Republican since then. Wisconsin, Michigan, and Pennsylvania were reliably Democratic states but flipped to support Donald Trump in 2016, then reverted to the Democratic candidate in 2020. And lastly, Arizona and Georgia flipped from red to blue in 2020 for the first time since the 1990s (Georgia in 1992 and Arizona in 1996).

## Voter ID and the Small State Bias

Finally, let's look at the overlap between the small states and voter ID laws. The small state bias has been a problem with the Electoral College since its inception in 1787. The Senate has also benefited from the small state bias, as each state, regardless of population size, has two Senators. This means that Wyoming, with its population of 581,348 as of the 2020 census, and California, with a population of 39.35 million people, have the same power in the U.S. Senate. That means that the number of voters represented by each of Wyoming's senators' votes is 290,674 compared to the 19.68 million voters represented by each of California's senators. In the Electoral College, this translates to one electoral vote per 193,783 voters in Wyoming, while in California, it is one electoral vote per 715,455 voters. That is a difference of 521,672 voters, a very wide discrepancy, and a lot of voters who are potentially unrepresented (or at the very least underrepresented) in the Electoral College. Depending on these states' voter ID laws, these voters might be even more underrepresented. The small states for the 2012, 2016, and 2020 presidential election cycles are highlighted in figure 4.5.

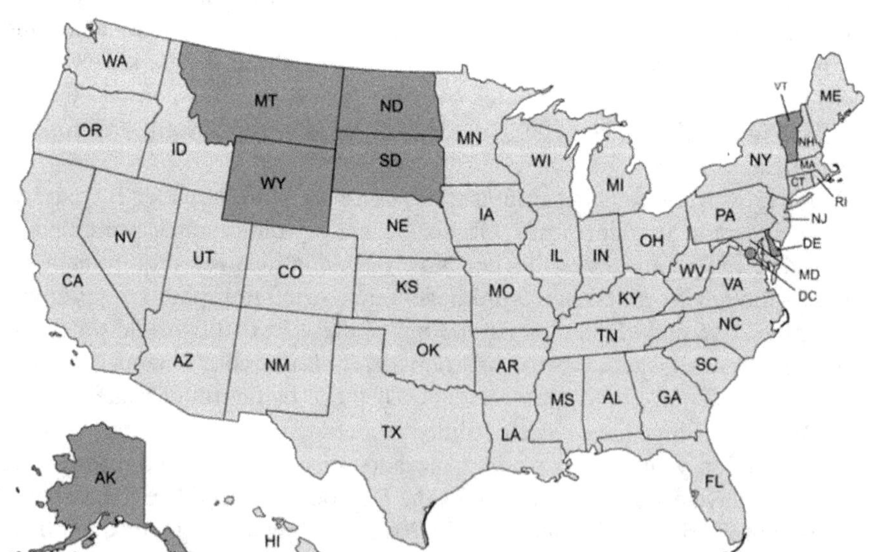


**Figure 4.5 Small States in the Electoral College for 2012, 2016, and 2020 Presidential Elections.** *Source*: The National Archives.

Among these small states, there is a mix of voter ID laws as well as partisan preferences. Delaware, Vermont, and the District of Columbia are solidly blue in the Electoral College, while Alaska, Montana, the Dakotas, and Wyoming are solidly red. The District of Columbia, Vermont, and Wyoming did not require any form of identification through the 2020 presidential election. However, Wyoming did adopt a strict, non-photo ID requirement in 2021, so they will likely still have that requirement on the books for the next presidential election. Alaska, Delaware, and Montana, all have a non-strict, non-photo ID requirement and have maintained that requirement since 2000 (except for Montana, which adopted that requirement in 2004). The Dakotas have changed their laws over the course of the past 20 years, with neither state requiring an ID in order to vote in 2000. Then, in 2004, North Dakota adopted a non-strict, non-photo requirement, and South Dakota adopted a non-strict photo requirement. South Dakota has maintained that requirement ever since, but North Dakota increased the standard to a strict, non-photo requirement for the 2020 presidential election. So, of the eight small states in the Electoral College, only one of them has a strict requirement, and that was just adopted for the 2020 election. An additional state has a non-strict photo requirement, while the other six have either no requirement or a non-strict, non-photo requirement (usually allowing a voter to cast a normal ballot if they sign an affidavit affirming their identity). Therefore, it seems as though voter ID laws are likely not inhibiting voters in these small states from taking part in elections, except for maybe North and South Dakota. However, given the fact that none of these states are battleground states, there is often less focus on whether or not the voices in these states are really being represented because they are regularly counted as safe Democratic or Republican strongholds in the Electoral College.

## DISCUSSION

Overall, state officials understand that voter ID laws tend to make it more difficult for minorities, less educated, and less wealthy citizens to vote. These officials also know that these voters tend to support Democratic candidates at higher rates than Republicans. More importantly, as demonstrated at the beginning of this chapter, we have elected officials on record admitting to the fact that voter ID laws tend to benefit the Republican candidate. This is also supported by rigorous, peer-reviewed research (see Hajnal et al. 2017). When we take all of this into conjunction with how the Electoral College works, we see that state-by-state voter ID requirements can have an extraordinary impact on national election results. In 2016, we saw a difference of less than 90,000 votes across three states (one with strict photo requirements, one with no ID requirements, and one in the middle with a non-strict rule) deciding the presidency, despite the popular vote winner nationwide receiving almost three million more votes. Voter ID laws would still impact presidential election results without the Electoral College present, as they would still disenfranchise voters without proper identification. The Electoral College, however, exacerbates the problems with these laws because the battles are waged at the state level, with the national trends largely meaningless.

As demonstrated throughout this chapter, the United States has a long history of trying to keep minorities from participating in elections—voter ID laws are just the latest way by which state officials are trying to disenfranchise these voters. Prior to the Civil War, many states simply outlawed Black participation in elections due to their slave status. Slaves were not considered citizens, so they were barred from participating in elections. This did not, of course, stop the slave states from trying to count the slaves as full citizens in order to artificially inflate their population size, giving them more representatives in the House and therefore a greater number of electoral votes. While the South was unsuccessful in counting their slaves as full citizens, they did succeed in including them in the population count, at least partially. The delegates to the Constitutional Convention compromised and agreed to count slaves as three-fifths of a person.

After the Civil War and the resultant Reconstruction era, the South still worked hard to keep former slaves disenfranchised despite the passage of the 13th, 14th, and 15th Amendments. They passed a series of laws aimed specifically at keeping Black people from voting. These efforts included poll taxes, literacy tests, grandfather clauses, and white primaries. In addition to these legal barriers, there were practices in place to attempt to intimidate Black people from even trying to register to vote. These efforts often involved the Ku Klux Klan. In some Southern states, Black people who successfully registered to vote had their addresses published in local newspapers, so Klan members knew exactly who to target. So while the 13th Amendment granted citizenship to Black residents and former slaves and the 15th Amendment granted all citizens the right to vote regardless of race, there were still policies in place to keep Black people from meaningfully participating in elections. Importantly, with the passage of the 13th Amendment, these newly admitted Black citizens were able to be counted as full residents for population purposes, increasing the population of the South, giving the South a greater number of representatives, and a higher number of electoral votes. Even so, it is clear that these new citizens were still prevented from voting or enjoying any real aspect of citizenship. Once again, the pattern was obvious: these states wanted to be able to maximize their population size by including Black citizens as part of the population, but they did whatever it took to keep them from meaningful participation. This period culminated in the Civil Rights movement, in which most of these discriminatory behaviors were outlawed. Poll taxes and literacy tests were legislated out of existence, while courts overturned grandfather clauses and white primaries. With these changes, many Black people were able to participate in elections for the first time in their lives. Yet, once again, history would repeat itself, and steps would be taken to prevent Black Americans from voting.

After the Civil Rights era, many states took part in practices in which Black voters were discriminated against with various tactics, including voter purges, intimidation tactics, and voter ID laws. On the surface, all of these tactics seem to apply equally to all voters regardless of race or ethnicity. However, when we scratch the surface, the racial motivations behind these actions become much clearer. In order to be purged from the voter rolls, a voter must have died, moved, or become ineligible to vote (e.g., been convicted of a felony or been declared mentally incapacitated). There are several examples of state officials using faulty lists to purge voters from the rolls. The Ohio secretary of state was set to purge 235,000 voters from the rolls in 2019 when he opted to let voting rights organizations examine the list for errors; these groups found 40,000 names that did not belong on a purge list (Vasilogambros 2019). Oklahoma has what is sometimes referred to as a "use it or lose it law," where voters who have not participated in the previous two elections have their voter registration revoked if they do not respond to a postcard confirming their address (Brown 2019). These "use it or lose it" laws tend to impact low-income and minority voters more than white voters and those in higher income brackets (Smith 2020). Now, these types of laws are not in use in all states but have been increasing as of late (Vasilogambros 2019).

Inactive voting is not the only reason why a voter may be purged from the rolls: death, moving, and a felony conviction also come into play. It is this last reason that also has a racialized component, as Black Americans are more likely than white Americans to have a felony conviction. In fact, while eight percent of all U.S. adults held a felony conviction in 2010, that rate was much higher (33 percent) among Black men. So, Black men are being disenfranchised at higher rates than white men due to the racial disparities in felony convictions in the United States.

Lastly, voter ID laws are also more likely to impact Black voters more than white voters. While identification requirements are on the rise throughout the country—the number of states requiring some form of identification in order to vote has risen from 13 to 35 over the past 22 years—they are highly concentrated in southern states, where discriminatory policies have a long history of impacting access to electoral participation. Additionally, these laws seem to overlap quite well with battleground states. In states where elections are likely to be highly competitive and hinge on small margins of victory, these voter ID laws can easily make a difference in election outcomes. This is especially true given the Electoral College, which causes candidates to wage elections on a state-by-state basis. Importantly, the voters that tend to be disenfranchised by voter ID laws are minorities, the less wealthy, and the less educated (Barreto et al. 2009). And even more, we know that these groups of voters tend to be more Democratic than Republican (Pew Research Center 2016). There are even politicians willing to admit that voter ID laws benefit the Republican Party over the Democrats. In response to the 2012 election, the Pennsylvania GOP chairman stated,

> We probably had a better election. Think about this: we cut Obama by five percent, which was big. A lot of people lost sight of that. He beat McCain by ten percent; he only beat Romney by five percent. And I think that probably photo ID helped a bit in that. (quoted in Blake 2016)

Notably, many do not mention the racial discrimination inherent in these laws, but they freely admit that the laws favor one party over the other. Yet, once in a while, there is an official who acknowledges the racism inherent in these voter ID laws. In a 2013 clip from the *Daily Show*, a Republican precinct chairman said, when asked about the potential negative impacts of voter ID, "If it hurts the Whites so be it. If it hurts a bunch of lazy Black people that want the government to give them everything so be it" (quoted in Gabbatt 2013). While he does not necessarily speak to the racist effects of voter ID laws, he does show himself, as a voter ID proponent, to be a racist. Regardless, these voter ID laws are increasing the likelihood of a Republican candidate winning the Electoral College because they are preventing reliably Democratic voters from participating in elections, and many of these reliably Democratic voters are minorities.

What should be clear is that the disenfranchisement of minority voters is not new. Nor is the impact of this disenfranchisement on the Electoral College. In fact, it was part of the original discussion of the Founders at the Convention. James Madison

> contended that States were divided into different interests not by their difference of size, but by other circumstances; the most material of which resulted partly from climate, but principally from (the effects of) their having slaves. . . . It did not lie between the large & small States: it lay between the Northern and Southern. (quoted in Farrand 1937, vol. 1, p. 486)

The Founders agreed to compromise on the personhood of slaves in order to get the Constitution adopted. This compromise, as well as the division in the United States over slavery, led to institutions embedded in our governmental system that are tinged with racist origins. This fact alone should justify reforming the Electoral College to ensure that any racist law or restriction could not possibly impact a presidential election result. However, this has not been the case. Instead, when one racist law or practice is repealed or abolished, another appears to take its place. Currently, states are adopting voter ID laws under the guise of election integrity and the effort to prevent voter fraud. Yet, several studies have demonstrated that voter fraud is not a cause for alarm. The laws have racist, and clearly partisan, intentions. Considering the fact that these laws do not seem likely to be repealed or rescinded any time soon, it is time to reform the Electoral College in such a way that these laws will have less of a direct impact on the overall election result. Many reform ideas have been introduced before. It is these reform ideas to which we now turn.

# *Chapter 5*

# We've Tried This Before

## *Analyzing the Major Reform Proposals*

When Janeway (1972) wrote, "If there is nothing more powerful than an idea whose time has come, there is nothing more ubiquitously pervasive than an idea whose time won't go," she was not talking about Electoral College reform. Yet the spirit behind her statement on women's equality is acutely applicable to it anyway. The idea of Electoral College reform is nothing new—as noted in chapter 3, it is something that has been introduced in bills on the floor of Congress more than 700 times. Not only that, it was introduced as early as 1800, just 13 years after the Constitution was adopted. Even James Madison, dubbed the "Father of the Constitution" and one of the authors of the *Federalist Papers*, acknowledged the haste in which the Electoral College was decided. In a letter to George Hay in 1823, Madison (1823) writes,

> The difficulty of finding an unexceptionable process for appointing the Executive Organ of a Govt. such as that of the U.S. was deeply felt by the Convention; and as the final arrangement of it took place in the latter stage of the Session, it was not exempt from a degree of the hurrying influence produced by fatigue & impatience in all such bodies.

Despite the long history of attempts at Electoral College reform, the institution has been able to endure with relatively little modification. Looking through the reform attempts, there are several that have received notable attention and have been discussed and debated quite thoroughly. The Automatic Plan, The District Plan, The Proportional Plan, and Direct Vote Plan have been the most prominent of the reform plans, though over the past couple of decades, the National Popular Vote Interstate Compact (NPVIC) has been gaining traction (not enough, however, to become a serious threat to the Electoral College). The Automatic Plan leaves the Electoral College as the official mechanism by which the president is elected but eliminates the physical electors. The electoral votes each state has would be awarded to the state's popular vote winner automatically upon certification of the state's election results. The District Plan calls for awarding electoral votes based on the popular vote totals in congressional districts, bringing the selection process closer to the people. The Proportional Plan calls for awarding electoral votes in proportion to the amount of popular votes won in each state, in an effort to make all voters feel heard in an election. The Direct Vote Plan calls for abolishing the Electoral College and electing the president based on the national popular vote. And finally, the NPVIC calls on states to agree to award their electoral votes to the winner of the national popular vote, regardless of the state-level popular vote results. In this chapter, I will discuss each of these reform plans: how they work, the benefits they bring, along with the drawbacks and challenges each possesses. For each reform plan, the drawbacks outweigh the benefits, signaling the need for a new reform plan—the Constant Two Plan, which will be fully detailed and defended in the next chapter.

## THE AUTOMATIC PLAN

"It is hardly worth cranking up the complex and protracted amendment process to accomplish so little—it would be almost like chasing a fly with an elephant gun" (Senator Sam Ervin, quoted in Peirce 1968). The Automatic Plan was never popular among members of Congress. Many of them had the same view as Senator Ervin: it would be a lot of work for very little gain. The Automatic Plan calls for keeping the Electoral College, with each state still receiving electoral votes equal to the sum total of its senators and representatives, but doing away with the office of elector. On election day, voters cast their ballots, and each state would award their electoral votes to the winner of the state's popular vote. The "automatic" part of the plan is that the electoral votes are awarded to the popular vote winner automatically, as the electors have been removed from the process. Each candidate is expected to still win 270 votes in order to win the presidency, and the contingency process stays the same. In other words, pretty much everything stays the same, except the physical electors are eliminated. The Automatic Plan ensures that a faithless elector (or group of faithless electors) cannot not sway an election result. It removes the deliberative nature of the Electoral College and places the decision-making responsibility in the hands of each state's voters.

The Automatic Plan has been introduced in Congress many times and has been supported by many notable politicians. Thomas Jefferson, while he did not have the name of the reform plan, offered support for the idea of doing away with physical electors and allocating all of a state's electoral votes to the presidential ticket that won the most votes in a state. John F. Kennedy supported it while he served in the Senate and during his time in the White House, and Lyndon B. Johnson offered his support for it when he assumed the presidency after Kennedy. Senator Birch Bayh, the author of two other constitutional amendments, also supported the Automatic Plan, leading many to think its time had come. Since Bayh had been successful in championing two amendments through Congress and ratification, many assumed he would be successful a third time. However, Bayh eventually pulled his support for the Automatic Plan in favor of the direct vote and Electoral College abolition altogether. Bayh said,

> It may well be that mere procedural changes in the present system would be like shifting around the parts of a creaky and dangerous automobile engine, making it no less creaky and no less dangerous. What we may need is a new engine, because we are in a new age. (Senator Evan Bayh, quoted in Peirce 1968)

Many point to the fact that the Automatic Plan prevents faithless electors as the major benefit of the plan. Faithless electors are those who vote against their state's popular vote winner. These electors, thus choose to ignore their state's voters and vote for their preferred candidate. The spirit of the Automatic Plan largely goes against what the Founders intended to happen with the Electoral College, as they actually supported the idea that the electors would debate and discuss the merits of those they considered worthy of the presidency (Alexander 2019). So, there is a great deal of irony in advocating for the Automatic Plan while also advocating for keeping the Electoral College in place because it preserves what the Founders set up. The Founders set up a system in which the electors would debate and decide which candidate to support; electors were designed to be free agents and had the right to deliberate and make their own decisions.

Overall then, the Automatic Plan, while a "simple" fix, is actually a fairly big change in the mechanics of how the Electoral College would work. Implementation of this reform would require a constitutional amendment because it eliminates the role of the elector, despite retaining the electoral votes. More importantly, this plan fixes problems that are not really problems. For one, as just discussed, faithless electors actually behave as the Founders expected all electors to behave. And more importantly, there has never been an instance in which a faithless elector has altered the result of a presidential election. While we have several examples of the national popular vote and electoral vote not aligning, none of the results have been altered by the actions of a singular (or group of) faithless elector(s). There have been notable faithless electors, but none have shifted the presidency from one candidate to another. Had the "Hamilton electors" movement, as discussed in chapter 2 been successful in triggering the contingency election process in 2016, that would have been the first time in which the expected action of the Electoral College would have been altered (Wegman 2020). However, it is difficult to predict how the House would have acted and whom it would have selected as president under such a scenario; it very well could have ended with Donald Trump still ascending to the presidency over both Hillary Clinton and John Kasich.

In terms of faithless electors, we witnessed a record number (seven) in 2016. Five of these seven electors were supposed to vote for Hillary Clinton but instead supported other candidates (i.e., Colin Powell, Bernie Sanders, and Faith Spotted Eagle), while two voted against Donald Trump and in favor of John Kasich and Ron Paul (Boccagno 2016). Other remarkable elections include those of 1872, in which 66 Democratic electors changed their votes from Horace Greeley to various other candidates after Greeley died prior to the Electoral College voting, and 1808, when six Democratic–Republican electors refused to support James Madison (FairVote 2020). All other elections, at least when looking at just the electoral votes for president, saw at most a singular faithless elector. In 2004, we saw an elector accidentally vote for John Edwards for both president and vice president, giving John Edwards the distinction of being only the second vice presidential candidate to receive more electoral votes than the Presidential candidate (Berg-Andersson 2021). In the 2000 election, a District of Columbia elector purposefully abstained from voting to highlight the district's lack of meaningful representation in Congress (i.e., the representative has no voting power). The 1988 election saw an elector flip the president and vice presidential candidates, so Lloyd Bentsen received an electoral vote for president while Michael Dukakis received a vote for vice president. During the 1976 election, a Republican elector supported Ronald Reagan, Gerald Ford's nomination challenger, over Ford with their electoral vote. A Republican elector opted to support the Libertarian candidate, John Hospers, over Richard Nixon in 1972, while a Republican elector supported George Wallace over Nixon in 1968. Notably, in 1968, George Wallace did win 46 electoral votes, but he won 45 of those votes by winning the popular vote in Alabama, Arkansas, Georgia, Louisiana, and Mississippi. In 1960, a Republican elector opted for Harry Flood Byrd Sr. over Richard Nixon, while a Democratic elector in 1956 opted for an Alabama state judge over Adlai Stevenson. Finally, in 1948, a Democratic elector from Tennessee voted in favor of Strom Thurmond of the Dixiecrat Party over Harry Truman.

Faithless electors are clearly few and far between—and with several states having adopted laws that bind their electors to the state popular vote, these numbers are likely going to decline even further. Because of the rarity of faithless electors, the Automatic Plan never really gained traction. Members of Congress largely viewed pursuing this plan as a waste of time, as absolutely no presidential election would have been altered due to this plan. And more importantly, it does not remedy any of the instances in which the popular vote winner loses the presidency. In none of those elections does an elector make the decision to support the national popular vote winner over their state's popular vote winner. However, what this reform plan does guard against is what Donald Trump attempted to do with slates of fake electors in the 2020 election. The Automatic Plan would prevent a fake elector scheme, as it eliminates the physical electors. In order to manipulate the electoral vote, an individual would need to manipulate the popular vote. While Trump did pressure the Georgia secretary of state to find him 11,800 more votes to tip the electoral vote in his favor in 2020, that would require much more organization given the process by which votes are tallied. It is not the case that a state's secretary of state can just add a certain number of votes to a candidate's total. Ultimately, despite the fact that it would guard against a scheme involving fake electors, it seems Senator Ervin was correct in his assertion that the Automatic Plan really was like "chasing a fly with an elephant gun" (quoted in Peirce 1968).

## THE DISTRICT PLAN

Next to simply relying on the national popular vote to determine the winner, the District Plan may be the easiest for American voters to understand because two states—Maine and Nebraska—use the district system to award their electoral votes. The District Plan calls for awarding electoral votes in accordance with both the state's preferences and each congressional district's preferences. Two of each state's electoral votes would be awarded to the candidate who won the state's popular vote, while the remainder would be awarded to the candidate who won each congressional district's popular vote. So, each state's electoral votes would potentially not go to a singular candidate but instead be split among the candidates in the race. These votes would likely be split just between the top two, but the door is certainly open to third-party candidates, who have a higher chance of winning a plurality of votes in a congressional district than a plurality in a statewide contest.

Notably, James Madison writes that this more closely resembles the intentions of the Founders than what was ultimately adopted. In his letter to George Hay, he writes,

> The district mode was mostly, if not exclusively in view when the Constitution was framed & adopted; and was exchanged for the general ticket & Legislative election, as the only expedient for baffling the policy of the particular States which had set the example. (Madison 1823)

So, by adopting the District Plan, we would be adopting the electoral system preferred by many of the Founders. But what other benefits might accompany the District Plan? Upon considering the setup, it seems the District Plan should more closely reflect the will of the voters and open the contest up more to third parties than the current system. The District Plan theoretically brings the election closer to the people. The electoral vote is not dependent on the statewide vote but rather on the congressional district vote. So, even in reliably blue New York and California, there will be a few districts won by the Republican candidate for president. The Democratic candidate will still win more votes in these two states, but they will likely not win all of the votes. The splitting of the electoral vote in this way demonstrates some of the appeal of this plan. Republicans in blue states and Democrats in red states are more likely to see at least a vote or two go to their preferred candidate rather than all of their state's electoral votes go to the candidate they oppose, as usually happens under the current system.

By awarding votes piecemeal rather than en bloc, voters may feel better represented under the District Plan than they do under the current Electoral College system. At the very least, they should feel their vote matters more than it does under the current system. In the 2020 election, for example, we saw Nebraska's second congressional district award its electoral vote to Democratic candidate Joe Biden while the remaining four votes went to Republican Donald Trump. Douglas County, in which Omaha is located (the largest city and the most populous metropolitan area in this district), voted for Biden over Trump 54 percent to 43 percent, and because of that, this district's electoral vote reflected the popular vote. Perhaps a better example of how the District Plan may better resemble the diversity of voices within a state is the example of Illinois in 1960. Abbott and Levine (1991) show that while Kennedy won Illinois by a total of 8,858 votes (or 0.18 percent), Nixon actually won the popular vote in more districts than Kennedy did. So, of Illinois's 27 electoral votes, Nixon would have won 14 to Kennedy's 13 under the District Plan; however, under the current structure of the Electoral College, Kennedy won all 27 votes. The district plan, therefore, has the power to break up some of the power held by the "big" states of the Electoral College. Importantly, however, it does nothing to eliminate the small state bias discussed in chapter 2. For example, by winning a state like Wyoming, South Dakota, North Dakota, Delaware, or any state with just three electoral votes, by winning the state's popular vote, the candidate automatically wins all three electoral votes because the congressional district is the entirety of the state.

In addition to the benefit of awarding electoral votes more in-line with how a state's citizens vote, the District Plan opens the door to third-party candidates. This door may not be open wide, but it is wider than under the current system. Take the 1992 election, for example, in which Bill Clinton and George H. W. Bush, the two major party candidates, were challenged by independent businessman H. Ross Perot. Perot ended up receiving almost 19 percent of the national popular vote but was never really seriously in contention for the presidency. His best showing was in Maine, where he finished in second place behind Clinton by roughly 8 percentage points. However, he came within roughly 15,000 votes of winning an electoral vote in Maine's second congressional district. Had the rules been different in other states, with votes awarded by congressional districts, we may have seen other voters persuaded to support a third-party candidate over one of the major party candidates. Looking back further, we see that in 1968, George Wallace won 45 electoral votes under the current Electoral College structure, but under the district system, his total would have increased to 53. This increase comes from picking up congressional district wins in South Carolina (two districts), Tennessee (four districts), Texas, and Virginia (two districts), but losing two votes with district losses in Louisiana and Arkansas; taken together, this would have netted Wallace seven additional electoral votes. We also see two electoral votes cast for a third-party candidate in South Carolina in 1956 and five cast for a third-party candidate in Mississippi in 1960. In both of these cases, voters supported "unpledged" electors over the major party candidates to give the electors the ability to support whoever they wanted. This also sent the obvious signal that voters were unhappy with both the Democratic and Republican candidates in these elections.

In order to implement the District Plan, a constitutional amendment is not needed; instead, all that is needed is a change in state law (Adkins and Kirwan 2002). The Electoral College still follows the structure and mechanics as outlined in the Constitution, all that is changing is how the electoral votes are allocated. That is why we have seen this plan instituted in Nebraska and Maine—any state can determine how it wants to allocate electoral votes. So, this plan is arguably easier to adopt because states can undertake the reform on their own—they are not dependent upon Congress to pass an amendment or go through the ratification process.

The biggest problem associated with the District Plan is gerrymandering. With reapportionment every 10 years, we see states regularly redraw their congressional district lines to benefit the majority political party within the state. The incentive to gerrymander congressional districts would be even greater under an Electoral College in which all votes would be allocated according to the District Plan (Adkins and Kirwan 2002; Best 1996; Longley 1975). When we look at the results of the 2020 redistricting process, 350 out of the 435 congressional districts were coded as solidly partisan according to the *Cook Political Report* (162 solidly Democrat and 188 solidly Republican), with 27 districts likely to favor one party over the other and an additional 26 rated as leaning toward one of the two major parties ("2022 House Race Ratings" 2022). That leaves U.S. congressional elections with approximately 32 competitive, or toss-up, districts—roughly 7 percent of all congressional contests (Levine 2022). In other words, 93 percent of our congressional elections are noncompetitive and largely predictable. That is not to say that some of the "leaning" and "likely" districts cannot swing to the other party in any given election cycle based on the political stances of the parties and candidates. We do indeed see elections in which 40 or so seats change parties, but again, 40 out of 435 is not a very large number, highlighting the fact that gerrymandering is rampant across the country. If we make the outcome of a presidential election dependent on the partisan division of congressional districts, the impulse to gerrymander congressional districts becomes even greater.

An argument can be made that if a majority of residents of a particular district are overwhelmingly Democratic or Republican, they should absolutely be represented by someone who shares their partisan preference. However, when we see elections like Wisconsin's 2018 gubernatorial race, gerrymandering's impact is on full display. In that contest, the Democratic candidate for governor (Tony Evers) defeated the Republican incumbent (Scott Walker) by one percentage point—admittedly a slim margin. Simultaneously, however, Walker won a plurality of votes in 63 of the state's 99 Assembly districts, giving the Republican Party a 63–36 advantage in the state Assembly, despite the Republican Party losing every single statewide elective office on the ballot that year (Gilbert 2018). While this level of gerrymandering remains a consistent issue, the District Plan is likely to continue to meet resistance from those trying to better align the electoral vote with the popular will.

In addition to the Wisconsin example, Alabama's redrawing of congressional district lines after the 2020 census is illuminating as well. In 2021, Alabama released its newly redrawn congressional district map with just a single district in which Black voters held a majority over White voters, despite the fact that the state is 27 percent Black. Upon reviewing a lawsuit, a federal district court ordered the congressional districts redrawn and mandated that two districts be drawn in which Black voters would be in the majority, or at least close to it. Alabama redrew its congressional districts, but refused to add a second district in which Black voters held a majority. In response, the same federal district court that originally ordered the districts redrawn mandated they be redrawn again—and this time appointed a special master to do the redrawing (Bisaha 2023). In doing so, a second district was created with a Black majority in place. While this example does not impact the Electoral College today, as Alabama does not use the District Plan to award electoral votes, it highlights the pivotal role gerrymandering plays in the congressional redistricting process today. If these districts helped determine the presidency, the problem of gerrymandering would no doubt grow exponentially.

## THE PROPORTIONAL PLAN

The Proportional Plan relies on the concept of proportional representation to allocate electoral votes. Under this system, candidates would receive electoral votes in proportion to the percentage of the popular vote they won. So, if a candidate wins 60 percent of a state's popular votes, they would win 60 percent of that state's electoral votes, rounded to the nearest one-thousandth of a percent. According to Peirce (1968, 165), rounding to the nearest one-thousandth of a percent has been standard practice in these computations since Representative Jordan Cravens introduced it in 1877. To exemplify this, let's look at the Pennsylvania vote in the 2020 election, in which 6,940,449 total votes were cast across the state. Of the total votes, Joe Biden received 3,461,221 while Donald Trump received 3,379,055. To calculate each candidate's proportional haul of electoral votes, we multiply each candidate's vote total by 20 (69,224,420 for Biden and 67,581,100 for Trump). Then, each of those numbers gets divided by the total number of votes cast (6,940,449). Therefore, each candidate's proportional allocation would be 9.974 electoral votes for Biden and 9.737 for Trump. This proportional allocation system shows how very closely the Pennsylvania voters were split between Biden and Trump, with Biden receiving just 0.237 electoral votes more than Trump. Under the current system, Biden won all 20 of Pennsylvania's electoral votes because he won the plurality of votes. The current system does not demonstrate nearly as clearly as the proportional system how closely divided these Pennsylvania voters were in 2020.

As demonstrated, one of the clear benefits of the Proportional Plan is how clearly the electoral vote mimics the attitudes of the voters in that particular election. Taking just the example of Pennsylvania in 2020 shows how lopsided the current structure of the Electoral College can make elections seem. Pennsylavania voters supported Biden over Trump by a margin of just 1.18 percent. This is indeed a Biden victory, but not a landslide by any stretch of the imagination. However, when we look at the allocation of electoral votes, by winning by just over a single percentage point, Biden received 20 electoral votes compared to Trump's zero. Under the Proportional Plan, Trump and Biden would have almost evenly split the state's 20 electoral votes, with Biden receiving just slightly more. This is much more representative of how Pennsylvania voters behaved in the 2020 election. By adopting a system that splits electoral votes in this fashion, it makes voters of both the winning and losing candidates feel heard. The voters who supported Biden know that Biden won slightly more votes than Trump, but the voters who supported Trump can also see that Trump is able to claim almost as many votes as Biden did because of how close he finished to Biden in the state's popular vote. These feelings of having your voice heard can lead to increased feelings of political efficacy, which can lead to increased levels of voter turnout (Rosenstone and Hansen 2003). So, there is much to be gained from finding a way to split up a state's electoral votes to make voters feel as though their vote does indeed matter.

An additional benefit of the Proportional Plan—at least a benefit to those who support third parties or the idea of the United States adopting a multiparty system over the current two-party system (Drutman 2020)—can be found by looking at the electoral vote totals of third-party candidates. Extending the look at Pennsylvania voters in the 2020 election, 79,445 votes were cast for Jo Jorgensen, the Libertarian Party's candidate. While her number of voters pales in comparison to the millions received by Biden and Trump, she still would have earned 0.229 electoral votes, as the computational math calls for rewarding electoral votes to any candidate that earns at least one one-thousandth of a vote (Abbott and Levine 1991; Peirce 1968).

An even clearer example would be a closer look at Utah's 2016 presidential election vote. Because Utah Republicans were largely split on how they felt about Donald Trump, Evan McMullin entered the presidential race to provide Utahn Republican voters with someone to vote for besides Trump or his Democratic challenger, Hillary Clinton. McMullin was an intelligence officer for the Central Intelligence Agency and worked for the Republican Congressional Caucus; it was through this work that he was able to establish himself as a traditional Republican that appealed to many Utahn Republican voters. Thus, in the 2016 election, we saw him pull in 243,690 votes, compared with 515,231 for Trump and 310,676 for Clinton. While McMullin won zero electoral votes under the current system, he would have won 1.278 under the proportional system. This may not seem like a big haul, but in comparison to the 2.703 and 1.630 votes Trump and Clinton would have won, respectively, it does not seem so small. Again, under this plan, each candidate wins a proportional amount of electoral votes, helping all voters feel heard in an election.

The Proportional Plan also helps ameliorate some of the small state bias. While the constant two votes are still given to each state (the votes that correspond to the number of senators each state has), these votes are no longer awarded en masse but will be distributed according to the proportion of the popular vote won by the candidate. Taking Montana and its three electoral votes as an example, if we look at the breakdown of their popular vote, Trump won 343,602 votes while Biden won 244,786 votes. This translates to 1.708 electoral votes for Trump and 1.216 votes for Biden under the Proportional Plan. Again, this does not completely wipe away the small state bias, but it does help lessen its effects.

While there appear to be many benefits to the Proportional Plan, there are a few limitations it brings with it. For those who want to defend the federal nature of the Electoral College, the allocation procedure under the Proportional Plan largely eradicates this aspect. As Best (1996, 34) explains,

> The presidential election system operates according to both the state equality and the federal districting provisions of the federal principle. . . . Each state has two electoral votes to match the state equality principle of the Senate, plus one electoral vote for every representative the state has in the House.

While she is correct in her assertion that this is where the number of electoral votes for each state comes from, as demonstrated in chapter 1, her justification is off. The Founders were clearly not concerned with the federal principle (Edwards 2004); they were looking for enough agreement on how to select an executive in order to close the Convention. Madison (1823) says as much to George Hay in his letter, when he also clearly laid out that the intention for many of the Founders was actually to institute something that resembles what we now refer to as the District Plan. Yet, if the federal principle is the sticking point for many in the camp of defending the Electoral College, the federal principle should be acknowledged. To not acknowledge it leaves us with little chance of reform. For these defenders, the Proportional Plan is likely a nonstarter, as the two votes assigned to the "state equality" provision of the federal principle, as Best calls it, are not awarded according to "state interest." Instead, they are simply lumped in with all of the electoral votes and divided up according to the state's popular vote.

Best (1996) also offers the critique that calculating the decimal place out to the one-thousandth place is too complicated. This is a blatantly absurd critique, as we clearly have technology capable of quickly calculating such totals; election results would not be delayed due to this type of calculation. Fon (2008) provides a much more solid critique in this vein: it is difficult to justify this level of exactness in calculation while preserving the physical elector element of the Electoral College to get around the need for a constitutional amendment in order to enact this reform. In order to keep the calculation to the one-thousandth decimal point, an amendment would be needed, making this a more difficult reform to enact. Constitutional amendments are hard. Fon (2008) offers what she calls the Integral Proportional System to get around this rounding scheme. In this plan, the calculation stays exactly the same, the rounding is what changes. So, we would see the candidate's vote total multiplied by the number of electoral votes in that state, then divided by the total number of votes cast in that state. Then, the top vote-getter would have their number rounded up to the nearest whole number, while the second-place candidate would see their number rounded down to the nearest whole number. Should any electoral votes remain, they would be allocated in much the same way. However, when we look at the 2020 Pennsylvania numbers again, we see that under the proportional calculation, Biden would have won 9.974 votes to Trump's 9.737. So, Biden's total gets rounded up while Trump's total is rounded down: Biden gets 10, Trump gets 9. That leaves 1 for Jorgensen? But Jorgensen's total was 0.229. It seems a stretch to argue that Jorgensen's total should be rounded up from 0.229 to one, when Trump's total was rounded down from 9.737.

This highlights one of the earliest critiques of the Proportional Plan: it harms the two-party system firmly entrenched in the United States (Peirce 1968). Some may argue that the United States would benefit from adopting a multiparty system along with proportional representation (Drutman 2020), but the existing major parties are going to be strongly resistant to it, and there are many electoral mechanisms in place that firmly root the two-party system in place. So, there is clearly going to be resistance to the Proportional Plan from those who support the two-party system. While the proportional system has several benefits in its favor, there is enough resistance to make this reform unlikely to be adopted.

## THE DIRECT VOTE PLAN

The Direct Vote Plan is likely the easiest reform plan for Americans to understand, as many believe this is how our president is chosen already. This reform calls for the abolition of the Electoral College altogether, with the president chosen by the national popular vote. The direct election of a country's executive is quite common in global democracies. Amorim Neto and Strom (2006) show that of Europe's 46 separate states, 32 have parliamentary systems with directly elected heads of state, with the remaining either indirectly elected or using a different governing system (e.g., a monarchy). So, if the United States were to decide to do away with the Electoral College and rely just on the national popular vote, they would join a long list of other democracies that do the same.

George Edwards has long been a vocal proponent of direct election of the president. In extolling the benefits of direct election he writes,

> Counting all votes equally (and making all votes equally valuable to the candidate) would not only strengthen political equality but also provide an incentive for candidates to clarify their stances rather than hedging them to persuade only the undecided in competitive states. (Edwards 2004, 154)

Edwards highlights two benefits of direct election: strengthening of political equality and incentivizing national campaigning. As demonstrated in the previous chapter of this book, the Electoral College has a racialized history and still, to this day, has disparate impacts across racial groups. As Edwards (2004) makes clear throughout his book, because the Electoral College exists, not all votes count the same. The small state bias clearly shows how small states vastly overpower large states (size here determined by population, not geographic size)—at least in terms of electoral power. So, the fewer residents a state has, the more power that state holds in the Electoral College. Despite the historic commitment to democracy in the United States, the Electoral College has meant that not all votes are equal. Under a direct vote system, all votes would count the same—at the end of election day, all votes would be counted, and the candidate with the most votes would win. This leads to Edwards' second point about electioneering activities among presidential candidates. Right now, under the Electoral College system, candidates are mostly incentivized to campaign heavily in battleground states and mostly ignore the states that are traditionally safe for them as well as states they are likely to lose. Under a system that relies on the national popular vote, candidates would be incentivized to campaign in all states in order to run up their vote totals as much as possible in as many states as possible. Of course, the natural critique of this is "to run a sectional campaign, to promise everything to the populous Eastern megalopolis; run up the score, run up the votes with them, and to hell with the rest of the country" (Best 1996, 24). However, this is not likely to happen. It is clear that even in deeply red and blue states, there are pockets of opposition voters. So, if Democrats have an advantage in the Northeast and the West Coast, Republicans have a similar advantage in the South and Plains states. So there does not seem to be a particular geographic advantage that clearly favors one party over the other, and despite the fact that one party might have an advantage in a particular region, that does not mean that the opposition party does not have supporters there. Candidates should rather be incentivized to campaign to run up their vote totals across the country—not just in the geographic region they may hold an advantage in.

Really, with the Direct Vote Plan, we see that all problems with the Electoral College are completely removed, as the Electoral College would cease to exist. That means: no more small state bias, no more examples of the popular vote winner not becoming president, and no more concerns over faithless electors. All of these benefits that come with enacting direct election of the president should bring with them an increase in presidential legitimacy and in turnout (Wegman 2020). We would expect this because voters should begin to feel as though their vote matters despite where they live or for whom they vote. They will know that their vote has been counted, as all that matters at the end of the day are those votes. This should bring with it increased feelings of political efficacy and with that an increase in voter turnout (Rosenstone and Hansen 2003).

So, given all of these potential benefits, why has direct election failed to become law? There are two main reasons we have seen this movement fail: (1) amendments are difficult to pass, and (2) the persistent belief that the federal principle is necessary in the election of the president. As discussed in chapter 3, there have been hundreds of attempts to either reform or completely abolish the Electoral College, yet none were able to muster enough support to pass. Amendments require the support of two-thirds of both houses of Congress and then the support of three-fourths of the states. Since the passage of the 12th Amendment, no amendment to reform the Electoral College has passed Congress with the necessary two-thirds majority. Amending the Constitution was designed to be difficult in an effort to prevent unnecessary amendments from passing and being codified in law. The Founders did not want the passions of the public to change the Constitution on a regular basis; they wanted amendments to be rare and to address major gaps or changes in understanding of the law. Due to this difficulty, the Constitution has only been amended 27 times since its ratification. Notably, the first 10 amendments, collectively known as the Bill of Rights, were passed and ratified by 1791, just three years after the Constitution was officially ratified. Since then, we have seen just 17 amendments passed (one of which simply repeals a previous amendment). This slow, difficult, and deliberative process is part of the reason the direct election of the president was never passed.

Secondly, the main critique of the Direct Vote Plan is the fact that it ignores the federal nature of the Electoral College. Judith Best has long been one of the Electoral College's biggest supporters, and her long-standing support relies solely on the federal principle on which she claims this institution rests. In her major defense of the Electoral College, *The Choice of the People?*, Best (1996) lays out the importance of federalism in the Constitution, all of which she claims supports retaining the Electoral College. First, given the vastness of the United States, federalism helps balance both local and national interests. The Electoral College forces the president to win a majority of states in order to govern the entirety of the country, helping to ensure small factions (localities or states) do not overpower the larger national will (Best 1996, 35). Second, federalism ensures that the national interest is defined by majorities, which Best (1996, 36) argues are simply coalitions of minorities (in her understanding, the individual states). So, again, because the president is required to compete at the state level, she argues that the federal system ensures that the policies the president supports will be appealing to a majority of citizens. And lastly, federalism is an important component to the separation of powers system embedded in the Constitution. Best (1996, 41) argues that federalism ensures that representatives, senators, and the president all "represent somewhat different interests and therefore are competitors who must compromise." While some of these rationales are stronger than others, it is important to remember that none of them were used when actually creating the Electoral College (see Edwards 2004 for a strong rebuttal of the federal nature of the Electoral College). Instead, these are all the rationales Electoral

College defenders have projected onto the institution itself. However, reformers must acknowledge these arguments if reform is to move forward. By simply ignoring these objections, resistance to reform will undoubtedly continue. So, while the Direct Vote Plan is indeed the most democratic and brings with it several benefits, it remains unlikely to survive the amendment process and become the mechanism used to select the president.

## A FEW MORE ATTEMPTS AT REFORM

One of the most popular reform plans currently is the NPVIC. This compact supports the direct election of the president,but acknowledges the difficulty of the amendment process. So, the organizers behind this movement call on states to pass individual laws that preserve the office of elector but award the state's electoral votes to the winner of the national popular vote regardless of what the results of the state's popular vote are. So, for instance, if New York were to enter into this compact, New York would agree to award its 28 electoral votes to the winner of the national popular vote rather than to the candidate who won the popular vote in New York state. The clear benefit of the NPVIC is that it would elect the national popular vote winner while at the same time eliminating the need for a constitutional amendment, as none of the structure of the Electoral College is actually changing, all that changes is how the votes are allocated (Lucas 2017). Currently, 15 states plus the District of Columbia have signed on to this compact, representing a total of 195 votes (National Popular Vote 2017). However, the compact does not go into effect until the sum of the electoral votes of the states that have signed on to the it equals 270.

As of now, all of the states that have signed on have a more liberal bent than those that have not, meaning this compact stands little chance of passage. In all cases of a mismatch between the electoral and popular vote, the Republican Party has always benefited, meaning states with a Republican tint have little incentive to sign this compact. Additionally, the NPVIC removes the federal principle associated with the Electoral College (Rathbun 2008). The electoral weight of each state would be removed if the state signs on to the compact. The current structure of the Electoral College works to maintain a balance between the state and federal governments; it also serves as an undemocratic institution, as the Founders were not favorable toward a popularly elected president (Goidel 2013). Williams (2012) points out that the federal intentions are also seen in the fact that state legislatures are supposed to select slates of electors to represent state, not national, interests. In addition to the removal of the federal principle, the NPVIC faces several legal challenges. Rathbun (2008) points to the compact Clause in Article 1, Section 10, which states that Congress must consent to any compact entered into by states (see also Gaines 2010). Considering the fact that none of the 15 states nor Washington, D.C., have received congressional approval of their compact, there is a good chance this will lead to years of legal dispute.

The National Bonus Plan was designed to preserve the federal nature of the Electoral College but also acknowledge the winner of the national popular vote with a bonus of 102 votes (see Schlesinger Jr. 2000). These votes would be in addition to the 538 electoral votes that currently exist. This preserves the Electoral College as it is currently structured but provides a bonus to those candidates who have won the popular vote composed of two votes for each state and Washington, D.C. Schlesinger Jr. (2002, 27) writes, "The national bonus plan is a basic but contained reform. It would fit comfortably into the historic structure." While this is indeed true, it would require a constitutional amendment to be enacted, as it changes the number of overall electoral votes available to candidates. It also does not fix what is inherently wrong with the current structure. The small state bias still exists, for example; it is just less visible, as the candidate who wins the national bonus is largely guaranteed the presidency.

## WHAT HAPPENS IF REFORM PASSES?

The obvious answer is that we allocate electoral votes differently. The interesting answer is that we don't know, and we can't be sure! This is due to the fact that if we were to change the rules of the Electoral College, candidates would adjust strategies and campaigns differently. But, we can look back over previous elections in an effort to see which candidate would have won and what those victories would have looked like if any of these various reform plans were enacted. Doing so lets us see what happens if candidates do not adjust their campaign strategies or what is likely to happen if similar strategies are employed. In order to do this, I have compiled the data that allows us to examine which candidate would have won under both the Proportional and District plans to compare with the current structure of the Electoral College as well as the popular vote results. Relying on several editions of *The Almanac of American Politics*, I was able to compile the raw vote totals and the electoral count of each state to calculate each candidate's share of the electoral votes under the Proportional Plan as well as a breakdown of the presidential vote by congressional district to determine the electoral vote distribution under the district allocation system. I have done this going back to the 1956 presidential election, giving us 17 elections to examine. The results can be found in table 5.1.

**Table 5.1 Comparing Electoral College Breakdown by Reform Plan (1956–2020)**

| | *Current Electoral College* | | | *District Reform Plan* | | | *Proportional Reform Plan* | | | *Direct Vote Plan** | | |
|---|---|---|---|---|---|---|---|---|---|---|---|---|
| | Dem | Rep | 3rd | Dem | Rep | 3rd | Dem | Rep | 3rd | Dem | Rep | 3rd |
| 1956 | 73 | **457** | 1 | 124 | **407** | 2 | 227 | **297** | 7 | **35.6** | 26.0 | 0.22 |
| 1960+ | **303** | 219 | 14 | 251 | **278** | 5 | 259 | 264 | 7 | **34.2** | 34.1 | 0.29 |
| 1964 | **486** | 52 | 0 | **466** | 72 | 0 | **320** | 214 | 4 | **43.1** | 27.2 | 0.21 |
| 1968 | 191 | **301** | 45 | 190 | **295** | 53 | 225 | 231 | 79 | 31.3 | **31.8** | 9.9 |
| 1972 | 17 | **520** | 1 | 64 | **474** | 0 | 198 | **331** | 10 | 29.2 | **47.2** | 1.1 |
| 1976 | **297** | 240 | 1 | **273** | 265 | 0 | **270** | 257 | 10 | **40.8** | 39.1 | 0.74 |
| 1980 | 49 | **489** | 0 | 142 | **385** | 0 | 221 | **273** | 35 | 35.5 | **43.9** | 5.7 |
| 1984 | 13 | **525** | 0 | 64 | **474** | 0 | 217 | **318** | 4 | 37.6 | **54.5** | 0.23 |
| 1988 | 111 | **426** | 1 | 160 | **378** | 0 | 244 | **288** | 5 | 41.8 | **48.9** | 0.43 |
| 1992 | **370** | 168 | 0 | **320** | 218 | 0 | 231 | 202 | 102 | **44.9** | 39.1 | 19.7 |
| 1996 | **379** | 159 | 0 | **345** | 193 | 0 | 263 | 220 | 49 | **47.4** | 39.2 | 8.1 |
| 2000+ | 264 | **271** | 0 | 245 | **293** | 0 | 258 | 262 | 15 | **51.0** | 50.5 | 2.9 |
| 2004 | 251 | **286** | 0 | 220 | **318** | 0 | 258 | **275** | 10 | 59.0 | **62.0** | 0.46 |
| 2008 | **365** | 173 | 0 | **305** | 233 | 0 | **279** | 246 | 10 | **69.5** | 60.0 | 0.74 |
| 2012 | **332** | 206 | 0 | 261 | **275** | 0 | **272** | 256 | 10 | **65.9** | 60.9 | 2.4 |
| 2016 | 227 | **304** | 7 | 251 | **287** | 0 | 258 | 247 | 34 | **65.9** | 63.0 | 7.1 |
| 2020 | **306** | 232 | 0 | **277** | 261 | 0 | **273** | 254 | 11 | **81.3** | 74.2 | 3.1 |

*Source*: Data compiled from various editions of Almanac of American Politics and CQ Almanac.
*Notes*: *Direct Vote Plan number is number of raw votes in millions; Bolded number indicates winner; +Indicates differing victor in Electoral College; Underlining indicates no majority winner; 3rd represents independent and third-party candidates.

I have omitted the Automatic Plan, the national popular vote interstate compact, and the Bonus Plan from the table. There is little to learn from their inclusion. The Automatic Plan would just bind electors to their state's popular vote, and as demonstrated earlier in this chapter, there have been very few faithless electors over the history of the Electoral College. Thus, while the numbers may change slightly under the Automatic Plan, the winner of the presidency does not. NPVIC would award the popular vote winner the Electoral College victory through the rules of the compact. And finally, the Bonus Plan would award the national popular vote winner a "bonus" of 102 electoral votes, all but guaranteeing the winner of the national popular vote would win the presidency. Looking at the Electoral College column in the table, adding 102 to each popular vote winner's total demonstrates that this would indeed be the case (under the Bonus Plan, a candidate would need at least 321 electoral votes to win). The results presented under both the district and proportional plans provide us with much more interesting information and evidence that neither of these plans should be enacted. Based on the data presented in table 5.1, it is clear that both the District and Proportional plans perform worse than the current Electoral College structure by creating even more uncertainty and inequality than already exists. The District Plan actually creates more mismatched winners than the current system, and the Proportional Plan produces results that would require the use of the contingent election process.

Looking first at the District Plan results, there are a few things to note. First, the District Plan results in lessened margins of victory in the Electoral College for most presidential candidates. Except for the elections of 2000, 2004, and 2012, the candidate that won the electoral vote under the current structure saw their electoral vote total decrease. The Electoral College tends to magnify a candidate's margin of victory in the popular vote, so a reform that lessens the electoral vote margin of victory likely brings it a bit more in-line with the popular vote. A second observation under the District Plan is that third-party candidates do not fare much better than under the current structure. While it is theoretically easier for a candidate to win the popular vote of a congressional district than that of a state, we see that it is still quite difficult for third parties to accomplish even that. table 5.1 shows that a third-party candidate has not won a single electoral vote since the 1968 election when George Wallace won several Southern states with his anti-integration platform.

Finally, and most importantly, the District Plan does not remedy the problem of mismatched winners in the electoral and popular votes in 2000 and 2016; in fact, it adds 1960 and 2012 to the list. Even worse, both the 1960 and 2012 elections were won by candidates that won both the popular and electoral votes, whereas the District Plan would have awarded the presidency to a candidate that did not win the popular vote. So in these two incidents, the Electoral College got it right; the reform plan got it wrong.

In 1960, Richard Nixon and John Kennedy were in a heated election, where Nixon (Eisenhower's vice president) relied on his experience and Eisenhower's popularity, while Kennedy relied on his youthfulness, energy, and good looks, as well as his running mate Lyndon Johnson's popularity in the South. Kennedy also focused his campaign activity on the swing states, while Nixon campaigned more broadly. As a result, Kennedy won the popular vote by just 112, 827 votes, or 0.10 percent of the vote (the second slimmest margin in U.S. history, behind the 1880 election). Despite this narrow margin of victory in the popular vote, he won the electoral vote decisively with 303 votes compared with Nixon's 219, a 15.6 percent margin of victory. Yet, had the District Plan been in place, Kennedy would have lost the electoral vote. Under the District Plan's allocation rules, Kennedy would have won only 251 electoral votes compared to Nixon's 278.

Roughly 50 years later, we see a similar result. The 2012 election resulted in the reelection of Barack Obama with a decisive victory in both the popular vote and the Electoral College. Obama defeated Mitt Romney by roughly five million popular votes and bested him in electoral votes, 332 to 206. Yet, under the District Plan's rules, Romney would have defeated Obama in the Electoral College, winning 275 electoral votes to Obama's 261. So, in 2012, Romney would have won the presidency while losing the popular vote by roughly five million votes.

Finally, the District Plan does not correct the mismatched electoral and popular vote winners in 2000 and 2016. Under the District Plan, George W. Bush's electoral vote total actually would have increased from 271 to 293, despite losing the popular vote to Al Gore by roughly 500,000 votes. In 2016, Donald Trump's electoral vote victory would have dropped from 304 to 287, but he still would have won the presidency despite losing the popular vote by almost three million votes. Under the district plan, therefore, Bush and Trump still would have won the presidency despite having lost the popular vote. This is in addition to the finding that Kennedy would have lost his election in 1960 and Obama would have lost his reelection bid in 2012.

Overall, these are concerning findings and should result in no longer taking the District Plan seriously as a mechanism for Electoral College reform. These results should also highlight the potential problems that would follow from the impact of gerrymandering on the District Plan. Gerrymandering is a problem that has been around for a while, originating in a Massachusetts district drawn by then-Governor Elbridge Gerry to benefit a friend in 1812. However, gerrymandering has increased over the past couple of redistricting cycles, with Republicans instituting "Operation REDMAP" prior to the 2010 reapportionment process (Daley 2017), in which the Republican Party spent millions of dollars to win majorities in state legislatures and gubernatorial seats in an effort to ensure control over the redistricting process. If the District Plan were instituted, these efforts would be increased, as parties would be incentivized to draw as many partisan districts as possible in order to have a greater impact on the presidential election results. As discussed earlier, Alabama ignored a federal court order to draw a second majority Black congressional district through their reapportionment process after the 2020 census. After the Supreme Court rejected Alabama's appeal, the federal court appointed a special master to assist the cartographer in redrawing Alabama's districts (Bisaha 2023). Similar legal battles would likely be waged across the country if congressional districts were crucial to success in presidential elections. Thus, between the problems associated with gerrymandering and this reform plan creating more "wrong winners" than the current Electoral College structure, it seems prudent to abandon the District Plan as a potential solution to the problems associated with the Electoral College.

Turning now to the Proportional Plan, there are, as expected, a number of noticeable benefits that accompany it. The biggest benefit, I would argue, of the Proportional Plan is that under this plan, the Electoral College better reflects both the popular vote and the competitiveness of the election. Looking over the results of the 17 different elections listed in table 5.1, there is no election in which any candidate wins more than 331 electoral votes; in fact, there are few elections in which any candidate wins more than 300 electoral votes. Lyndon Johnson won 320 in 1964, Nixon won 331 in 1972, and Reagan won 318 in 1984. In all of the other elections examined here, no candidate exceeded 300 electoral votes, demonstrating the fact that many of our presidential elections are relatively competitive—at the very least, very few of them are landslide victories. The three cases we do have were all reelection campaigns in which the incumbent president was quite popular and handily won the popular vote. In 1964, Johnson defeated Barry Goldwater by nearly 16 million votes, a significant show of support for Johnson—albeit not significant enough to support the Electoral College landslide victory of 486–52. In 1972, Richard Nixon easily defeated George McGovern by 18 million votes, which was again magnified in the Electoral College with Nixon winning 520 of the 538 electoral votes (McGovern won just the District of Columbia and Massachusetts). This is, again, a margin of victory that seems to unnecessarily exacerbate a candidate's popularity among the voting public. Finally, in 1984, Ronald Reagan soundly defeated Walter Mondale by approximately 17 million votes; Mondale, in fact, was able to win a plurality of votes in just Washington, D.C., and his home state of Minnesota, giving him just 13 electoral votes to Reagan's 525. In each of these elections, it is clear which candidate the majority of Americans supported, yet in each case the margin of victory awarded to the president by the Electoral College far exceeded the actual level of support he won in that election. The Proportional Plan brings these margins of victory more in line with their respective victories in the nationwide popular vote.

One of the reasons the electoral votes awarded under the Proportional Plan better reflect the national popular vote is because it awards electoral votes to third-party candidates. In each of the elections examined here, third-party candidates received at least a few electoral votes. Looking at the 1992 election, in which Ross Perot received 19.7 million votes (almost 19 percent of the total votes cast), he would have won 102 electoral votes under the Proportional Plan. Under the current system, he won zero. While Perot did not have a realistic chance of winning the presidency, he presented the strongest third-party challenge to the major parties since Teddy Roosevelt created the Bull Moose Party to challenge William Taft and Woodrow Wilson for the presidency in 1912. In most of the elections analyzed here, third-party candidates were not as successful as Perot was in 1992, but there were electoral votes awarded to third-party candidates in each of them. There were clearly elections in which there was a slight uptick in interest in third-party candidates, as more than ten or so votes would have gone to a third-party candidate (1968, 1980, 1996, 2000, and 2016), but this number would likely increase if the Proportional Plan were adopted. If adopted, voters would likely be more open to voting for a third-party candidate, knowing that their candidate stood a chance of receiving electoral votes. Under the current system, the only way a non-major party candidate would receive an electoral vote is through the actions of a faithless elector—at least since 1968. This support for third-party candidates under the Proportional Plan will likely be seen as a benefit by some and a drawback by others. Regardless of how it is viewed, it is a clear effect of the Proportional Plan.

The biggest challenge presented by the Proportional Plan is the fact that several of the elections analyzed here trigger the contingent election process—something almost all reformers seem to be opposed to given its undemocratic nature. Of the 17 sets of election results presented in table 5.1, six of them would have required the House of Representatives to select the president and the Senate to select the vice president. The elections of 1960, 1968, 1992, 1996, 2000, and 2016 all would have resulted in no candidate receiving a majority of electoral votes, meaning that 35 percent of all elections since 1956 would have been decided by Congress rather than the public. This is an alarming number; however, each of those elections was either very competitive or included a strong third-party candidate. The 1960 election ended with Kennedy defeating Nixon by just over 100,000 votes, and in 1968, Nixon defeated Hubert Humphrey by just over 500,000 votes. The 1968 election also saw George Wallace pose a strong third-party challenge (and win several electoral votes) in the South. Wallace ran on an anti-integration platform and won over Southern voters; between Wallace's campaign and the competitiveness of the race in the rest of the country, none of the candidates would have been able to win a majority of electoral votes in 1968. The 1992 and 1996 elections saw Ross Perot challenge Bill Clinton and his Republican opponents (George H. W. Bush and Robert Dole, respectively). Given the strength of Perot's challenge in each of these elections, he prevented either of the major party candidates from reaching a majority in the Electoral College under the proportional allocation rules. The 2000 election saw George W. Bush narrowly defeat Al Gore in the Electoral College, despite Gore's approximate 500,000 vote lead in the popular vote. Ralph Nader did not pose an exceptionally strong challenge as a third-party candidate, but he did perform more strongly than expected in the tightly contested state of Florida. In this election, the Proportional Plan actually slightly increased George Bush's lead in the Electoral College from 271 to 275. Finally, in 2016, Hillary Clinton bested Donald Trump by roughly three million popular votes but lost the Electoral College with only 227 votes to Trump's 304. The 2016 election also saw a higher-than-normal amount of public interest in third-party candidates given both Trump's and Clinton's unpopularity. This is fully displayed in the Proportional Plan results: Clinton receives a slight advantage with 258 to Trump's 247 electoral votes, both of which are short of the necessary 270 majority, partially due to the fact that 33 votes would have gone to third-party candidates Gary Johnson and Jill Stein. So, under the Proportional Plan, when an election is highly competitive and/or a strong third-party candidate emerges, we are likely to see the need for a contingent election.

Now, the main problem with the contingent election process is that the public is completely excluded from the process. In the House of Representatives, each state is tasked with voting for a presidential candidate rather than each Representative voting individually. So, each state's delegation votes as a whole. This means that gerrymandering once again comes into play. Should a contingent election be held, it is likely to benefit the Republican candidate over the Democratic candidate, as there are more states with a Republican-majority delegation sent to the House. Take 2016, for example. Under the Proportional Plan, Trump would have won 247 electoral votes, Clinton 258, Gary Johnson 18, Jill Stein 6, and Evan McMullin 2. According to the 12th Amendment, the House would be able to choose from among the top three finishers. Given the Congressional delegations at the time of the election, it is clear Trump would have been chosen by the House, and his running mate Mike Pence would have received the support of the Senate. While we cannot be sure that this is how Congress would vote, given the increasing partisanship of Congress over the past several decades (McCarty, Poole, and Rosenthal 2006; Lee 2009), we can be fairly sure that there will not be many (if any) crossover voters.

In addition to the increased polarization in Congress, invoking the contingent election process once again raises questions about the problem of gerrymandering. If the House is charged with selecting the president and the House is gerrymandered, it necessarily follows that gerrymandering will then impact the selection of the president. While gerrymandering certainly does not cause polarization, it is important to note that both of these factors will impact the presidential selection process should the contingent election process be needed. Given that the Proportional Plan regularly results in the contingent election process being used, the Proportional Plan is an unacceptable alternative to the current Electoral College structure. Despite the benefit of bringing the margin of victory in the Electoral College more in line with the margin of victory in the popular vote, the cost of regularly cutting the public out of the presidential selection process is too high to justify adopting the Proportional Plan. A Proportional Plan without a majority requirement to become president may be a plausible solution, but one that would require an amendment in order to enact. Additionally, even if this were the case, Bush still would have won in 2000 while simultaneously losing the popular vote.

## CONCLUSIONS

Reforming the Electoral College to bring it more in line with what voters actually want is not a new initiative. There have been reform efforts in Congress since 1800, and some have even been met with support from some of the Founding Fathers who participated in the design of the structure that still survives to this day. The Automatic Plan would eliminate electors and automatically award electoral votes to each state's popular winner, violating the spirit of what the Founders intended when they created the Electoral College. More importantly, this is a plan that solves a problem that doesn't really exist: no faithless elector has ever overturned the results of a presidential election. Nor have faithless electors ever come close to altering the winner of a presidential election; the opportunity was present in 2016, but even then, it failed. Part of this failure was due to several individual state laws binding electors to the state popular vote; these laws specify that if an elector votes against the state's preference, they are replaced with an elector that will uphold it. All of this strongly suggests that the Automatic Plan is completely unnecessary.

The District Plan would award two electoral votes in accordance with the state's popular vote but divide the remaining votes based on the popular vote in each of the state's congressional districts. Supporters of this plan argue that this allocation of votes brings presidential elections closer to the people (i.e., better reflects the will of the voters). Yet when we look at what would have happened had the District Plan been in place over the past 17 elections, we see that gerrymandering would have created even more wrong winners than the current structure does. Any plan that performs worse than the current structure at making sure the popular vote winner becomes president deserves no more consideration than it has already received.

Finally, the Proportional Plan sounds great theoretically. It brings down lopsided victories in the Electoral College, provides a voice for third-party supporters, and ensures the national popular vote winner consistently wins a plurality in the Electoral College. But, if instituted, the Proportional Plan would have resulted in several contingent elections over the past 70 years because the plurality winner would not have regularly won a majority of electoral votes. Given the highly competitive nature of several presidential elections in our recent past, in addition to the presence of a few strong third-party candidates, about 35 percent of the elections held since 1956 would have ended with Congress deciding who would control the executive branch. Here again, the problem of gerrymandering presents itself. While the Proportional Plan does better represent the will of the people, if it prevents the people from actually picking the president, there is no reason to consider its implementation any more than has already happened.

The only reform plan that guarantees the popular vote winner becomes president is the Direct Popular Vote plan. Admittedly, the NPVIC does as well, but there seems to be little chance of this plan being implemented given the fact that the compact has not been signed on by a single red state, or even a battleground state for that matter. The National Bonus Plan would also almost certainly guarantee the national popular vote winner would become president as well, but it would require an amendment to the Constitution in order to be implemented. And if effort is going to be expended on an effort to reform the Electoral College via amendment, the Direct Vote Plan seems the most worthy candidate, as it is easily understood and many Americans already believe that this is how the president is selected. So, why not the Direct Vote Plan? For one, we have been down this road before. There have been many attempts to pass such an amendment, but it has failed to get the support needed in order to pass it. Second, there is absolutely no chance that Congress would pass such an amendment today. Given the increased partisanship in both houses of Congress, there is little chance the Republican Party would support switching from the Electoral College to the direct election of the president, as the Electoral College has proven several times to favor the Republican Party over the Democratic Party. The intensity by which Congress is divided, the increased polarization, and gerrymandering make a two-thirds majority vote in either the House of Representatives or the Senate seem impossible. Given this calcification in polarization has also spread to the U.S. population at large (see Sides, Tausanovitch, and Vavreck 2022), the odds are also that a direct vote amendment would also fail to achieve ratification in three-fourths of the states.

What is needed is a new plan for reform. This plan must avoid the need for a constitutional amendment and must make every effort to ensure the winner of the popular vote becomes president. It should also be as parsimonious as possible so that it is easy for American voters to understand. Any reform that performs worse than the current structure or is overly complicated and confuses voters should be eliminated from consideration. All reform efforts need to be focused on better aligning the electoral vote with the popular vote. The voters of the United States should be in charge of selecting their executive leader, and reform efforts should seek to ensure that happens—especially without relying on a contingent election. To that end, I offer my alternative in the following chapter. I believe the Constant Two Plan offers a practical alternative to other reform plans offered, while also preventing the need for a constitutional amendment. The Constant Two Plan helps balance concerns about federalism with the desire to incorporate the national popular vote. This plan is outlined next.

# Chapter 6

# A Novel Approach

## *Joining the Federalist Ideal with the National Will through the Constant Two Plan*

On the eve of the 2016 presidential election, most Americans believed that Hillary Clinton would become the next president of the United States. Despite the many ups and downs of the 2016 election and the inevitable tightening in the polls as election day drew closer, polling showed her consistently ahead of Donald Trump. The elections betting market had much higher odds for Clinton defeating Trump, and the approval rating for the incumbent Democratic president, Barack Obama, was slowly increasing as his term came to a close—a good sign for a Democrat seeking the White House. Clinton also had an impressive political resume: she was First Lady of both Arkansas (1979–1981, 1983–1992) and the United States (1993–2001), she served as a Senator from New York (2001–2009), and she served as the secretary of state throughout Obama's first term in the White House (2009–2013). Trump, on the other hand, had absolutely no political experience. He actually used his lack of political experience as a selling point: he was not beholden to the normal Washington, D.C., elite or their money because that was not his world. Instead, he came from the business world. This business background, he argued, would make him a better economic leader for the country. Yet many remained skeptical of his political abilities.

Additionally, several scandals rocked the 2016 election. Just one month prior to the election, a recording of Trump talking to Access Hollywood's Billy Bush was released in which Trump made statements tantamount to sexual abuse and harassment (Arrowood 2016). With this, Trump's polling numbers dropped even lower, and many assumed his campaign was over. However, just three weeks later (and less than two weeks prior to election day), FBI director James Comey sent a letter to Congress informing them that more of Clinton's emails from her time as Secretary of State were found on the computer of Anthony Weiner (then-husband of longtime Clinton aide Huma Abedin) while they were searching Weiner's computer on an unrelated charge (Goldman and Rappeport 2016). Clinton was investigated (and ultimately cleared of wrongdoing) by the FBI for potentially compromising sensitive government information earlier in 2016 due to her use of a private email server while she served as secretary of state. After examining these newly found emails, Comey again cleared Clinton of wrongdoing just two days before the election. While this news excited Clinton supporters, for her opponents, it still provided enough reason to support Trump or sit out the election altogether (Wise and Hosenball 2016). Also, considering this investigation of Clinton occurred within the last two weeks of the election season, this means that early voting was already underway. This means most, if not all, of the 47 million voters who voted early in 2016 did so knowing that one of the major party's candidates was under an active FBI investigation (Lange 2020). Despite all of the ups and downs of the 2016 election, Clinton was still heavily favored to win the presidency.

Instead, the presidential election of 2016 provided Americans with the latest example of the Electoral College undermining the national will. For the second time in less than two decades, the popular vote winner failed to win a majority in the Electoral College. In fact, Hillary Clinton bested Donald Trump by almost three million votes but failed to achieve a majority of votes from the Electoral College, winning only 227 votes out of the necessary 270. In addition to the 2016 contest, the 2000, 1888, 1876, and 1824 presidential elections also present cases in which there were mismatches in popular and electoral vote winners. With these five discrepancies, several reform plans have been offered to better match the electoral and popular vote winners. However, all reform plans come with drawbacks that have slowed their chances of successfully reforming the Electoral College. The Constant Two Plan, unveiled here, aims to provide a new approach to Electoral College reform, accounting for the popular vote winner, while also preserving the federal ideal often associated with the Electoral College. Importantly, it does not require a constitutional amendment in order to be enacted, eliminating that hurdle to reform.

As discussed in chapter 3, reforming the Electoral College has been the focus of roughly one-tenth of the constitutional amendments that have been proposed since the Constitution was ratified. The Automatic Plan, District Plan, Proportional Plan, and Direct Vote Plan have all been proposed as potential reforms of the Electoral College several times. Considering there was little enthusiasm for the Electoral College among delegates to the original Constitutional Convention, evidenced by the fact that it was the result of several compromises based on over 30 different votes, there should be little surprise that the Electoral College has been subject to many attempts at reform (Edwards 2004; Farrand 1937; Robertson 2005; Slonim 1986). Despite these attempts at reform—including several by the original constitutional convention delegates—the Electoral College, frustratingly, remains in its original form.

Here, I offer a novel, practical solution to the problem of awarding the presidency to the candidate who lost the national popular vote. This plan involves reconfiguring how electoral votes are allocated while keeping the number of electoral votes at 538, requiring 270 in order to win the presidency, therefore avoiding the need for a constitutional amendment. The Constant Two Plan would require each state and Washington, D.C., to award two electoral votes to the winner of the national popular vote while awarding the remaining electoral votes to the statewide popular vote winner. This plan remedies all five mismatched elections (those in which the popular and electoral vote victors did not align) and fixes several problems associated with the current Electoral College design.

## MISMATCHED ELECTIONS AND OTHER PROBLEMS UNDER THE ELECTORAL COLLEGE

What should be clear from the previous chapters of this book is that problems with the Electoral College have been pointed out since before the Constitution was ratified (see also Rogers 2010 for a full discussion). In fact, Edwards (2004) details the confusion and consternation that existed during the original constitutional drafting about how to select a president. These early debates about presidential selection were also detailed in chapter 1. The Electoral College was devised through several compromises and over thirty votes taken at the convention, with the intent behind it left entirely unclear. As Edwards (2004) further points out, even the *Federalist Papers* are unclear about how the Electoral College should function, with the Founders referencing the choice of the people while defending an institution that is wholly anti-democratic. Others argue that the Founders intended for electoral votes to be decided at the congressional district level, as Nebraska and Maine currently operate (Dewey 1962; Adkison and Elliot 1997; Anon. 2001). In fact, James Madison wrote a letter in 1823 in which he advocated for a constitutional amendment to change the allocation of electoral votes from the state level to the congressional district level (Kurland and Lerner 1987). Yet, by the election of 1800 and the rise of national political parties, most states had moved to award their electoral votes en bloc to the statewide popular vote winner (Larson 2007). This method of electoral vote allocation has remained since, with Nebraska and Maine being the exceptions.

The largest cause of consternation with the Electoral College is the mismatch that occasionally occurs between the winner of the Electoral College and the winner of the national popular vote. In fact, the original structure of the Electoral College makes it an inherently anti-majoritarian institution. The original construction of the Electoral College involved the appointment of electors—non-Congress members who were to remain independent of partisan persuasion and not rely on public pressures—who were to decide the next president. These electors were to be chosen in a manner decided on by state legislatures. In 1824, a majority of states (18 out of 24) allowed the public (at least those who were legally allowed to vote) to vote for electors (Edwards 2004, 58). In this election, Andrew Jackson won the popular vote as well as a plurality of electoral votes—besting John Quincy Adams by roughly 37,000 popular votes out of a total of approximately 366,000 total votes cast and 15 electoral votes. However, Jackson failed to reach a majority in the Electoral College by votes. This result necessitated a contingent election in which the House elected Adams to the presidency, while John C. Calhoun was elected to the vice presidency by the Electoral College without issue.

After this incident, it was not until 1876 that a president would be elected without the support of a plurality of voters. In this election, we saw Rutherford B. Hayes, a Republican from Ohio who had served in both the House of Representatives and as governor of Ohio, defeat Samuel Tilden, the Democratic governor of New York. Tilden won a majority of the popular vote with 50.92 percent but lost the electoral vote to Hayes. In fact, Hayes won 185 electoral votes compared with Tilden's 184. Hayes, therefore, won the bare minimum number of electoral votes needed to secure the presidency. However, Hayes securing 185 electoral votes was not seen as a likely outcome after ballots were cast, as the election closed with neither candidate winning a majority of electoral votes due to contested results in four states: Florida, Louisiana, Oregon, and South Carolina (Morris Jr. 2004). Notably, just one vote in Oregon was disputed, while the entire slate of electors was disputed in the three Southern states (Holt 2008). Both Tilden and Hayes submitted slates of electors to be counted, leaving Congress to determine which slates should be counted as part of the official total. Given the unprecedented nature of this, Congress decided to establish a bipartisan commission consisting of 15 members: five members from the House of Representatives, five members from the Senate, and five Supreme Court Justices, seven of whom were to be Republicans, seven Democrats, and one Independent (Holt 2008). The singular Independent was Supreme Court Justice David Davis from Illinois who ultimately resigned his seat on the court (and thus the commission) because the Illinois state legislature appointed Davis to the U.S. Senate. The Illinois legislature believed their actions would ensure Davis supported Tilden over Hayes, but Davis resigned from the commission after his appointment and, given the lack of any more independents on the court, was replaced by a Republican. So, the commission split down party lines in each case, awarding Hayes the electoral votes in each of the disputed states by a vote of 8–7. In addition to this, a much-disputed account from Woodward (1951) alleges that Hayes was buoyed by Democratic support in the South after he agreed to demands to end Reconstruction in what some have referred to as the Compromise of 1877. Yet many historians dispute this "compromise" and argue Reconstruction was well on its way to being ended prior to this election (Holt 2008; Polakoff 1973). Regardless of the dispute, Hayes became president by the slimmest margin ever recorded in the Electoral College—just one vote.

Just 12 years after the disputed 1876 election, the United States once again witnessed the presidency go to the loser of the popular vote. The 1888 election resulted in Benjamin Harrison defeating Grover Cleveland, an incumbent president, in the Electoral College but losing the popular vote. Cleveland served as president for four years, prior to which he was the Democratic governor of New York. Harrison was a Republican senator from Indiana and the grandson of William Henry Harrison, the ninth president of the United States. Cleveland won a plurality in the popular vote (48.6 percent) compared to Harrison's 47.8 percent, while Harrison bested Cleveland in the Electoral College 233–168. So, while Harrison narrowly lost the popular vote, he won a decisive victory in the Electoral College. Edwards (2004) explains this by pointing out that Harrison won several states by slim margins, while Cleveland won many of his states by large margins, thus driving up his popular vote numbers but not his electoral vote numbers. There are several accusations of corruption levied at the 1888 election, causing many to question who the rightful winner of this election should have been. John Garraty, an American historian said, "Corruption was perhaps more flagrant than in any other presidential election" (quoted in Baumgardner 1984, 416). There were voter suppression and disenfranchisement accusations throughout the Black communities in the South (Baumgardner 1984). Many looked at Indiana's "blocks of five" voting as a way for Harrison to buy votes in his home state. "Floaters" was the term given to voters who would float between parties across elections to the highest bidder (i.e., they would vote for whichever candidate's party would pay them the most) (Ackerman 1998). Each election ward in Indiana had a boss, and each boss was given instructions to break the floaters into "blocks of five" to ensure they would support Harrison. So, this was clearly a Republican Party-sponsored scheme, not a state-sponsored one. Yet, with the accusations of corruption and vote-buying, it is hard to say who the rightful winner of this election should have been. Regardless, in the end, Harrison became president because he won the Electoral College, and Cleveland earned the distinction of becoming the first and (as of this writing) only president to serve one term, lose his reelection bid, and then win a second term four years later, as he defeated Harrison in a rematch in 1892.

Much ink has been spilled in an effort to understand the 2000 election result, in which Al Gore won the popular vote but lost the electoral vote to George W. Bush. Gore was the vice president to Bill Clinton for eight years and previously served as a Democratic Senator from Tennessee. Bush was a former Republican governor of Texas and the son of George H. W. Bush, the 41st president. Gore won the popular vote by roughly 500,000 votes, while Bush won the Electoral College with 271 votes—just one more than the necessary 270. However, on election night, neither candidate won the electoral vote, as Florida remained "too close to call." With Gore at 267 electoral votes and Bush at 246, Florida's 25 electoral votes would determine which candidate would become president. By the close of election night, the networks had called Florida for both Gore and Bush, retracted both calls, and labeled it too close to call. The following morning, Bush was ahead by approximately 1,300 votes, a slim enough margin to trigger an automatic machine recount. Additionally, concerns were raised about the butterfly ballot used in Palm Beach County, in which third-party candidates overperformed expectations (Fineman 2000; Van Natta Jr. 2000). Pat Buchanan, specifically, received approximately 2,800 more votes than expected in Palm Beach County alone based on projections and data available from other Florida counties (Wand et al. 2001). These votes for Buchanan came from Democratic strongholds, so many of these votes likely should have gone to Gore, making him the winner. In fact, in their analysis, Wand et al. (2001) demonstrate Gore to be the likely rightful winner of the 2000 election. Regardless, because of the reported voter confusion with the butterfly ballot used in the election, the Gore campaign requested a hand recount of the ballots in four Florida counties: Palm Beach, Broward, Miami-Dade, and Volusia (all of which are typically strong Democratic counties).

These recounts hit a number of snags along the way. Many lawsuits were filed and court rulings were handed down from various state and federal courts in November and December, leaving those in charge of the recounts confused about whether or not they should be proceeding or not, effectively causing many starts and stops over these two months (see Brady et al. 2001). In addition to the confusion sparked by the various court rulings, there were several disputes about chads and whether or not the individuals recounting ballots really knew a voter's intent (Fessenden 2000). A chad is the small circular piece of paper that is punched out of a paper ballot by the voting machines used throughout Florida at the time. In fact, these chads sparked a whole new set of lingo for election watchers in 2000, including hanging chads (those that were not fully punched out but slightly attached) and dimpled chads (those that were slightly punched but not torn from the ballot).

Regardless of the expanded election vocabulary, the 2000 election was finally brought to a close on December 12, 2000, when the U.S. Supreme Court ruled in a 5–4 decision that there were constitutional problems with some of the recounts ordered and must be halted. With the halting of the recount, Bush was ahead by 537 votes, giving him all of Florida's 25 electoral votes for a total of 271. Bush therefore became the 43rd president with his victory in the Electoral College solidified.

Just sixteen years later, the United States got yet another example of a popular vote winner not getting to become president—and this time the popular vote margin of victory was almost three million votes. Hillary Clinton, the first female to receive the nomination of a major party, bested Donald Trump in the popular vote by more than two percent (or 2.87 million votes). Clinton had years of political experience under her belt, serving as First Lady of Arkansas, First Lady of the United States, a Democratic Senator for New York, and secretary of state during Barack Obama's first term. Despite this lengthy resume, Clinton lost the electoral vote to Donald Trump 304–227. Trump possessed no political experience, bringing with him, instead, years of experience dealing with business and real estate transactions. Again, a good amount of research has been done to unpack the reasons Clinton lost and Trump won, including the obvious gendered attitudes and expectations; yet without the Electoral College in place, the United States would have elected its first female president.

So, how did Clinton lose the Electoral College while winning three million more popular votes than Trump? By losing three normally reliable blue states by very slim margins. Wisconsin, Michigan, and Pennsylvania had been won by the Democratic candidate in every presidential election since 1992, with Wisconsin also having supported Michael Dukakis over George H. W. Bush in 1988. In 2016, each of these states went red instead of blue, but only by small margins. Trump did not have landslide wins in these states; instead, he won by less than one percent in each of them. In Wisconsin, Trump won the statewide popular vote by just 22,748 votes; in Michigan, he won by 10,704; and in Pennsylvania, he won by 44,284. So, with a combined vote total of 77,736 votes across these three traditionally blue states, Trump eked out a victory in the Electoral College. Notably, each of these states reverted back to their "blue" status in 2020. In addition, voter identification laws, as discussed in chapter 4, were at play in these states. Wisconsin has a strict voter ID law, meaning you have to show an ID in order to cast a ballot. Michigan required anyone unable to show an ID to vote via an affidavit ballot so that the voter's identification could be verified. Pennsylvania had a strict photo ID requirement for the previous election in 2012, but it was overturned by the Pennsylvania Supreme Court just two years later. So while Pennsylvania did not require voters to produce identification in 2016, many voters may have been under the assumption that they would need to provide one, just like they did four years prior. Thus, the 2016 election resulted in a candidate who lost the national popular vote by three million votes taking over the presidency because he won roughly 78,000 more votes across three states. This really highlights the absurdity of the Electoral College.

These five elections soundly violate democratic norms. Dahl (2000, 37) tells us that treating people as politically equal is central to the democratic process, writing that "every member must have an equal and effective opportunity to vote, and all votes must be counted as equal." The current structure of the Electoral College certainly does not measure up to that standard, as we have five examples in which an individual has become president without winning a plurality of support from voters. Reforming the Electoral College should be focused on making sure democratic norms are centered in American elections. The Constant Two Plan will do just that—it will ensure the national popular vote winner becomes president in every election.

Another problem with the Electoral College is the small state bias inherent in its original form. Small states have a disproportionate amount of power in the Electoral College due to the number of voters each electoral vote represents (Adkins and Kirwan 2002; Siaroff 2010). Figure 6.1 shows the number of voters per electoral vote in all 50 states and Washington, D.C., under the current structure. What this shows is that small states have an overwhelming advantage in terms of how many voters are represented by each electoral vote a state has. Under the current Electoral College system, each electoral vote from Wyoming represents 193,105 voters, while in Texas, each electoral vote is worth 744,858 voters. This advantage given to small states is also in violation of the democratic norm of political equality—especially in terms of the equality of each individual's vote (Dahl 1989). The weighting of one state's voters over another creates an imbalance of electoral power across the United States. While many point to the electoral power of large states like California, Texas, and Florida—which, do indeed, have a large number of electoral votes—it is actually the small states that are advantaged under the current structure of the Electoral College.

Yet another critique of the Electoral College is that it creates an unequal distribution of campaign resources. Based on the current structure, it is common to see that battleground states receive the majority of attention from candidates in the form of advertisements and visits (Devine 2018; Doherty 2010; Johnson 2005; Shaw 1999, 2004). States that are reliably Republican or Democratic are often ignored by candidates because they are assumed to already be in support of their party's nominee. Instead, candidates spend their time and money trying to increase turnout and their vote share in battleground states. These battleground states are seen as "make or break" wins for the candidates seeking office, and their residents often tire of hearing

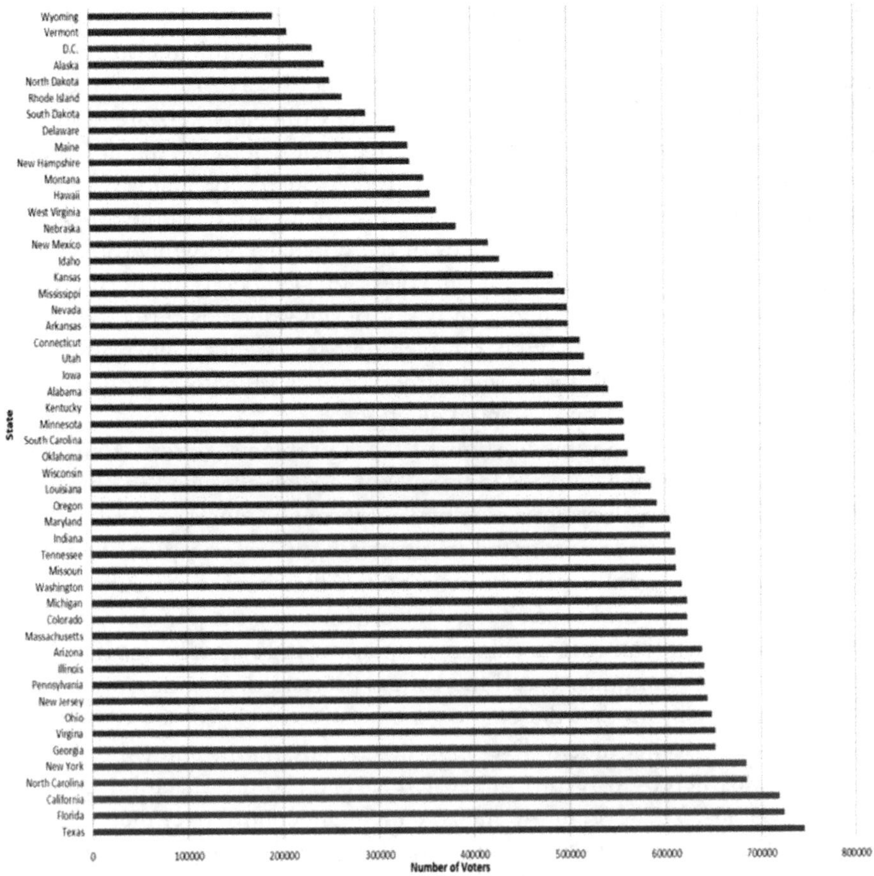


**Figure 6.1 Number of People Per Electoral Vote Under the Current Electoral College.** *Source*: Number of Electoral Votes Taken from the National Archives; State population take from the 2010 U.S. Census.

about the candidates by the end of the election. In contrast, states that are considered safely ensconced in one of the candidates' columns receive very little attention from the candidates running for president (Johnson 2005). Very little is spent on advertising, and very few (if any) visits are made to these states because, even before we have presidential nominees, we know how these states are going to vote. Because candidates need to win states under the current Electoral College system, they are incentivized to focus on the battleground states, as those are the ones that will tip the election in their direction. Thus, the Electoral College encourages candidates to ignore the voters that live in these safe states in order to court the voters found in battleground states.

All of these criticisms of the Electoral College taken together create a political arena in which turnout is depressed due to lower political efficacy. Voters who feel like their vote does not matter are not likely to show up to vote. Due to the undemocratic nature of the Electoral College, voters are reminded every election night that the popular vote does not determine the next president, but rather how the electoral votes are allocated. For many voting-age Americans, in addition to the 2016 results, they can also recall the 2000 election, giving them two recent examples of the popular vote winner losing the presidency. Additionally, Republican voters in Democratic-majority states and Democratic voters in Republican-majority states feel less effective in the voting booth, as the partisan winner in each state is largely known prior to any votes being cast. Overall, the current structure of the Electoral College does little to inspire turnout in presidential elections.

So, in order to try to remedy some of these problems, reform plans have been proposed, debated, and voted upon. Yet, as demonstrated in chapter 3, none of these reform plans have ever made it through Congress. And perhaps more importantly, as demonstrated in chapter 5, the reform plans that have been attempted generally perform worse than the current structure. If the reform plan does not move the country toward ensuring the popular vote winner becomes president, it is not a reform plan worth considering. If Americans are going to continue to call the United States a democracy, we should work toward ensuring that the country's executive is chosen by the people. Anything short of that fails to live up to democratic norms and expectations. To that end, I hereby offer my suggested revision to the Electoral College. These revisions, I believe, allow states to maintain control over their election systems (thus preserving the federalist ideal) while also ensuring the popular vote winner becomes president. The Constant Two Plan, as I refer to it, is outlined next.

## THE CONSTANT TWO PLAN

While several reform plans have been offered, they all present a unique set of challenges to implement. Thus, what is needed is a plan that eliminates the main impediments to reform and aligns the popular vote with the electoral vote. The Constant Two Plan outlined below would do just that. It does not change the number of electoral votes awarded to each state or eliminate physical electors. It simply changes how electoral votes are distributed, thereby eliminating the need for a constitutional amendment and necessitating only a change in state law. Under this plan, the nationwide popular vote winner would receive the votes of the Constant Two electors (the two votes from each state that correspond to the number of Senators each state has), thus guaranteeing that candidate 102 electoral votes. Each of the remaining electoral votes would be allocated according to each state's current rules. Thus, if Candidate X wins the nationwide popular vote, they would receive two electoral votes from each state and Washington, D.C., totaling 102 electoral votes. The remaining 436 electoral votes would be allocated according to the statewide popular vote, as they currently are (save Nebraska and Maine, which use the district system to award electoral votes).

The Constant Two Plan fixes many of the problems associated with the other reform plans discussed above. First, it remedies all five cases in which the popular vote and electoral vote winners did not align. Table 6.1 highlights these elections, while a breakdown of all U.S. elections can be found in Appendix A. These data demonstrate that Hillary Clinton, Al Gore, Grover Cleveland, Samuel Tilden, and Andrew Jackson all would have won the presidency in the years in which they won the popular vote. Taking the 2016 presidential election as an example, we see that under the current structure of the Electoral College, Hillary Clinton won 227 electoral votes and the popular vote in 20 states and Washington, D.C., whereas Donald Trump won 304 electoral votes and the popular vote in 30 states, with various write-in candidates having won seven electoral votes due to faithless electors. Under the Constant Two Plan, Clinton would have received an extra 60 electoral votes, and Trump would lose 60 votes (the constant two votes from the 30 states Trump won) to give Clinton the new total of 287 votes to Trump's 244. Under this metric, Clinton would have surpassed the 270 electoral vote threshold needed to win the presidency, aligning the electoral vote with the popular vote. These new totals also reflect the closeness of the popular vote, as Clinton bested Trump by roughly three million popular votes. Applying the same metrics to the other 49 presidential elections in which there was a popular vote, we see that all candidates who won the popular vote would have received an Electoral College victory as well.

Historically, the Constant Two Plan would thus have a perfect record of aligning the popular vote with the electoral vote. While the Electoral College is largely an anti-majoritarian institution, the Constant Two Plan would include a mechanism in which the nationwide popular vote winner receives 102 votes, better aligning it with democratic norms as it takes into account the preferences of the country's voters. The United States has a long history of democratizing elections: expanding the franchise to include minorities, women, and young voters between the ages of 18 and 21, granting Washington, D.C., electoral votes, providing for the direct election of U.S. Senators, eliminating poll taxes, removing literacy tests, and creating a meaningful vote in the presidential nominating process, among many other examples. However, the Electoral College, a staunchly undemocratic institution, remains. The Constant Two Plan would help democratize presidential elections by

**Table 6.1 Mismatched Popular Vote and Electoral College Results Under the Current Structure and the Constant Two Plan**

| *Year* | *Party* | *Candidate* | *Original E.C. Total* | *Number of States Won* | *Net Change in E.C. Vote* | *New E.C. Total* |
|---|---|---|---|---|---|---|
| 2016 | Democrat | Hillary Clinton | 227 | 21 | 60 | 287 |
| | Republican | Donald Trump | 304 | 30 | –60 | 244 |
| | Various | Write-Ins | 7 | 0 | 0 | 7 |
| 2000 | Democrat | Al Gore | 266 | 21 | 60 | 326 |
| | Republican | George W. Bush | 271 | 30 | –60 | 211 |
| | Democrat | Abstention | 1 | 0 | 0 | 1 |
| 1888 | Democrat | Grover Cleveland | 168 | 18 | 36 | 208 |
| | Republican | Benjamin Harrison | 233 | 20 | –36 | 193 |
| 1876 | Democrat | Samuel Tilden | 184 | 17 | 40 | 224 |
| | Republican | Rutherford B. Hayes | 185 | 20 | –40 | 145 |
| 1824^ | Democratic–Republican | Andrew Jackson | 99 | 5 | 38 | 127 |
| | Democratic–Republican | John Quincy Adams | 84 | 7 | –14 | 70 |
| | Democratic–Republican | William Crawford | 41 | 1 | –2 | 39 |
| | Democratic–Republican | Henry Clay | 37 | 3 | –6 | 31 |
| | Republican | Unpledged | 0 | 0 | 0 | 0 |
| | Others | | 0 | 0 | 0 | 0 |

*Source*: Number of electoral votes taken from the National Archives.
^Denotes that DE, GA, LA, NY, SC, and VT did not hold popular vote, electors chosen by state legislature

creating a mechanism to award the nationwide popular vote winner with 102 electoral votes, only 168 electoral votes short of a majority, making it nearly impossible to win the popular vote but lose the presidency with an Electoral College loss.

Additionally, the Constant Two Plan helps lessen the small state bias associated with the current structure of the Electoral College. Under the current structure, the value of each electoral vote depends on the number of Representatives and Senators that represent a state. Figure 6.1, shown prior, depicts how many voters each electoral vote represents under the current structure, while figure 6.2 shows the relationship between voters and electoral votes under the Constant Two Plan. Switching to the Constant Two Plan would help alleviate some of this small state bias, with each electoral vote in Rhode Island representing 529,820 voters and each electoral vote in Montana representing 1,050,493 voters. Under the Constant Two Plan, Rhode Island would have two electoral votes to award to the state's popular vote winner, while Montana would have just one (though after the 2020 census, Montana gained an additional electoral vote, which will be added to its total for the 2024 presidential election and onward). This is largely due to the fact that the Senate is a malapportioned body (Griffin 2006; Johnson and Miller 2023). Because the Senate requires equal representation for states, the proportion of Senators to voters across the United States leads to Senators from less populated states having more voting power in the Senate than those in heavily populated states, leading to political inequality throughout the chamber (Griffin 2006). The Constant Two Plan removes the electoral votes that correspond to the two senators from each state and awards them to the nationwide popular vote winner, which largely removes the malapportionment problem associated with the Senate, which is really the cause of the small state bias in the Electoral College. While this still does not create complete equity among all 50 states and Washington, D.C., it does significantly narrow the discrepancies between the states at either extreme. In fact, only seven states fall outside the 600,000 to 800,000 voters per electoral vote range. This range includes the average congressional district population size and helps create a more level playing field in terms of political power across the United States. At the time of this book's publication, the average congressional district would be approximately 765,000 people (Chinni 2023). Under the distribution of electoral power in the current structure, only 20 states fall within that range, and there is, in fact, no 200,000 range of voters per electoral vote in which a majority of states fall. The Constant Two Plan thus goes a long way toward creating equity in electoral power in the Electoral College by significantly reducing the small state bias.

Under the Constant Two Plan, the federalism ideal currently associated with the Electoral College is preserved. While Edwards (2004) clearly

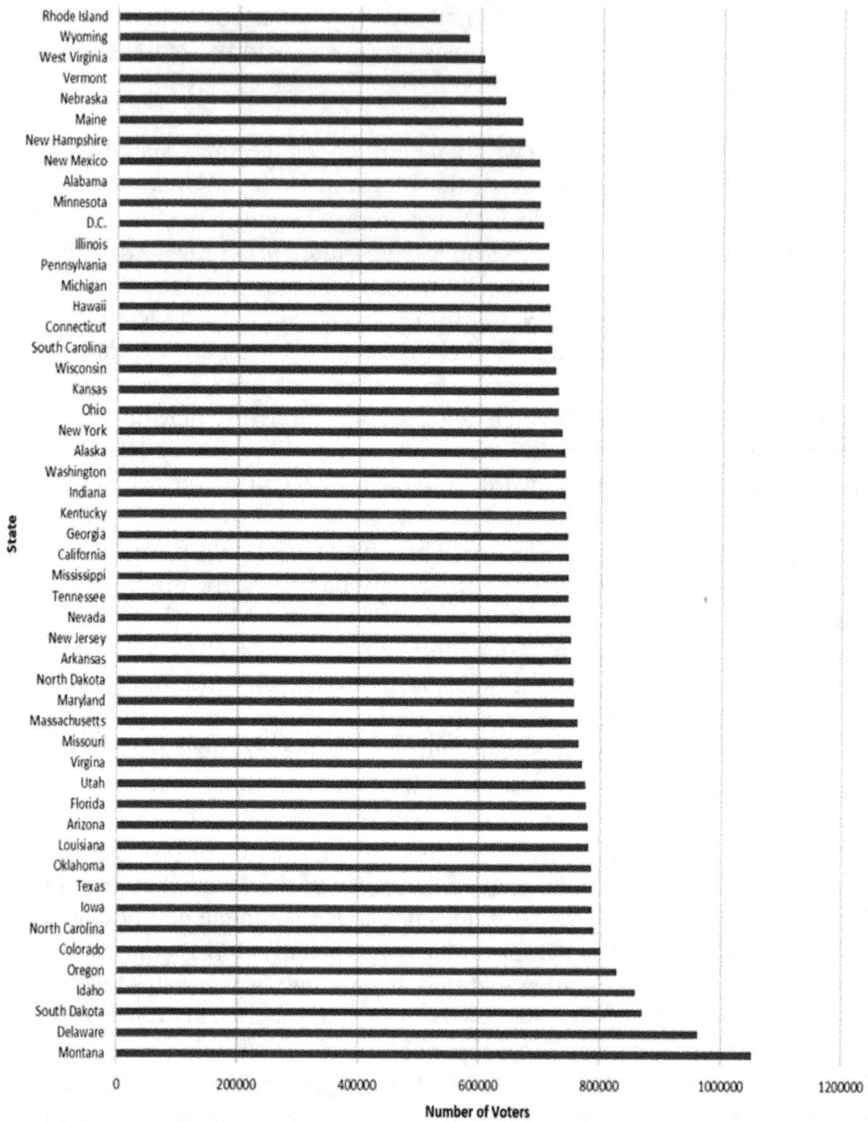


**Figure 6.2 Number of People Per Electoral Vote Under the Constant Two Plan.** *Source*: Number of Electoral Votes taken from the National Archives; State population Taken from the 2010 U.S. Census.

articulates that this federalist ideal was not intentionally intertwined with presidential selection, it is nonetheless an important part of the current discussion regarding Electoral College reform. In fact, the Founders were not concerned with federalism when creating the Electoral College. They were more focused on preventing tyranny and being able to return home from the convention. Instead, federalism is an importance we have since placed on the institution. Electoral College supporters frequently point to federalism as a reason to keep the Electoral College as is (see Best 1996; Kimberling 1992). The Constant Two Plan would keep presidential elections ultimately waged at the state level, while incorporating a mechanism by which a candidate also receives votes for winning the national popular vote. Each state would still retain electoral votes to award to the candidate who received a plurality of votes in that state but also award two votes to the candidate who won the overall national popular vote, thus helping marry the Federalist principle with the national will.

For the Constant Two Plan to go into effect, a constitutional amendment would not be needed. Instead, what would be needed would be for states to change their laws regarding how electoral votes are allocated, similar to the District Plan and National Popular Vote Interstate Compact (NPVIC). However, unlike under the District Plan, gerrymandering will not impact how a state allocates its electoral votes. Congressional districts do not enter into the metric for the Constant Two Plan. Further, unlike under the proportional plan, the Constant Two Plan does not create the need for more contingent elections. Under the Proportional Plan, Congress has been given the opportunity to officially elect the president and vice president six times since 1956. Under the Constant Two Plan, contingent elections would still exist because eliminating them would require a constitutional amendment, but in the 49 elections in which a popular vote was held, a contingent election would not have been needed. In all of them, the Electoral College awarded the popular vote winner a majority of electoral votes. This means that in all of these elections, American voters would be in charge of selecting their president, and the contingent election process would largely become defunct.

Under the Constant Two Plan, candidates vying for the presidency would also be encouraged to campaign nationwide, as winning the national popular vote would earn them 102 electoral votes. It is likely that elections would still produce battleground states in which neither candidate has a clear advantage of winning the presidency, but due to the electoral votes associated with winning the national popular vote, candidates will be more encouraged than they currently are to increase turnout no matter the ideological preferences of a state. Under the current structure of the Electoral College, candidates are largely focused solely on battleground states, increasing their travel and advertising expenditures in these toss-up states (Shaw 1999, 2004). That generally leaves reliably blue and red states largely ignored by presidential candidates (Doherty 2010). While Stonecash (2010) argues that this behavior actually makes candidates broaden their electoral strategies to include groups of voters outside of their base, it still does not encourage candidates to campaign across the entirety of the country. Candidates still do not spend resources in states where they know they will not win. The Constant Two Plan would encourage campaign activity throughout the United States in an effort to drive up candidates' vote shares, as they actually would be incentivized to compete to win the nationwide popular vote.

Some will argue that creating a way to include a "reward" for winning the popular vote will increase campaign attention to cities, causing candidates to focus mainly on the most densely populated areas where their supporters are located. This may indeed be the case. Instead of focusing on battleground states, we may see an increase in battleground cities. However, this all seems to comport with democratic norms. Candidates should be focused on attracting voters, and in order to do so, they need to wage their campaigns where the voters are. Compare Los Angeles, CA, with the entire state of Wyoming, for example. According to the 2020 census, Los Angeles, CA, is home to just under four million people while the entire state of Wyoming is home to 581,348 people. If a candidate is trying to attract as many voters as possible, it makes the most sense that they would focus on the more heavily populated areas. Despite the fact that cities are more heavily Democratic, they are not completely homogenous. According to a 2014 Pew Research Report, approximately 29 percent of Los Angeles voters identify as Republicans. Thus, out of almost four million voters, over one million identify as Republicans. So even the Republican candidate for president would be well served by campaigning in Los Angeles in an attempt to mobilize these Republican voters. The same logic applies to Wyoming, where approximately 25 percent of voters identify themselves as Democrats (Pew Research 2014). So, if the Democratic candidate would spend some time trying to mobilize Wyoming Democrats, there are approximately 145,000 voters who may be receptive to those activities. Nonetheless, there are more voters to mobilize in larger cities for members of both parties, so there is a good chance we will see an increase in urban campaign mobilization activities. But these activities should increase across the entire United States if winning the national popular vote is rewarded, not just in a handful of battleground states.

Taken together, all of the benefits of the Constant Two Plan should increase turnout. Voters in presidential elections will know that the nationwide popular vote winner will be guaranteed to receive 102 electoral votes. With this knowledge, voters will know that even if their preferred candidate loses their state's popular vote, he or she will at least receive two electoral votes from each state should they win the national popular vote. Additionally, they will know that the state's popular vote winner will also receive electoral votes. This is unlike the NPVIC in that states will not be expected to award all of their votes to the national popular vote winner, in some cases completely overturning a state's popular vote. Under the current structure of the Electoral

College, Democratic voters in red states and Republican voters in blue states feel less inclined to turn out, as they know the likelihood of their vote changing their state's Electoral College vote is slim, despite the partisanship of the candidate who wins the national popular vote (Cebula and Murphy 1980). However, were the Constant Two Plan adopted, these voters would know that their vote would matter in terms of the overall national popular vote. Thus, if a Republican candidate were to win the popular vote, Republican voters in a reliably blue state (e.g., Vermont) would know that the Republican candidate would win at least two of that state's electoral votes. Democratic voters in Mississippi, for example, would also know that the Democratic candidate would win two votes from their state should they win the national popular vote. In addition, Mississippi's Republican voters would also know the Republican candidate would win the state's four remaining electoral votes. Overall, then adoption of the Constant Two Plan should increase turnout in presidential elections because voters know that the winner of the national popular vote will be rewarded with 102 votes. Thus, even if a candidate loses a state, if that candidate wins the national popular vote, they will still get two votes from that state, making their supporters in that state feel heard. At the very least, voters should feel more heard under this structure than under the current structure.

## THE POLITICS OF PROPOSALS

Any discussion of Electoral College reform would be incomplete without discussing the politics behind the passage of the proposed reform. An important question to consider regarding Electoral College reform is whether or not a constitutional amendment is needed. In the cases of the Automatic, National Bonus, Proportional, and Direct Vote Plans, the answer would be in the affirmative. In the cases of the District Plan, NPVIC, and the Constant Two Plan the answer would be in negative. The amendment process is slow and deliberately difficult. We have seen several amendments proposed to alter the Electoral College in some capacity, and two have succeeded: creating separate votes for president and vice president via the 12th Amendment (ratified in 1804) and allocating three electoral votes to Washington, D.C., via the 23rd Amendment (ratified in 1961). I assume here that adopting a reform that does not require a constitutional amendment is an easier reform than one that does. The last time an amendment was successfully ratified was in 1992, however, the 27th Amendment was actually written and passed by Congress in 1789. This particular amendment contained no sunset clause and was the focus of a Texas graduate student's research, who ultimately led a successful ratification campaign, culminating in the amendment being added to the Constitution in May 1992 (Largey 2017). Yet, today, there has been a steady increase in partisan polarization, meaning Americans have gotten better at aligning their ideology and partisanship (Abramowitz and Saunders 1998; Fiorina et al. 2011). The same holds for Congress, as Democrats and Republicans have continued to move farther and farther apart from each other (McCarty, Poole, and Rosenthal 2006). Given this increased partisan division, the likelihood of a two-thirds majority in Congress supporting a constitutional amendment to alter the Electoral College is seemingly zero. Congress also needs to approve interstate compacts, leading to doubts that the NPVIC stands any chance of passage for the same reasons. The Constant Two Plan does not rely on an amendment, nor does it require all states to enter into a compact, thus also avoiding the need for Congress to ratify it.

Another large obstacle that stands in the way of reform is the partisan slant of each of the states. It is clear from the two most recent examples of the mismatch between electoral and popular votes that Republicans have benefited from the Electoral College and will likely be reluctant to embrace reform. This may be for one of two reasons. First, many Republicans like to raise concerns about the elimination of the federalist principle found in the Electoral College. This concern holds little water with respect to the Constant Two plan, as this plan acknowledges the federalist principle by allowing each state the right to allocate their electoral votes—save two—according to state law. Two of a state's electoral votes would be allocated to the national popular vote winner, while the remaining electoral vote(s) would be determined by the popular vote in a state (with the exceptions of Nebraska and Maine, which currently award their votes according to congressional district results). Thus, objections on the grounds of the elimination of the federalist principle in the Constant Two Plan would be largely unfounded.

In addition, any traditional Republican strongholds may be loath to embrace a reform plan that seems to benefit the Democratic Party. Admittedly, there is little incentive for Republican-majority states to embrace Electoral College reform because the current structure has awarded the Republicans the presidency in all four elections since 1824, in which the popular vote and electoral vote did not align. However, there is reason for Republicans to consider supporting some form of Electoral College reform. The demographics of the United States are shifting in such a way that Texas will become a battleground state rather than remain a reliable Republican stronghold in the Electoral College (Jackson 2019). Without being able to rely on Texas' 36 electoral votes, Republicans have reason to be concerned about their long-term ability to win presidential elections (Anuzis and Steele 2019). Al Gore winning Texas would have guaranteed him the presidency over George W. Bush in 2000, and it would have narrowed the 2016 election considerably, with Clinton receiving 263 and Trump receiving 268. Thus,

2016 would have resulted in either a contingent election or the seven faithless electors deciding the outcome. If we look at how those faithless electors voted, we see that five were Clinton electors while two were Trump electors, though these two Trump electors were from Texas. It is hard, however, to be sure how these faithless electors would have voted had Clinton actually won and by how many electoral votes she won. So, with Clinton winning Texas, the 2016 election would have ended with Trump receiving 270 electoral votes to Clinton's 268. While this does not give Clinton a win over Trump, it makes the election much closer than it was with Trump winning Texas.

In addition to Texas likely becoming a battleground state due to changing demographics, both Arizona and Georgia are likely to become battlegrounds as well (Barron-Lopez 2019). In fact, we saw Arizona and Georgia flip from red to blue in the 2020 presidential election. Importantly, it was not just the electoral votes of these states that the Democrats won. Both states have each sent two Democrats to serve in the Senate since 2018. Arizona elected Kirsten Sinema to a full six-year term in 2018, and Mark Kelly was elected in 2020 to finish John McCain's term after he passed away. Kelly went on to win a full six-year term in 2022, playing up Arizona's shift from red to blue. Georgia elected both Jon Ossoff and Rafael Warnock to the Senate in 2020, with Ossoff winning a full six-year term and Warnock just two years, as he won a special election to fulfill the rest of Kelly Loeffler's term (Loeffler herself was initially appointed to finish the term of Johnny Isakson, who resigned in December 2019). Warnock, too, was elected to a full six-year term in 2022, further solidifying Georgia's shift from red to blue. All of this highlights the shifting demographics in these two states, setting them up to be battleground states in future electoral cycles. Winning one of these two states, along with Texas, would have easily given Clinton the presidency over Trump.

While changing Texas' Electoral College results is a purely hypothetical exercise, it will not always be hypothetical. The demographics of the United States are shifting in a way that will benefit the Democratic Party in the long term and spell electoral losses for Republicans (Anuzis and Steele 2019). This idea is confirmed by the electoral shift witnessed in Arizona and Georgia in the 2018, 2020, and 2022 election cycles. These two states flipped their electoral votes from their traditionally Republican roots to the Democratic candidate (Georgia for the first time since 1992 and Arizona for the first time since 1996). Because of these demographic shifts, Republicans should begin to consider reform plans (outside of voter suppression) that help level the playing field—especially considering the evidence from Arizona and Georgia. The Constant Two Plan presents a way to balance both the federalist principle embodied by the current structure of the Electoral College while also accounting for the national popular vote, something that would not inherently benefit either major American political party. In fact, it would encourage both major parties to compete for as many votes as possible across the country, regardless of the state in which a voter resides.

A related obstacle is the fact that the Constant Two Plan would eliminate the small state bias, thus creating the possibility for small states to protest this reform. In addition, several of the small states are also traditionally Republican states so they may be doubly hesitant to embrace such a plan. The states with only three electoral votes are Alaska, Delaware, Montana, North Dakota, South Dakota, Vermont, and Wyoming, along with Washington, D.C. From this list, we can see that five of these states are traditional Republican strongholds while the remaining three reliably vote Democratic. They are not uniformly representative of one political party, so there is a low chance of all of them banning together to protest this plan on partisan grounds. However, there is still a chance they will oppose this due to their small state status. While this is admittedly possible, it does seem to be less of a concern than the partisan obstacle, as these states banning together would not alter the election results under the Constant Two plan.

The 2016 election is the closest election we would have had under the Constant Two plan, as seen in table 2 (Trump would have received 244 electoral votes to Clinton's 287). If we altered those results even further to accommodate a small state refusal to comply with the Constant Two Plan we would still see a Clinton victory, ensuring the popular vote and electoral vote winners were the same candidate. In 2016, Trump won five of those states, while Clinton won three. So if we allocate those 24 electoral votes according to the current Electoral College structure while allocating all other electoral votes according to the Constant Two Plan, Clinton would have received 278 electoral votes to Trump's 254. There would only have been a net change of 50, rather than 60, in the electoral vote since five of the 30 states Trump won were small states that were exempted from the rules of the Constant Two Plan in this example. Thus, if all small states were to uniformly reject this plan, there are no historical examples in which this would alter the anticipated winner of the presidency.

## WHY REFORM AND WHY NOW?

According to a Pew Report released in September 2023, 65 percent of the American public favors abolishing the Electoral College and relying on the popular vote to select the president, while only 33 percent favor keeping the current system (Kiley 2023). The number of Americans who favor abolishing the Electoral College has fluctuated a bit since 2000 (the previous example of a mismatch between the electoral and popular votes) but has consistently maintained majority support. This data can be seen in figure 6.3 below.

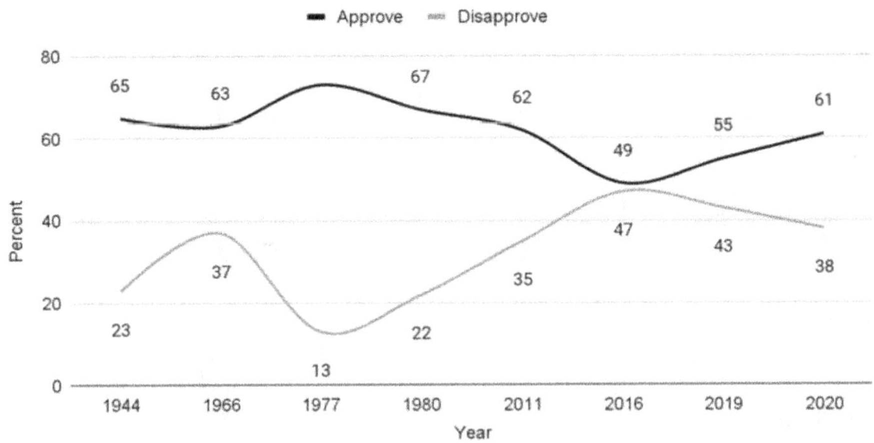


**Figure 6.3 Public Support for Abolishing the Electoral College.** *Source*: Gallup Polling data as reported by Brenan (2020).

According to Pew's polling, 61 percent of Americans were supportive of abolishing the Electoral College in 2000, but support dipped to 51 percent in 2016 and then increased to 60 percent by 2020 (Kiley 2023). This is largely mirrored by Gallup's polling, which found 60 percent of Americans in favor of eliminating the Electoral College in 2000, dipping to 49 percent in 2016, and then increasing to 61 percent in 2020 (Brenan 2020). Combined, it seems that there has been consistency in American attitudes toward the Electoral College over the past two decades. While there has been some fluctuation, there has been a constant plurality (mostly majority) in support of getting rid of the Electoral College. Taken together, this highlights the fact that more Americans want to abolish it than keep it, so it seems the American public would rally behind a large push for reform.

However, when we explore some of the underlying data, there is a clear partisan pattern that raises concerns. Since 2000, Democrats have more strongly supported eliminating the Electoral College than Republicans (Brenan 2020; Kiley 2023). Looking at the data presented by the Pew Research Center, a whopping 82 percent of Democratic voters would like to see the Electoral College eliminated, but among Republican voters, that number only reaches 47 percent (Kiley 2023). Democrats have been fairly steady in their support for eliminating it, moving from 75 percent in 2000 to 69 percent in 2012, with a gradual increase to 82 percent in 2023 (Kiley 2023). Considering the Democrats lost both the 2000 and 2016 elections, their strong dislike of the Electoral College is not surprising. It also explains why Republicans are more hesitant to embrace the abolishing of the Electoral College. Support among Republicans has grown over time but still has not reached majority support. According to the Pew data, Republican voters have moved from 46 percent in support of abolishing the Electoral College in 2000 to a low of 27 percent after the 2016 election, but have since seen a steady increase toward 47 percent in 2023 (Kiley 2023). These numbers do not quite align with what Gallup has found—especially among Republican voters. Democrats were found to be even more strongly in support (89 percent in 2020), but Gallup reports that only 23 percent of Republican voters felt favorable toward abolishing the Electoral College in 2020 (Brenan 2020). This discrepancy may be due to the fact that Gallup disentangled independents from their partisans and leaners, while Pew included leaners in their party data.

What we see are clear partisan patterns in attitudes toward eliminating the Electoral College—a big reason why passing an amendment to abolish the Electoral College will continue to be incredibly difficult to do. Due to the partisan nature of this debate, it seems highly unlikely that any sort of reform mechanism that relies on a constitutional amendment would pass. Any reform plan that stands a chance at passing likely needs to not require an amendment. While there are some of these reform plans out there, that does not mean they are not polarizing, as they indeed are. As demonstrated in the Pew Data, Republican voters are just not supportive of reforming an electoral institution with which they win. Currently, that is a smart strategic move. However, this reluctance to embrace reform will likely hurt the party in the long run—in fact, we are starting to see the effects now. As discussed earlier, with states like Texas, Arizona, and Georgia trending blue, the advantage Republicans currently hold in the Electoral College will shift, and so should the party's support for electoral reform. Recent elections in Arizona and Georgia have helped underscore the fact that these shifts are indeed happening. Both of these reliably red states have now elected two Democrats to the U. S. Senate, with Kyrsten Sinema and Mark Kelly elected in Arizona in 2018 and 2020, respectively, and Rafael Warnock and Jon Ossoff elected in Georgia in 2020. Additionally, both states went blue in the 2020 presidential election, and Arizona elected a Democratic governor in 2022. The projected shift in electoral competitiveness based on demographic changes in these states has largely come to fruition. This implies that the projected shift in Texas will eventually take hold as well. In order to remain competitive, political parties will need to respond to these changing demographic trends—especially the Republicans. By remaining resistant to electoral reform in light of these changes, the Republican Party is setting itself up for failure in future presidential elections. The Republicans have been successful in winning the presidency thanks to the Electoral College—having won just one election's popular vote (2004) since 1992. Yet, out of those eight presidential elections, Republicans have taken the presidency in three of them. This is in large part due to the fact that Republicans have an advantage in the Electoral College, and Republican presidential campaigns have put together strategies focused on winning the necessary 270 electoral votes rather than the popular vote.

Based on these data, it seems unlikely that the public would ratify an amendment that abolishes the Electoral College and institutes the popular vote as the sole determinant of a presidential election. Yet the Republican Party should see that future presidential elections are unlikely to end in their favor under the current system. They ought to embrace reform to ensure that they can remain a competitive party in these future elections. While an amendment is unlikely to be ratified by the public, given the polarization found among the electorate, it also seems impossible that Congress would pass such an amendment. The polarization found among the electorate mirrors the polarization found in Congress, as Congress has been becoming increasingly polarized over time (Lee 2015). In fact, the American political system has become so polarized that it has calcified (Sides, Tausanovitch, and Vavreck 2022). Many voters are clinging to their partisanship and refusing to support a candidate of the opposite party or a policy that was sponsored by the opposition. This calcification is preventing meaningful governance, increasing animosity in our political system, and creating an atmosphere ripe with "us vs. them" mentality.

This, of course, is not to say that reform efforts in the past have failed solely because of logistics or more noble reasons than partisan gridlock. In fact, partisanship was indeed a reason for the failure of Electoral College reform in the past as well. The biggest push for the Direct Vote Plan came in 1969, when all of the pieces of the reform puzzle seemed to be coming together. Birch Bayh was seen as the "amendment wizard" by many political operatives given his history of steering two amendments through the process prior to his taking up the Direct Vote reform plan (Wegman 2019). Yet Strom Thurmond, a Republican Senator from South Carolina led the filibuster that ultimately ended the push for the Direct Vote plan. Thurmond's filibuster was motivated by partisan concerns, namely concerns over the uptick in political and racial minority participation that would likely accompany reform, thereby shaking up the constituency of Thurmond and all of his congressional colleagues. So, because Thurmond and his Republican colleagues were nervous about an increase in participation among likely Democratic voters, they were successful in killing the amendment via filibuster.

We also saw a strong push for the Proportional Plan by Henry Cabot Lodge Jr. throughout the mid-1900s, which also had partisan motivations. Lodge favored a national popular vote but saw no practical way to pass such an amendment (Wilmerding, Jr. 1949). So, believing in electoral reform, Lodge partnered with Ed Gossett, a Democratic member of the House of Representatives, and together they pushed for the Proportional Plan. Yet, Keyssar (2022) notes that Gossett's motivations were very different from Lodge's; Gossett wanted to ensure the Democratic stronghold in the South continues—mostly at the expense of minority groups. Silva (1950) demonstrates clearly that the Democratic Party would have benefited from this reform plan, while the Republican Party would have been hurt—even to the extent of Democrats being able to win the electoral vote while losing the popular vote. This was largely due to the stronghold the Democratic Party had in the southern states at the time. Silva (1950) shows that in the 1948 election, electoral votes in the South were each "worth" approximately 40,000 popular votes, while electoral votes outside of the South translated to about 108,000 popular votes. Additionally, the more "solid" the South was, the better the Democratic candidate would fare under the Proportional Plan (Silva 1950). Much of this, however, had not been brought to light while the Proportional Plan was debated by the Senate and Lodge. A Republican senator from Massachusetts was able to get the Proportional Plan through the Senate with the required two-thirds vote. After Gossett's more partisan motivations were exposed in the House of Representatives, the Proportional Plan met its defeat (Keyssar 2022).

The lesson to be taken from these previous reform attempts is that any effort at electoral reform will no doubt face partisan attacks and accusations. As a result, the real question becomes: Is right now the best time to attempt to reform the Electoral College? Taken together, the preceding pages clearly establish that the Electoral College is in dire need of reform. However, do we have politicians and an electorate that will allow reform to happen? Right now, reform is possible—it just needs to be done carefully and purposefully. An amendment will simply not pass. We are too polarized as a country to come together and pass an amendment of this magnitude. There is little chance of getting 290 Representatives and 67 Senators to agree to pass an amendment eliminating the Electoral College and sending it to the states for ratification. And even if they did, for the reasons discussed above, the amendment is likely to go unratified, as 38 states are unlikely to sign off on such a bill.

In response, the reform taken up needs to be one that does not lean on the amendment process but can be passed piecemeal throughout the country. This is similar to the path taken by reformers who have pursued the NPVIC. The Constant Two Plan would fit that bill. It does not require an amendment to be enacted; it can be passed state-by-state across the country. This is unlikely to be an easy task, as it will not work unless the red and purple states sign off on it. Blue states already award all of their electoral votes to the Democratic candidate, so if all blue states signed on to the Constant Two Plan, those votes would already be going to the popular vote winner (at least the popular vote winner of the 2000, 2008, 2012, 2016, and 2020 presidential elections). In addition, many of the blue states have signed on to the NPVIC, signaling their willingness to support reform. It is the non-blue states that need to agree to adopt the Constant Two Plan. Again, given the shifting demographics of the United States, the red and purple states are going to need to shift their policy preferences in order to form winning coalitions for Republican candidates, or they are going to need to embrace electoral reform in order to remain a competitive party in future U. S. elections. The Constant Two Plan seems like a good compromise then for these states that want to allow Republican candidates to remain competitive. It would not require red states to hand over all of their electoral votes to the Democratic candidate if the Democrat wins the popular vote, and it would preserve some state power in selecting the president, as a majority of the electoral votes would be allocated to the state's popular vote winner.

The only other option for red states to remain competitive in future presidential elections would be to cheat: work on voter suppression techniques, sew misinformation to confuse voters or make them stay home, and/or lob accusations of voter fraud—just to name a few examples. While we have certainly seen some of this activity over the past couple of election cycles, the vast majority of American voters still view this as wrong. In fact, a majority of Americans do acknowledge that Donald Trump deserves at least some of the blame for the January 6, 2021, insurrection on Capitol Hill (Galston 2023)—arguably our most prominent example of trying to cheat the American public out of the rightfully elected presidency of Joe Biden. With that said, while reform will no doubt be challenging, the time has come to once again push for Electoral College reform. The Constant Two Plan provides a path to a system in which the federalist ideal associated with the Electoral College is acknowledged while simultaneously ensuring the election of the national popular vote winner. This would bring our presidential elections more in line with democratic norms and values, all but guaranteeing a win for the candidate who wins the majority of the national popular vote.

## CONCLUSION

It is clear that the Electoral College is in need of reform. We have seen democratization in all other levels of elections, yet for presidential elections, the United States continues to rely on an undemocratic institution to select the winner. A candidate losing the popular vote and not becoming president because not all votes are weighted equally runs counter to the norm of political equality (Dahl 1989, 2000). When not all participants in an election have an equal voice in that election, it is clear that democratic norms suffer. Now armed with five examples of presidents winning the electoral vote, while losing the popular vote it is past time to debate the necessity of Electoral College reform.

In chapter 5, I offered critiques of several reform plans already devised and have here offered a novel solution to the problem of electoral and popular vote misalignment. The Automatic Plan does little to change the functionality of the Electoral College and does not remedy any of the five elections in which the popular and electoral votes did not match. The District Plan does not provide any acknowledgment of the national popular vote winner, raises concern about the accuracy of the results given the increasing problem of gerrymandering, and does not remedy the small state bias. The Proportional Plan makes some strides toward democratizing presidential elections but fails to eliminate the small state bias and regularly relies on the contingent election process, in which the House of Representatives would elect the president. While this is a feature of the current Electoral College, a contingent election has only been needed in the election of 1824—the first time a popular vote was held. Since then, contingent elections have not been needed. As highlighted in the previous chapter, The Proportional Plan would have caused six contingent elections from 1952 through today, including the 2016 election. The NPVIC does well in its attempt to award the nationwide popular vote winner the presidency, yet it ignores the federalist principle associated with the Electoral College and is logistically unlikely to come to fruition. The examples in which the popular vote winner lost the electoral vote all resulted in Republican presidencies. This means that the Republican Party has little incentive to support the NPVIC, and thus the reliably Republican-leaning states will be reluctant to vote for such a plan, let alone bring it up in a state legislative session. It also stands little chance of passing a Congressional vote—a necessity, given Congress' responsibility to vote on all interstate compacts.

In contrast to these already-offered reform plans, the Constant Two Plan outlined here offers a new, practical solution to the problems associated with the Electoral College. It should prove more palatable to even Republican-leaning states, which are currently the most hesitant to change the current structure. The Constant Two Plan acknowledges the federalist nature of the Electoral College that many of its defenders appreciate, while also providing an avenue through which the national popular vote winner receives votes for receiving support from a plurality—if not majority—of voters across the country. While the federalist nature of the Electoral College may not have been the intention of the Founders, it has come to be appreciated by defenders of the Electoral College and cannot be wholly dismissed if reform is to be seriously considered. Importantly, I demonstrate that the Constant Two Plan awards the presidency to the popular vote winner in all elections in which a popular vote was held. This brings the Electoral College more in line with democratic norms, helping to ensure the candidate with the most votes wins the presidency. The small state bias is also remedied under the Constant Two

Plan, with the power of each electoral vote more evenly distributed across the 50 states and Washington, D.C. While it does not ensure complete equity, only seven states fall outside of the 600,000–800,000 voters per electoral vote range. Under the current structure, there is a much larger variance across states in terms of the power of their electoral votes. The more populous states would thus no longer be punished for having larger populations under the Constant Two Plan. Additionally, the Constant Two plan encourages candidates to compete across the country for votes, as the nationwide popular vote winner will be awarded 102 electoral votes. While there will still be battleground states (or cities) that receive more attention than others, there is no reform plan that would result in a completely equal playing field across the United States. The Constant Two Plan would encourage candidates to expend some resources in all states to drive up their vote shares in areas of support, even if that state's partisan bent is not in their direction. With these benefits of the Constant Two Plan, we should anticipate increased electoral participation in presidential elections. The popular vote winner will receive a large share of electoral votes under this reform plan, helping to ensure feelings of political efficacy in voters, which should increase turnout.

The Constant Two Plan offers a new solution to the problems with the Electoral College as it is currently structured. It is time for the United States to better enshrine democratic norms in the presidential selection process. The nomination process, for example, has democratized greatly, allowing voters to have a strong voice in selecting a party's nominee—much to the dismay of some. These democratic norms should now be extended to the actual election of the president while at the same time acknowledging the federalist principle implicit in the Electoral College. Instead of relying on a mechanism which can subvert—and indeed has subverted—the public's will, it is time to take Electoral College reform seriously and adopt a reform plan that ensures the candidate with the most support nationwide actually becomes president. The Constant Two Plan would do exactly that.

## *Chapter 7*

# Beyond Time for Reform

## *Evaluating the Constant Two Plan*

I concluded the first chapter of this book by quoting Thomas Paine, who warned us against complacency—specifically that we should not just accept something as best practice just because of historical precedent. Yet this is exactly what we have done. With the exception of the 12th Amendment, which was ratified in 1804, the Electoral College has persisted in much the same way as the Founders designed it. The electors are much more partisan than the Founders had intended, the votes more predetermined, but the institution still functions as it was originally designed. Each state's legislature decides how electors are appointed, those electors meet in their respective state capitals and cast their votes for president, those votes are sent to the District of Columbia where they are counted in the presence of both Houses of Congress and the sitting vice president in early January. The candidate who reaches a majority of at least 270 votes is then declared the winner. Those are the basic mechanics outlined by the Founders at the Constitutional Convention in 1787. It is these mechanics that have been followed in every presidential election since.

To say that historical precedent is driving the use of the Electoral College is an understatement. It seems highly unlikely that anyone asked how best to select a president would suggest such a convoluted system. Instead, most people would likely suggest we hold a vote and that the person with the most votes be declared the winner. Yet we continue to rely on a system that does not guarantee the winner receives even a plurality of votes. We have done exactly what Paine urged us not to do: we have let historical custom convince us to keep using an institution that has outlived its usefulness.

The American public knows this. Looking at public opinion toward the Electoral College, it is clear that it does not have a lot of supporters among the American public. It has some, but a majority of Americans have supported abolishing, or at least reforming, the Electoral College dating as far back as 1944 (with a brief exception in 2016). As was discussed more thoroughly in the previous chapter and shown in figure 6.3, there has definitely been a fluctuation in attitudes toward the Electoral College, but overall, Americans want to see the Electoral College changed or eliminated. This data paints an incomplete picture, as this question is not asked every year but mostly when the Electoral College is a topic of public discussion. In fact, Gallup did not ask about the Electoral College from 1980 until after the 2000 presidential election, in which George W. Bush won the Electoral College but lost the popular vote. Regardless of the inconsistent polling, this still gives us some insight into how Americans feel about the Electoral College. Support for reform hit a high of 81 percent in 1968, in the run-up to 1969, when the United States came the closest it had ever come to eliminating the Electoral College (Saad 2011). In 1969, the House of Representatives passed a direct vote amendment with the requisite two-thirds majority. President Nixon said he would sign such a bill, but the Senate failed to get past a filibuster on the amendment. Based on public opinion, it seems the amendment would have stood a good chance of passing ratification votes in three-fourths of the country. Since then, public attitudes toward the Electoral College have continued to support reform and have mostly hovered between 55 and 60 percent (Brenan 2020).

As discussed in the previous chapter, this signals that an amendment is unlikely to pass, so a reform plan is needed that avoids an amendment. While a Direct Vote Plan makes a lot of sense and aligns with democratic norms and principles, the chance of instituting this via an amendment is not politically feasible currently. Given our continued partisan calcification, a reform plan that requires action by two-thirds of Congress and three-fourths of the American public is unthinkable. A plan that avoids these hurdles is needed if we are to see successful Electoral College reform. The Constant Two Plan all but guarantees the popular vote winner will become president—and it does this while avoiding the need for an amendment, requiring only a majority vote in each state. While this still will not be accomplished easily, it will nonetheless be easier than passing an amendment abolishing the Electoral College and instituting direct election of the president.

Why, then, has so much ink been spilled over Electoral College reform without any actual change to this archaic institution? One answer, of course, is that change is difficult. Historical precedence is a strong force in American politics, and overcoming it is challenging—and in the case of the Electoral College, it has been impossible. An even bigger obstacle is the fact that reforming the Electoral College has become politicized over time. Looking over the cases in which the electoral and popular vote did not align, Republicans have been the beneficiaries in every single instance. While it is disingenuous to compare the Republican Party today with that of 1876 and

1888, when we last saw the popular vote and electoral vote won by different candidates prior to 2000, focusing on just the presidential elections of 2000 and 2016 still highlights the Republican advantage in the Electoral College. The Republican Party has an advantage when it comes to the small state bias, as five of the eight states with just three electoral votes are reliable red states. The Republican advantage can also be seen when comparing the national popular vote advantage with how close the outcomes are in just a handful of battleground states. The 2020 election was decided in Biden's favor due to roughly 43,000 voters spread across three states: Arizona, Georgia, and Wisconsin. All of these voters could easily fit into most major sports arenas in the United States. The 2016 election went in Trump's direction due to roughly 78,000 voters across the states of Michigan, Pennsylvania, and Wisconsin. While this number does require a larger stadium, all 78,000 voters would easily fit into several stadiums—including Lambeau Field, the home of the Green Bay Packers.

While these elections were incredibly narrow victories in each of these states, nationally, the races were not that close. In 2016, Donald Trump lost the national popular vote by roughly three million votes. In 2020, he lost it by roughly seven million votes. These are both decisive victories for the Democratic candidates in the popular vote, yet only Biden was able to become president due to the archaic rules of the Electoral College. Looking back over the past eight presidential elections, only one of them saw the Republican candidate win the national popular vote. Yet, three of the last eight elections awarded the presidency to the Republican candidate. George W. Bush won the popular vote in 2004 for the first time since his father won it in 1988, and he has been the last Republican candidate to win it since then. All together, it is clear that Republicans have an advantage over the Democrats in winning the presidency as long as the Electoral College remains intact; thus, we see Republicans largely coming to its defense and Democrats calling for its elimination.

Despite the difficulty and increased politicization of Electoral College reform, many plans have been offered and considered since its adoption. Yet none of these reforms have been adopted, and there have been only small tweaks to the Electoral College over time. If a reform plan is ever to be adopted, it is obviously good for that plan to be fully understood in an effort to try to prevent any unforeseen problems. In Gary Bugh's edited volume on Electoral College reform, Paul Schumacher (2010) lays out nine criteria for use in evaluating the Electoral College as well as any reform ideas. He argues that there are some ways in which the Electoral College performs reasonably well. Because the Electoral College ensures a majority winner (in electoral votes), it generally confers legitimacy to the winner and preserves and protects the two-party system, which many Americans have come to view as the best (Schumaker 2010). Yet, he also acknowledges that there are many ways in which the Electoral College can be deficient, so he develops an evaluative system in an effort to best assess the potential performance of any proposed reform. There are nine criteria he suggests using: simplicity, equality, sincerity, neutrality, participation, legitimacy, governance, inclusiveness, and feasibility (Schumaker 2010, 206). He evaluates the Electoral College, the popular plurality system, and instant runoff voting (IRV) and concludes that a national popular vote system with Instant Runoff would likely be the best way to select a president. However, given the infeasibility of passing a constitutional amendment to that effect, this is an unlikely outcome. Schumacher (2002) also evaluates the Automatic, District, and Proportional plans and points to the fact that the Electoral College generally performs better along these criteria than any of these alternatives. So, to conclude this book, I will analyze the Constant Two reform plan using the criteria developed by Schumaker to demonstrate why I believe it is a workable alternative to all of the reform plans proposed to date. A summary of my evaluation of the Constant Two Plan vis-à-vis the Electoral College can be found in table 7.1.

## EVALUATING THE CONSTANT TWO PLAN

Schumaker (2010, 206) encourages us to evaluate Electoral College reform plans by examining each while keeping the following criteria in mind: simplicity, equality, sincerity, neutrality, participation, legitimacy, governance, inclusiveness, and feasibility. Simplicity refers to both its understandability as well as its use. Can voters understand it? And are the mechanics of the process easy to use? Equality looks at the value of each voter in the electoral system, with the more equal voters are treated, the better the system is. Sincerity looks at how sincere voters are in the voting booth. Are voters choosing sincerely, or are they voting for the candidate they dislike the least because their favorite candidate has only a small chance of winning? A system that encourages voters to select a candidate most closely aligned with their sincere preferences would get a better score than one that does not. In order for a system to be viewed as neutral, it must not favor any candidate or voter. An electoral system should be as neutral as possible, it should treat all candidates and voters equally. Electoral systems should also encourage participation in them, not encourage them to sit out an election. The system should also be viewed with legitimacy. Voters should accept the outcome of an election, helping to preserve the long tradition of peaceful transitions of power from one president to another, except for the insurrection prior to the peaceful inauguration of President Biden in 2020. The governance criterion encourages

**Table 7.1 Evaluative Comparison of Electoral College and the Constant Two Plan**

| *Criterion* | *Electoral College* | *Constant Two Plan* |
|---|---|---|
| Simplicity | Moderately complex; National popular vote does not matter, only state popular votes determine winner | Moderately complex; both national and state popular votes used to determine winner |
| Equality | Does not treat voters equally—small states have more power than large states | Treats voters more equally—better distribution of power across states |
| Sincerity | Does not encourage voters to participate sincerely—feel need to pick among major party candidates, ignore third Parties | Allows voters to participate more sincerely—makes the popular vote matter more than under the Electoral College |
| Neutrality | Not neutral—battleground states are more important than safe states | Relatively neutral—reduces the importance of battleground states |
| Participation | Does not encourage participation in safe states, only in battlegrounds | Will encourage participation nationwide |
| Legitimacy | Confers legitimacy, but because of historical precedence | Confers legitimacy through popular vote victory |
| Governance | Preserves two-party system; should have less fragmentation and make governance easier | Governance should be easier; popular vote winner will be president, should carry some mandate to govern accordingly |
| Inclusivity | Not very inclusive; winner take all allocation rules ensure winner gets all electoral votes regardless of victory margin | Inclusivity is improved because electoral votes may be split between national and state popular vote winners |
| Feasibility | If this system were proposed today, it likely would not be viewed as a feasible electoral system | More feasible than many reform plans—amendment not required |

*Source*: Table created by the author.

us to consider how easily it will be to govern after the use of the electoral system. Will leaders selected under it be able to pass policies that address the problems society is facing? Or will it leave the system deadlocked? With the inclusiveness criterion, we are asked to consider how well the electoral system treats the diversity of interests and ideas in the organizations and individuals tasked with governing. Finally, we are tasked with answering the question of whether or not the proposed system is feasible—can it be passed? So, how does the system that would be created under the Constant Two Plan compare with the existing Electoral College system?

First, let's look at simplicity. The simpler the electoral system is, the easier it is for voters to understand how to use it and for candidates to understand how to campaign within it. The Electoral College is not simple. Sure, candidates understand how to campaign within the current system, but many Americans have little understanding of how the Electoral College works, even after they have voted in presidential elections. In fact, according to a 2008 study, 43 percent of Americans do not know the Electoral College is constitutionally mandated—rather, they think it is a group of people that train others on how to run for office or supervise presidential debates (NBC Los Angeles 2008). So, the current system used is not that simple. Admittedly, the Constant Two Plan is not overly simple either; however, the added component to the system is one that many will easily understand. Under the Constant Two Plan, two votes from each state would be given to the national popular vote winner—a concept that many Americans do understand; some Americans believe the popular vote is the mechanism by which we select our president already, so the concept will definitely be understandable to them. The remainder of each state's electoral votes are allocated according to the rules that currently exist, something the American public may not fully understand but is at least aware of. So, the change in rules is one that should be easily understood by both candidates and voters. The District and Proportional Plans are also fairly simple to understand as well, though admittedly none of these reforms are as simple as the direct vote plan. However, both of these plans have significant drawbacks that I outlined in chapter 5. They would also make candidates and voters learn a completely new system, except for the voters in Nebraska and Maine. The Constant Two Plan does change the rules and adds some complexity to the way in which we choose our presidents. However, it is a rules change that brings together both the national popular vote and state preferences, thus preserving the federalist principle that many use to justify the existence of the Electoral College. It is also a rules change that would lead to the national popular vote winner regularly winning the presidency—a simple concept that we already know many Americans understand and approve of. Thus, while the Constant Two Plan may be a bit more complex than the current system, the result of a president who wins the popular vote is much more easily understood than when the popular vote winner fails to win the presidency.

Next, when we consider the second criterion—equality—the Constant Two Plan is an improvement over the Electoral College. The Electoral College is very clearly unequal. Because the Senate is disproportionate, this disproportionality translates to the Electoral College. Figures 6.1 and 6.2 highlight the equality problem under the Electoral College and how the Constant Two Plan helps in remedying it. Under the Electoral College, small states like Wyoming, Vermont, Washington, D.C., Alaska, and the Dakotas have one electoral vote for roughly every 300,000 voters or less. At the other end of the spectrum, large states like Texas, California, Florida, North Carolina, and New York all have one electoral vote for almost every 700,000 people. Under the Constant Two Plan, states on the lower end (Rhode Island, Wyoming, West Virginia, and Vermont) have one electoral vote for roughly every 600,000 voters. Those on the upper end (Oregon, Idaho, South Dakota, Delaware, and Montana) have one electoral vote for roughly every 900,000 voters. Montana is the outlier with one vote for every 1,000,000 voters, but they were awarded an additional electoral vote after the 2020 redistricting process, which would give them one vote for roughly every 570,000 voters under the Constant Two Plan.

Now, if we use the U.S. population to calculate what the average number of voters per electoral vote should be, it is approximately 617,000 voters. The Constant Two Plan has only seven states that fall outside of the 600,000–800,000 voters per electoral vote range, meaning that 44 fall within that range. The population-based average falls in this range, underscoring the fact that the Constant Two Plan is more equitable than the Electoral College. Under the Electoral College, only 20 states exceed 600,000 votes, leaving 31 that fall below the population-based average. This highlights the fact that, due to the small state bias found in the Electoral College, the number of voters per electoral vote is largely unequal. This problem is vastly improved upon with the Constant Two Plan because the small state bias is eliminated. The electoral votes corresponding to the state's Senators are removed from the state-allocated electoral votes. Instead, those votes are awarded to the winner of the national popular vote. The Constant Two Plan, thus is an improvement on the Electoral College in terms of equality, our second evaluative criterion.

The third evaluative criterion is sincerity. As part of his evaluation of the Electoral College, Schumaker (2010) compares the current system with what presidential elections would look like under IRV. With IRV, voters are asked to rank the candidates in order of their preference, and if no candidate wins a majority of votes after the initial tallying of votes, the candidate with the fewest votes is eliminated from consideration, and those votes are redistributed to the voter's second preference. This process then continues until one candidate crosses the 50-percent threshold, resulting in a winner capturing a majority of support—at least among the ballots counted in the final round of tallying. This is likely the most sincere form of voting, as voters are able to convey their sincere feelings in their ranking. Even if they do not believe the Libertarian candidate will win the presidency, for example, they are able to rank that candidate first if they are the voter's first preference, and then rank the remaining candidates they find to be acceptable alternatives should the Libertarian candidate be eliminated from consideration over the rounds of tallying. The current system uses plurality voting, so voters are only able to vote for one candidate. Voters may therefore fall victim to the wasted vote mentality and not cast their ballot for their most preferred candidate, choosing instead to vote for the major party candidate they deem most acceptable because there is almost no chance that a third-party candidate will win the presidency under the Electoral College. The Constant Two Plan, admittedly, does not match the sincerity offered by IRV. Yet, I would argue it offers more sincerity than the current Electoral College because electoral votes will be allocated based on both the national popular vote winner and the state's preferred candidate. This likely will not help third-party candidates much, if at all, but because both the national and state popular votes would be used to allocate electoral votes, it may encourage voters to behave more sincerely in the voting booth. At the very least, it should convince voters who may have sat out previous elections because they believed their vote would not count because they do not share their state's usual partisan bent to turn out and cast a ballot since there is a chance some electoral votes will go to the national popular vote winner.

Next, how neutral is the Constant Two Plan? Does it favor any particular candidate or voter? Overall, it should be viewed as more neutral than the Electoral College. Under the current Electoral College system, most states are easily predicted even before we know who the candidates are. This has not always been the case, but since Reagan's landslide victory in 1984, the electoral map has been rather predictable. Except for a handful of battleground states, most states have predictable outcomes (e.g., most Northeastern states will go blue and most Southern states will go red in a presidential election). While this is not necessarily a bad thing, it does highlight how battleground states are prioritized over other states. Battleground states get the most attention, the most campaign stops, the most campaign spending, and the most press coverage (Hillygus and Shields 2009; Holbrook 1996; Huber and Arceneaux 2007; Johnston et al. 2004; Shaw 1999, 2006). So the Electoral College is not neutral: it causes candidates to favor the battleground state voters and ignore "safe state" voters. The Constant Two Plan would award two electoral votes to the winner of the national popular vote, which would encourage candidates to compete for the national popular vote victory. This should encourage candidates to compete for votes nationwide—including in "safe" states. Even Democratic candidates may want to compete in reliably red states in an effort to maximize Democratic votes, while Republicans may want to drive up turnout in red areas within reliably blue states. The remaining electoral votes will be allocated according to the state's popular vote results, which will likely result in some continuation of battleground states, yet with the national popular vote winner guaranteed 102 electoral votes, these battleground states become less critical to a candidate's chances of winning. So ultimately, the Constant Two Plan creates a more neutral electorate than the Electoral College currently does. It is not completely neutral, like abolishing the Electoral College and relying just on the national popular vote would be, but it is a definite improvement in neutrality from the system we currently use to select our presidents.

How will participation be impacted by a shift from the current Electoral College to the Constant Two Plan? We should expect that the Constant Two Plan will increase participation from our current system. Again, aside from the battleground states, most states are reliably red or blue states in the Electoral College. The Northeast region of the United States is largely blue, while the southern region is largely red. While New Hampshire has been a battleground state, an electoral vote in Maine has been awarded to a Republican candidate because Maine uses the district allocation system, and Georgia has become a battleground state as of late. These two regions are still largely predictable in terms of electoral outcomes. While predictability is not inherently a bad thing, it does underscore the likely outcome of presidential elections, which can have participation effects. It can cause Republican voters in reliably blue states and Democratic voters in reliably red states to stay home. Why should they bother taking the time to cast a ballot if their state is going to award their electoral votes to the candidate they do not support? It can also cause complacency among Democratic voters in blue states and Republican voters in red states. As Alexander (2019) argues, where you live determines how much (or little) your vote will matter. If you believe your vote will not matter (either because your vote aligns with your state's partisan bent or because you live in a safe state of the opposite party), you may choose to not participate in an election. The Constant Two Plan, however, should encourage participation across all states, regardless of how red or blue a state normally votes. Two votes from each state will be awarded to the national popular vote winner, meaning that should a Democrat win the popular vote, even red states would award two votes to the Democratic candidate. Or, if a Republican were to win the popular vote, even blue states would award two votes to the Republican candidate. Voters, therefore, should not be complacent, but instead, they should be energized to vote for their preferred candidate. With the opportunity for candidates who win the national popular vote to receive 102 total electoral votes, there is a much greater incentive for all voters to participate under the Constant Two Plan regardless of the usual electoral color of their state. Increased participation would have the added benefit of strengthening the value of, and commitment to, democracy throughout the United States, as democracy relies on regular participation to function.

The sixth criterion asks us to look at how legitimate voters view the results of an election under the electoral system used. Despite the complicated nature of the Electoral College, most Americans actually accept the results as legitimate—even when the Electoral College winner did not also win the popular vote. In 2000 and 2016, the American public was upset that both George W. Bush and Donald Trump won the presidency, respectively, the results were viewed as legitimate. It is true that in response to the 2016 election, the hashtag #NotMyPresident trended in response to Trump's popular vote loss, and people marched throughout the country in protest, but the Obamas welcomed the Trumps to the White House in the transition period, and Trump was allowed to be inaugurated without any major violent incident. The transition of power was still conducted peacefully. The same cannot be said of the 2020 election, despite the fact that Joe Biden won both the popular and electoral votes. As discussed in the first chapter, there was an armed insurrection in Washington, D.C., for the first time in recent history. In response to the 2020 election, Donald Trump called the election fraudulent and urged his supporters to march on the Capitol and disrupt the counting of electoral votes (Broadwater and Schmidt 2022). This march on the Capitol resulted in millions of dollars in damage, members of Congress sheltering in their offices to escape these insurrectionists, and several deaths (Snowdon 2022). Despite this disturbing incident, a majority of Americans still recognized Biden as the rightful and legitimate winner of the 2020 election, rejecting the message of the insurrectionists. The Constant Two Plan should also confer legitimacy on the winner of the presidency; in fact, it should do better at conferring legitimacy than the Electoral College because some electoral votes are awarded to the national popular vote winner. When the national popular vote winner loses the electoral vote, we clearly see a drop in legitimacy for the presidency. In fact, a voter quoted in Thomson-Deveaux, Mithani, and Bronner (2020) stated, "That would be very upsetting. . . . I probably wouldn't vote again" in response to being asked about how he would feel if Trump won the presidency without the popular vote. The Constant Two Plan would help with some of this legitimacy problem by virtually assuring that the popular vote winner would become president. This allocation system will show voters that winning the national popular vote results in a candidate receiving *some* votes, while still allowing states to award their remaining votes according to state rules.

Next is governance—or the ability to enact policy after winning an election. Schumaker (2010) points to the preservation of the two-party system as a strength of the Electoral College and argues that a two-party system should lead to less fragmentation than a multiparty system, ultimately making governance easier under a two-party system. Others, like Drutman (2020), argue that a two-party system is what is causing problems throughout the United States, and a multiparty system would benefit from the negotiating and deal-making that would need to happen within it. Regardless, it seems as though both sides agree that the United States is stuck in a polarized state (Sides, Tausanovitch, and Vavreck 2022). Schumacher

(2010) also states that this polarization, in addition to fragmentation, leads to difficulty in governing. Looking at the current structure of the Electoral College, it is clear how the hyper-polarized nature of U.S. politics is creating governance problems. Abramowitz and Webster (2016) convincingly demonstrate the rise of negative partisanship and the challenges it brings with it to governing in the United States. With more Americans now disliking the opposition party more than they like their own party, elected officials have little incentive to work toward bipartisan solutions to problems. Sides, Tausanovitch, and Vavreck (2022) argue that these trends have led to the calcification of the U.S. electorate. Without a major shock to the system, we are likely to see little change in the partisan behavior of American voters. Will the Constant Two Plan change any of this? And will that make governing any easier? The answer to these questions is not clear, but considering the change in how electoral votes would be awarded, the Constant Two Plan should help with governance—if even slightly. Considering the allocation of two electoral votes from every state to the national popular vote winner, we should see an end to the examples of the popular vote winner not becoming president, which should help with governance. If the candidate who wins the most votes gets to become president, governing might not always be easy, but, as discussed above, it should be viewed as more legitimate and make governing a bit easier than under the current structure of the Electoral College.

Inclusiveness is the eighth criterion we are asked to use to evaluate electoral systems. Is the Electoral College inclusive? Does it allow for a diversity of interests to participate in the electoral process and then allow them to be meaningfully represented in the governance structure? Those who believe that states should be the main vehicles by which presidents are elected will likely argue that the Electoral College performs strongly in this regard. However, the Electoral College is not inclusive of all voices within a state. It awards all of a state's electoral votes to the winner of the state's popular vote, regardless of the margin of victory. So, a two-point margin or twenty-point margin does not matter, though regardless of the winning candidate's margin of victory, there are still some voters within a state who feel unheard after an election. Democratic voters in red states and Republican voters in blue states do not feel as though their votes matter. The Electoral College is not an inclusive institution. And importantly, it was not meant to be. It was designed to be an anti-democratic institution. It was supposed to ensure that the passions of the public did not elect someone unfit for office. The Constant Two Plan should be viewed as more inclusive than the Electoral College. Awarding two votes to the national popular vote winner and the remaining votes in accordance with the state's popular vote will make for a more inclusive electoral system. This will ensure that both the national will and state will are accounted for in presidential elections, creating a more inclusive process than what currently exists.

Lastly, we need to consider the feasibility of any proposed reform. The Electoral College, itself, would likely not be considered a feasible plan if it were introduced today. It is complex and anti-democratic—and it is not an institution that has been adopted by any other country in the world. It is a uniquely American electoral institution. Yet, this is the system we continue to use because we have used it for over 200 years. Schumacher (2010) argues that anything that requires a constitutional amendment is not a feasible reform plan. In today's hyper-partisan, calcified political system, there is no chance of Congress passing an amendment that will change the electoral system with two-thirds support. It is also unclear whether or not it would pass ratification in three-fourths of the states. So, a reform plan needs to be found that can be enacted without an amendment and that can be deemed palatable by even the red states. The Constant Two Plan does not require an amendment but rather a change in state rules governing how electoral votes are allocated.

Of course, feasibility means more than just the ability to get something passed; it also includes the ability for the proposed reform to attract support among the American public. Many Americans support reform, but they want reform that ensures the popular vote winner becomes president. As I've shown in chapter 5 the District Plan does not ensure the popular vote winner becomes president, and neither does the Proportional Plan. The Direct Vote Plan would likely have public support because it abolishes the Electoral College and ensures the popular vote winner becomes president, but it requires an amendment, making it infeasible. The national popular vote interstate compact (NPVIC) would ensure that the popular vote winner becomes president, but it ignores the federalist principle that many states want to see preserved, even if this principle was not part of the original intent behind the Electoral College. Additionally, the NPVIC does not go into effect until states that award at least 270 electoral votes altogether sign on to the compact, something that cannot happen without some battleground states signing onto the agreement—something that has not happened yet. Congress also needs to sign off on interstate compacts, and in today's political climate, that seems unlikely to happen. The Constant Two Plan does not require an amendment, does not require Congressional approval, nor does it require all states to sign a compact. It requires all states to change their laws and award two electoral votes to the national popular vote winner, while allocating the remainder of their votes however the state decides to do so. It preserves the federalist principle, while also taking into account the national will. The Constant Two Plan, therefore, does appear to be a feasible alternative to the Electoral College. That does not mean that its passage will be easy, as convincing 50 states plus Washington, D.C., to change their electoral vote allocation rules would be a difficult task. But, it does seem to be a feasible solution—at least more feasible than any of the proposed alternatives.

Overall, then, the Constant Two Plan seems to be a viable reform plan for the Electoral College. Taking into account the nine evaluative criteria set forth by Schumaker (2002, 2010), the Constant Two Plan appears to be an improvement on the current Electoral College structure. It is a fairly *simple* adjustment to the current structure—and one that most Americans would likely be supportive of. The Constant Two Plan seems to treat voters more *equally* and *neutrally* than the Electoral College, as battleground states seem less important with this proposed reform. In addition, the Constant Two Plan will likely improve upon *sincere* voting, increase *participation*, and should not impact how *legitimate* voters view the results of presidential elections, especially since the popular vote winner should always win the presidency. It is also clear that *governance* and *inclusiveness* should be improved upon—voters should feel more included in the electoral process and policymaking should be improved, as all presidents will be able to claim legitimate public support. And lastly, the reform is *feasible*. It does not require an amendment, nor does it require congressional approval. It just asks states to change their electoral vote allocation rules. The Constant Two Plan therefore seems to be a practical alternative to the Electoral College.

## IT IS BEYOND TIME TO REFORM THE ELECTORAL COLLEGE

The last serious attempt at reforming the Electoral College was made in 1969, over 50 years ago. Since that time, we have seen two presidents elected who have not won the popular vote. In fact, since 1992, the Democrats have won the popular vote in every single election except for 2004, yet the Republican Party has controlled the presidency for 12 out of these past 30 years. So, for almost half of the past 30 years, the party without even a plurality of votes has controlled the presidency—hardly a democratic outcome. This has brought with it many long-term consequences that should deeply trouble those committed to democratic governance. These minoritarian presidents have appointed five members of the nine-person U.S. Supreme Court, shifting the balance of power from fairly moderate to solidly conservative, resulting in the overturning of the landmark Supreme Court ruling in *Roe v. Wade*, an expansion of prayer in schools, and a limitation of a state's ability to prevent the carrying of firearms in public. These same presidents have also had veto power over actions taken by Congress. Altogether, this demonstrates the power presidents can wield even if they do not receive the support of a plurality of voters on election day. This can lead to the passage of policies that most voters are not actually supportive of or court decisions that are viewed as illegitimate, both of which threaten the stability of democracy. We need to ensure that the candidate who wins the popular vote also wins the presidency. The Constant Two Plan allows us to ensure that the popular vote winner will become president, and importantly, it does this without the need for an amendment. Relying on the amendment process for Electoral College reform has not worked since the passage of the 12th Amendment in 1804, despite the Founders not necessarily wanting the institution to continue to select the president.

Chapter 1 focused on the origins of the Electoral College. The Founders created this complex system because they wanted to prevent placing such a decision in the hands of a preexisting political body and did not believe the decision should be left to the public. However, they did not want the public to have a say because the technology at that time would not have allowed the public to be meaningfully informed, nor would voting have been easy. The country was too big for voters in New York to understand the concerns of voters in South Carolina or how candidates for the presidency would be able to address all of these concerns across the country. Today, technology is advanced enough to handle the vastness of the United States. There is nothing prohibiting voters from being able to be meaningfully informed about the candidates running for president. We also have technology available to conduct nationwide elections, unlike in 1787, we already voted on the same day across the country. The technology exists now to do what many of the Founders wanted to do back in 1787. If the Founders had had the technology that exists today back then, the Electoral College likely would not have been created—a popular vote almost certainly would have passed the Constitutional Convention.

In the second chapter, I examined some of the purported benefits that come with the Electoral College. While it should be clear that the Electoral College is in need of reform, it does have defenders. Its defenders generally point to the federalist nature of the institution, the fact that it forces candidates to compete outside of just the most populous areas of the United States, the decisive majoritarian victories, and the preservation of the two-party system. However, under scrutiny, these benefits do not hold up. After reviewing the records from the Constitutional Convention, the *Federalist Papers*, and the *AntiFederalist Papers*, it is clear that the Founders did not create the Electoral College in order to underscore the federalist system they created. Additionally, not everyone agrees with those who argue that the two-party system needs to be preserved—some would like to see a multiparty system adopted to replace it (Drutman 2020).

The Electoral College does not cause national campaigning but rather battleground-state-focused campaigning. There are states that get very little attention from candidates because they know they are safe in their support column or in their opponent's column. The majoritarian victories of the Electoral College do not always align with the popular vote, so presidents are not guaranteed a majority support of voters, just electoral votes. The number of states won by a candidate does not necessarily align with the popular vote either. When Trump won the presidency in 2016, he won a majority of electoral votes and a majority of the states (31), but he still lost the popular vote by almost three million votes. In 2000, when Bush won the majority in the Electoral College and lost the popular vote, he won a majority of states (30). When Jimmy Carter won in 1976, he won only 24 states but won a majority of popular votes and electoral votes. This highlights the problem with the argument that the states should have a role in selecting the president. A president is not elected to represent the states, but rather the people that live in those states. It is the people, then, that should elect the president, not the states. So, while there are a handful of things Electoral College defenders will point to in supporting its preservation, none of them withstands careful scrutiny.

The third chapter examined the main drawbacks of the Electoral College and presented a timeline of the more than 700 attempts at reforming this outdated electoral system. These drawbacks point to the potential for faithless electors to defy the will of the voters, contingent elections that blur the line between separation of powers and not relying on public input, candidates that are still not encouraged to compete nationwide, the popular vote winner still not being guaranteed the presidency, and the system not ensuring political equality among voters. Many states currently have laws to replace faithless electors, so that all electors will actually vote according to the state's popular vote. However, this is a break from what the Founders actually intended—they wanted lively debate among politically aware citizens in order to select the best president. Contingent elections are indeed a threat to democratic norms, as they allow the legislative branch to select the leader of the executive branch. Ultimately, there are several drawbacks to the Electoral College, many of which continue to threaten democratic stability across the country—if that were not the case, it likely would not have been the focus of over 700 bills on the congressional floor.

One of the biggest drawbacks of the Electoral College is the inherent racism found within it, which was the focus of the fourth chapter. This comes from the three-fifths compromise that was adopted at the same time as the Electoral College's formation. The South wanted to count their slaves as part of their population in order to increase their number of representatives in Congress. The North argued that slaves should not count as part of the population because they were not given any citizenship rights. So, in order to pass a new Constitution and send it to the states for ratification, the delegates compromised and decided to count each slave as three-fifths of a person for the purposes of calculating population size. This helped increase Southern representation a great deal (including in the executive branch—with each presidential ticket including a Southerner until Lincoln took the presidency in 1860). Southern representation further increased even more after slavery was abolished and each slave was counted as a full person. Despite the abolition of slavery, the South still found ways to keep its Black citizens from voting. This racism persists today when we look at voter ID laws. Research clearly demonstrates that minority voters, along with poorer and older voters, are least likely to have proper identification in order to cast a ballot. These voter ID laws have led to a rightward shift in voting patterns in states that have adopted them, causing some reliably blue states to become toss-ups or more solidly red than they were without the law.

In chapter 5, I examined the major reform plans that have been proposed. These include the District Plan, The Proportional Plan, the Automatic Plan, The National Bonus Plan, NPVIC, and the direct vote plan. While many of these plans sound like great alternatives to the Electoral College, all of them either create more problems than the current structure, cause very little change, or require the herculean task of passing a constitutional amendment. The automatic plan would eliminate electors and bind electoral votes to the state's popular vote. This would require an amendment, and many states already have passed laws that bind their electors to the popular vote. The District Plan falls victim to gerrymandering, creating even more elections in which the wrong winner becomes president (i.e., Mitt Romney would have defeated Obama in 2012 under the District Plan). The Proportional Plan would require contingent elections in six elections since 1956, effectively removing the popular vote altogether and allowing Congress to select the president and vice president. The National Bonus Plan also requires a constitutional amendment, so it stands little chance of passing. The same goes for the Direct Vote Plan. While both of these plans would guarantee that the popular vote winner selected the president, passing an amendment in today's hyper-partisan climate is not feasible. Lastly, in NPVIC, states would sign on to an agreement that they would all award their electoral votes to the national popular vote winner. This is a clever solution, as it avoids the need for an amendment, but so far no reliably red state or even a battleground state has signed off on the compact. This compact does not go into effect until enough states (those whose electoral votes total at least 270) sign on, and without some red and battleground state signatories, this compact is unlikely to ever be enacted.

This leads, then, to my proposal: the Constant Two Plan. The Constant Two Plan asks each state to award just two of its electoral votes to the winner of the national popular vote. The remainder of these votes would then be awarded to the winner of the state's popular vote, just as they are now. This plan avoids the need for a constitutional amendment and does not require all states to sign onto a compact. Instead, each state needs to just pass a law to change their allocation rules. State legislatures are given the authority to decide how their electoral votes are allocated, so the federal government has no authority in this realm. Nebraska and Maine, for example, award their votes according to the district method. Applying the Constant Two allocation metric to all previous presidential elections, we see that it always awards the presidency to the winner of the national popular vote. And as discussed at the outset of this chapter, it is a clear improvement on the current Electoral College system, based on the evaluative criteria developed by Schumaker (2002, 2010).

Clearly, Electoral College reform is not an easy task. It is the focus of much debate and analysis. However, the United States is past due for electoral reform. Given the outcomes of the 2000 and 2016 elections, in which we saw the popular vote loser become president, and the 2020 election, where Joe Biden bested Trump by seven million votes but narrowly won the electoral votes in a handful of states, there is a clear likelihood that we are in store for many more close elections. This is bolstered by the findings of Sides, Tausanovitch, and Vavreck (2022), who argue our politics are in a calcified state due to the increased negative partisanship throughout the American electorate. Until something changes to shake loose some of these calcified partisans, it is clear that elections like those in 2016 and 2020 will persist for years to come. That means small swings of votes (approximately 40,000 in 2020 and 78,000 in 2016) will determine the outcome of American presidential elections for the foreseeable future. I believe that the Constant Two Plan can help lead some of this change. With Democrats holding a clear advantage in the national popular vote and Republicans having an advantage in the Electoral College, neither side is likely to support a plan that helps one party more than the other. The Constant Two Plan does not inherently favor one party over the other. It does provide a significant number of votes for the winner of the national popular vote, but this will encourage national campaigning for as many partisan votes as these candidates can attract. With demographics trending in the Democrats' favor in Arizona, Georgia, and Texas, if these states were to become reliably blue states, Republicans would have a very small path to the presidency. Considering the Constant Two Plan does allow states to award some of their electoral votes according to state law, rather than nationalizing the whole election, this plan should be able to attract some Republican support. Arizona and Georgia both went blue in 2020, underscoring the fact that these trends will likely continue. With this possibility, in order for both major political parties to be competitive in a presidential election, electoral reform may be necessary. This means finding a reform plan that accounts for both the national popular vote and the federalist ideal that many people like about the Electoral College. The Constant Two Plan would do just that.

Thomas Paine told us, "A long habit of not thinking a thing wrong, gives it a superficial appearance of being right" (Conway 1894, 68). We have, for too long, accepted the Electoral College as the right way to select a president. And we have done so for no good reason, except for the fact that this is how we have always done it. It is time to take a serious look at reforming the Electoral College. It is beyond time for the reform of this archaic, complex, and undemocratic institution. It is time to adopt the Constant Two Plan.

# Appendix A

**Table A.1 Change in Electoral College Totals from Current Structure to The Constant Two Plan**

| *Year* | *Party* | *Candidate* | *Original E.C. Total* | *Number of States Won* | *Net Change in E.C. Vote* | *New E.C. Total* |
|---|---|---|---|---|---|---|
| 2020 | Democrat | Joseph R. Biden, Jr. | 306 | 26 | 50 | 356 |
| | Republican | Donald Trump | 232 | 25 | –50 | 182 |
| 2016 | Democrat | Hillary Rodham Clinton | 227 | 21 | 60 | 287 |
| | Republican | Donald Trump | 304 | 30 | –60 | 244 |
| | Various | Write-Ins | 7 | 0 | 0 | 7 |
| 2012 | Democrat | Barack Obama | 332 | 27 | 48 | 380 |
| | Republican | Willard Mitt Romney | 206 | 24 | –48 | 158 |
| 2008 | Democrat | Barack Obama | 365 | 29 | 44 | 409 |
| | Republican | John McCain | 173 | 22 | –44 | 129 |
| 2004 | Republican | George W. Bush | 286 | 31 | 40 | 326 |
| | Democrat | John Kerry | 251 | 20 | –40 | 211 |
| | Democrat | John Edwards | 1 | 0 | 0 | 1 |
| 2000 | Democrat | Albert Gore | 266 | 21 | 60 | 326 |
| | Republican | George W. Bush | 271 | 30 | –60 | 211 |
| | Democrat | Abstention | 1 | 0 | 0 | 1 |
| 1996 | Democrat | William Clinton | 379 | 32 | 38 | 417 |
| | Republican | Robert Dole | 159 | 19 | –38 | 121 |
| 1992 | Democrat | William Clinton | 370 | 33 | 36 | 406 |
| | Republican | George H. W. Bush | 168 | 18 | –36 | 132 |
| 1988 | Republican | George H. W. Bush | 426 | 41 | 20 | 446 |

| | | | | | | |
|---|---|---|---|---|---|---|
| | Democrat | Michael Dukakis | 111 | 10 | −20 | 91 |
| | Democrat | Lloyd Bentsen | 1 | 0 | 0 | 1 |
| 1984 | Republican | Ronald Reagan | 525 | 29 | 4 | 529 |
| | Democrat | Walter Mondale | 13 | 2 | −4 | 9 |
| 1980 | Republican | Ronald Reagan | 489 | 44 | 14 | 503 |
| | Democrat | James Carter | 49 | 7 | −14 | 35 |
| 1976 | Democrat | James Carter | 297 | 24 | 54 | 351 |
| | Republican | Gerald Ford | 240 | 27 | −54 | 186 |
| | Republican | Ronald Reagan | 1 | 0 | 0 | 1 |
| 1972 | Republican | Richard Nixon | 520 | 49 | 4 | 524 |
| | Democrat | George McGovern | 17 | 2 | −4 | 13 |
| | Libertarian | John Hospers | 1 | 0 | 0 | 1 |
| 1968 | Republican | Richard Nixon | 301 | 32 | 38 | 339 |
| | Democrat | Hubert Humphrey | 191 | 14 | −28 | 163 |
| | American Independent | George Wallace | 46 | 5 | −10 | 36 |
| 1964 | Democrat | Lyndon Johnson | 486 | 45 | 12 | 498 |
| | Republican | Barry Goldwater | 52 | 6 | −12 | 40 |
| 1960 | Democrat | John F. Kennedy | 303 | 22 | 56 | 359 |
| | Republican | Richard Nixon | 219 | 26 | −52 | 167 |
| | Democrat | Unpledged Electors | 15 | 2 | −4 | 11 |
| 1956 | Republican | Dwight D. Eisenhower | 457 | 41 | 14 | 471 |
| | Democrat | Adlai Stevenson | 73 | 7 | −14 | 59 |
| | Democrat | Walter Jones | 1 | 0 | 0 | 1 |

(Continued)

**Table A.1 Continued**

| *Year* | *Party* | *Candidate* | *Original E.C. Total* | *Number of States Won* | *Net Change in E.C. Vote* | *New E.C. Total* |
|---|---|---|---|---|---|---|
| 1952 | Republican | Dwight D. Eisenhower | 442 | 39 | 18 | 460 |
| | Democrat | Adlai Stevenson | 89 | 9 | –18 | 71 |
| 1948 | Democrat | Harry Truman | 303 | 28 | 40 | 343 |
| | Republican | Thomas Dewey | 189 | 16 | –32 | 157 |
| | State's Rights | J. Strom Thurmond | 39 | 4 | –8 | 31 |
| 1944 | Democrat | Franklin D. Roosevelt | 432 | 36 | 24 | 456 |
| | Republican | Thomas Dewey | 99 | 12 | –24 | 75 |
| 1940 | Democrat | Franklin D. Roosevelt | 449 | 38 | 20 | 469 |
| | Republican | Wendell Wilkie | 82 | 10 | –20 | 62 |
| 1936 | Democrat | Franklin D. Roosevelt | 523 | 46 | 4 | 527 |
| | Republican | Alfred Landon | 8 | 2 | –4 | 4 |
| 1932 | Democrat | Franklin D. Roosevelt | 472 | 42 | 12 | 484 |
| | Republican | Herbert Hoover | 59 | 6 | –12 | 47 |
| 1928 | Republican | Herbert Hoover | 444 | 40 | 19 | 460 |
| | Democrat | Alfred Landon | 87 | 8 | –16 | 71 |
| 1924 | Republican | Calvin Coolidge | 382 | 35 | 26 | 408 |
| | Democrat | John Davis | 136 | 12 | –24 | 112 |
| | Progressive | Robert LaFollette | 13 | 1 | –2 | 11 |
| 1920 | Republican | Warren G. Harding | 404 | 37 | 22 | 426 |
| | Democrat | James Cox | 127 | 11 | –22 | 105 |

| | | | | | | |
|---|---|---|---|---|---|---|
| 1916 | Democrat | Woodrow Wilson | 277 | 30 | 36 | 313 |
| | Republican | Charles Hughes | 254 | 18 | –36 | 218 |
| 1912 | Democrat | Woodrow Wilson | 435 | 40 | 16 | 451 |
| | Bull Moose/ Progressive | Theodore Roosevelt | 88 | 6 | –12 | 76 |
| | Republican | William H. Taft | 8 | 2 | –4 | 4 |
| 1908 | Republican | William H. Taft | 321 | 30 | 32 | 353 |
| | Democrat | William J. Bryan | 162 | 16 | –32 | 130 |
| 1904 | Republican | Theodore Roosevelt | 336 | 33 | 24 | 360 |
| | Democrat | Alton Parker | 140 | 12 | –24 | 116 |
| 1900 | Republican | William McKinley | 292 | 28 | 34 | 326 |
| | Democrat | William J. Bryan | 155 | 17 | –34 | 121 |
| 1896 | Republican | William McKinley | 271 | 23 | 44 | 315 |
| | Democrat | William J. Bryan | 176 | 22 | –44 | 132 |
| 1892 | Democrat | Grover Cleveland | 277 | 23 | 42 | 319 |
| | Republican | Benjamin Harrison | 145 | 16 | –32 | 113 |
| | Populist | James Weaver | 22 | 5 | –10 | 12 |
| 1888 | Democrat | Grover Cleveland | 168 | 18 | 36 | 208 |
| | Republican | Benjamin Harrison | 233 | 20 | –36 | 193 |
| 1884 | Democrat | Grover Cleveland | 219 | 20 | 36 | 255 |
| | Republican | James Blaine | 182 | 18 | –36 | 146 |
| 1880 | Republican | James Garfield | 214 | 19 | 38 | 252 |

(*Continued*)

**Table A.1 Continued**

| *Year* | *Party* | *Candidate* | *Original E.C. Total* | *Number of States Won* | *Net Change in E.C. Vote* | *New E.C. Total* |
|---|---|---|---|---|---|---|
| | Democrat | Winfield Hancock | 155 | 19 | –38 | 117 |
| 1876 | Democrat | Samuel Tilden | 184 | 17 | 40 | 224 |
| | Republican | Rutherford B. Hayes | 185 | 20 | –40 | 145 |
| 1872 | Republican | Ulysses S. Grant | 286 | 31 | 12 | 298 |
| | Democrat | Horace Greeley | 66 | 6 | –12 | 54 |
| 1868 | Republican | Ulysses S. Grant | 214 | 25 | 16 | 230 |
| | Democrat | Horatio Seymour | 80 | 8 | –16 | 64 |
| 1864* | Republican | Abraham Lincoln | 212 | 22 | 6 | 218 |
| | Democrat | George McClellan | 21 | 3 | –6 | 15 |
| 1860** | Republican | Abraham Lincoln | 180 | 17 | 30 | 210 |
| | Southern Democrat | John Breckenridge | 72 | 10 | –20 | 52 |
| | Constitutional Union | John Bell | 39 | 3 | –6 | 33 |
| | Democrat | Stephen Douglas | 12 | 2 | –4 | 8 |
| 1856** | Democrat | James Buchanan | 174 | 11 | 24 | 198 |
| | Whig | John Freemont | 114 | 18 | –22 | 92 |
| | Whig-American | Millard Fillmore | 8 | 1 | –2 | 6 |
| 1852** | Whig | Franklin Pierce | 254 | 26 | 8 | 262 |
| | Democrat | Winfield Scott | 42 | 4 | –8 | 34 |
| 1848** | Democrat | Zachary Taylor | 163 | 15 | 30 | 193 |
| | Whig | Lewis Cass | 127 | 15 | –30 | 97 |

| | | | | | | |
|---|---|---|---|---|---|---|
| 1844** | Democrat | James K. Polk | 170 | 15 | 22 | 192 |
| | Whig | Henry Clay | 105 | 11 | –22 | 83 |
| 1840** | Whig | William H. Harrison | 234 | 19 | 14 | 248 |
| | Democrat | Martin Van Buren | 60 | 7 | –14 | 46 |
| 1836** | Democrat | Martin Van Buren | 170 | 15 | 20 | 190 |
| | Whig | William H. Harrison | 73 | 10 | –20 | 53 |
| | Whig | Hugh White | 26 | 0 | 0 | 26 |
| | Whig | Daniel Webster | 14 | 0 | 0 | 14 |
| | Whig | Willie Mangum | 11 | 0 | 0 | 11 |
| 1832** | Democrat | Andrew Jackson | 219 | 15 | 18 | 237 |
| | National Republican | Henry Clay | 49 | 6 | –12 | 37 |
| | Independent Democrat | John Floyd | 11 | 1 | –2 | 9 |
| | Anti-Masonic | William Wirt | 7 | 1 | –2 | 5 |
| 1828+ | Democrat | Andrew Jackson | 178 | 14 | 20 | 198 |
| | Republican | John Quincy Adams | 83 | 8 | –16 | 67 |
| 1824^ | Democratic-Republican | Andrew Jackson | 99 | 5 | 38 | 127 |
| | Democratic-Republican | John Quincy Adams | 84 | 7 | –14 | 70 |
| | Democratic-Republican | William Crawford | 41 | 1 | –2 | 39 |
| | Democratic-Republican | Henry Clay | 37 | 3 | –6 | 31 |
| | Republican | Unpledged Electors | 0 | 0 | 0 | 0 |
| | Others | | 0 | 0 | 0 | 0 |

(*Continued*)

**Table A.1 Continued**

| *Year* | *Party* | *Candidate* | *Original E.C. Total* | *Number of States Won* | *Net Change in E.C. Vote* | *New E.C. Total* |
|---|---|---|---|---|---|---|
| 1820 | Democratic-Republican | James Monroe | 231 | | | |
| | Democratic-Republican | John Quincy Adams | 1 | | | |
| | Non-Voting | | 3 | | | |
| 1816 | Democratic-Republican | James Monroe | 183 | | | |
| | Federalist | Rufus King | 34 | | | |
| | Non-Voting | | 4 | | | |
| 1812 | Democratic-Republican | James Madison | 128 | | | |
| | Federalist | DeWitt Clinton | 89 | | | |
| | Non-Voting | | 1 | | | |
| 1808 | Democratic-Republican | James Madison | 122 | | | |
| | Federalist | Charles Pinckney | 47 | | | |
| | Democratic-Republican | George Clinton | 6 | | | |
| | Non-Voting | | 1 | | | |
| 1804 | Democratic-Republican | Thomas Jefferson | 162 | | | |
| | Federalist | Charles Pinckney | 14 | | | |
| 1800 | Democratic-Republican | Thomas Jefferson | 73 | | | |

| | | | |
|---|---|---|---|
| | Democratic-Republican | Aaron Burr | 73 |
| | Federalist | John Adams | 65 |
| | Federalist | Charles Pinckney | 64 |
| | Federalist | John Jay | 1 |
| 1796 | Federalist | John Adams | 71 |
| | Democratic-Republican | Thomas Jefferson | 68 |
| | Federalist | Thomas Pinckney | 59 |
| | Democratic-Republican | Aaron Burr | 30 |
| | Federalist | Samuel Adams | 15 |
| | Federalist | Oliver Ellsworth | 11 |
| | Democratic-Republican | George Clinton | 7 |
| | | Other | 15 |
| 1792 | Federalist | George Washington | 132 |
| | Federalist | John Adams | 77 |
| | Democratic-Republican | George Clinton | 50 |
| | Democratic-Republican | Thomas Jefferson | 4 |
| | Democratic-Republican | Aaron Burr | 1 |
| | Non-Voting | | 6 |
| 1789 | No Party | George Washington | 69 |
| | No Party | John Adams | 34 |
| | No Party | John Jay | 9 |

(Continued)

**Table A.1 Continued**

| *Year* | *Party* | *Candidate* | *Original E.C. Total* | *Number of States Won* | *Net Change in E.C. Vote* | *New E.C. Total* |
|---|---|---|---|---|---|---|
| | No Party | Robert Harrison | 6 | | | |
| | No Party | John Rutledge | 6 | | | |
| | No Party | Other | 14 | | | |
| | No Party | Non-Voting | 24 | | | |

*Source*: Table created by the author.
*Denotes 11 states seceded from the United States.
**Denotes South Carolina did not hold popular vote, and electors were appointed by state legislature.
+Denotes DE and SC did not hold popular vote, and electors were chosen by state legislature.
^Denotes DE, GA, LA, SC, and VT did not hold popular vote, and electors were chosen by state legislature.
*Note*: Popular vote winner listed first; Data taken from Dave Leip's U.S. Election Atlas.

# Bibliography


"2022 House Race Ratings." 2022. *Cook Political Report*. https://www.cookpolitical.com/ratings/house-race-ratings (September 7, 2022).

Abbott, David W., and James P. Levine. 1991. *Wrong Winner: The Coming Debacle in the Electoral College*. New York, NY: Praeger Publishers.

Abramowitz, Alan I., and Kyle L. Saunders. 1998. "Ideological Realignment in the U.S. Electorate." *The Journal of Politics* 60(3): 634–52.

Ackerman, S. J. 1998. "The Vote That Failed." *Smithsonian Magazine* (November). https://www.smithsonianmag.com/history/the-vote-that-failed-159427766/ (September 28, 2022).

Adkins, Randall E., and Kent A. Kirwan. 2002. "What Role Does the 'Federalism Bonus' Play in Presidential Selection?" *Publius* 32(4): 71–90.

Adkison, Danny M., and Christopher Elliott. 1997. "The Electoral College: A Misunderstood Institution." *PS: Political Science and Politics* 30(1): 77–80.

Alexander, Robert M. 2012. *Presidential Electors and the Electoral College: An Examination of Lobbying, Wavering Electors, and Campaigns for Faithless Votes*. Amherst, NY: Cambria Press.

———. 2019. *Representation and the Electoral College*. New York, NY: Oxford University Press.

Amiri, Farnoush. 2023. "How the Trump Fake Electors Scheme Became a 'Corrupt Plan,' According to the Indictment." *Sun Sentinel*. https://www.sun-sentinel.com/2023/08/02/how-the-trump-fake-electors-scheme-became-a-corrupt-plan-according-to-the-indictment/ (October 2, 2023).

Amorim Neto, Octavio, and Kaare Strøm. 2006. "Breaking the Parliamentary Chain of Delegation: Presidents and Non-Partisan Cabinet Members in European Democracies." *British Journal of Political Science* 36(4): 619–43.

Anon. 2001. "Rethinking the Electoral College Debate: The Framers, Federalism, and One Person, One Vote." *Harvard Law Review* 114(8): 2526–49.

Ansolabehere, Stephen, and Shanto Iyengar. 1995. *Going Negative: How Attack Ads Shrink and Polarize the Electorate*. New York, NY: Free Press.

Ansolabehere, Stephen, Shanto Iyengar, Adam Simon, and Nicholas Valentino. 1994. "Does Attack Advertising Demobilize the Electorate?" *The American Political Science Review* 88(4): 829–38.

Anuzis, Saul, and Michael Steele. 2019. "Why Republicans Should Get Behind a National Popular Vote, Too." *Politico Magazine*. https://politi.co/2Zvvdlz (April 16, 2020).

Arceneaux, Kevin. 2007. "I'm Asking for Your Support: The Effects of Personally Delivered Campaign Messages on Voting Decisions and Opinion Formation." *Quarterly Journal of Political Science* 2: 43–65.

Arrowood, Emily. 2016. "The Very Definition of Sexual Assault." *US News & World Report*. www.usnews.com/opinion/articles/2016-10-07/hot-mic-catches-donald-trump-bragging-about-sexual-assault (October 4, 2022).

Azari, Julia R. 2014. *Delivering the People's Message: The Changing Politics of the Presidential Mandate*. Ithaca, NY: Cornell University Press.

Barreto, Matt A., Stephen A. Nuño, and Gabriel R. Sanchez. 2009. "The Disproportionate Impact of Voter-ID Requirements on the Electorate—New Evidence from Indiana." *PS: Political Science & Politics* 42(01): 111–16.

Barrón-López, Laura. 2019. "Study: New Citizens Could Swing Battleground States in 2020." *Politico*. https://www.politico.com/news/2019/11/19/new-citizens-swing-battleground-states-071571 (April 16, 2020).

Bartley, Numan V. 1990. *The Creation of Modern Georgia*. Athens, GA: University of Georgia Press. https://ugapress.org/book/9780820311784/the-creation-of-modern-georgia (October 17, 2022).

Baumgardner, James L. 1984. "The 1888 Presidential Election: How Corrupt?" *Presidential Studies Quarterly* 14(3): 416–27.

Beard, Charles A. 1913. *An Economic Interpretation of the Constitution of the United States*. New York, NY: Macmillan.

Bennett, Robert. 2010. "Current Electoral College Reform Efforts Among the States." In *Electoral College Reform: Challenges and Possibilities*. Edited by Gary Bugh. London, England: Routledge, 187–201.

Beckett, Samantha. 2016. "Election Betting, Polling Miss Presidential Results 2016 for Equal Epic Fail." *Casino.org*. https://www.casino.org/news/election-betting-polling-miss-presidential-results-2016-for-equal-epic-fail/ (June 21, 2021).

Berg-Andersson, Richard. 2021. "Appointment of the 2020 Electors for President and Vice President of the United States." *The Green Papers*. thegreenpapers.com/G20/EC-Appointed.phtml.

Best, Judith A. 1996. *The Choice of the People? Debating the Electoral College*. Lanham, MD: Rowman and Littlefield.

Biegon, Rubrick. 2020. "Primary Primers: Why Minnesota Is – and Isn't – a Swing State." *London School of Economics Primary Primers*. https://blogs.lse.ac.uk/usappblog/2020/05/01/primary-primers-why-minnesota-is-and-isnt-a-swing-state/ (October 24, 2022).

Bisaha, Stephan. 2023. "Alabama Finally Has a New Congressional Map after a Lengthy Legal Fight." *NPR*. https://www.npr.org/2023/10/05/1203309716/alabama-2024-congressional-map (October 9, 2023).

Blake, Aaron. 2016. "Republicans Keep Admitting That Voter ID Helps Them Win, for Some Reason." *Washington Post*. https://www.washingtonpost.com/news/the-fix/wp/2016/04/07/republicans-should-really-stop-admitting-that-voter-id-helps-them-win/ (October 26, 2022).

Blake, William D. 2019. "'One Difficulty…of a Serious Nature': The Overlooked Racial Dynamics of the Electoral College." *The Forum* 17(2): 315–43.

Boccagno, Julia. 2016. "Which Candidates Did the Seven 'Faithless' Electors Support?" *CBS News*. https://www.cbsnews.com/news/which-candidates-did-the-seven-faithless-electors-support-election-2016/ (September 6, 2022).

Bouie, Jamelle. 2013. "Republicans Admit Voter ID Laws Are Aimed at Democratic Voters." *The Daily Beast*. https://www.thedailybeast.com/articles/2013/08/28/republicans-admit-voter-id-laws-are-aimed-at-democratic-voters (October 19, 2022).

Bowler, Shaun, David M. Farrell, and Robin T. Pettitt. 2005. "Expert Opinion on Electoral Systems: So Which Electoral System Is Best?" *Journal of Elections, Public Opinion and Parties* 15(1): 3–19.

Brady, Henry E. et al. 2001. "'Law and Data': The Butterfly Ballot Episode." *PS: Political Science and Politics* 34(1): 59–69.

Brater, Jonathan, Kevin Morris, Myrna Perez, and Christopher Deluzio. 2018. *Purges: A Growing Threat to the Right to Vote*. New York, NY: Brennan Center for Justice at NYU School of Law. https://www.scribd.com/document/384240977/Purges-A-Growing-Threat-to-the-Right-to-Vote (October 18, 2022).

Brenan, Megan. 2020. *61% of Americans Support Abolishing Electoral College*. Washington, DC: Gallup Inc. https://news.gallup.com/poll/320744/americans-support-abolishing-electoral-college.aspx (December 4, 2022).

Brennan Center for Justice. 2006. *Citizens Without Proof: A Survey of Americans' Possession of Documentary Proof of Citizenship and Photo Identification*. New York, NY: Brennan Center for Justice at NYU School of Law. file:///C:/Users/JWendland/Downloads/download_file_39242.pdf.

———. 2016. *When Politicians Tell the Truth on Voting Restrictions*. New York, NY: Brennan Center for Justice at NYU School of Law. https://www.brennancenter.org/our-work/research-reports/when-politicians-tell-truth-voting-restrictions (October 19, 2022).

Broadwater, Luke, and Michael S. Schmidt. 2022. "Trump Urged Armed Supporters to Capitol, White House Aide Testifies." *The New York Times*. https://www.nytimes.com/2022/06/28/us/politics/trump-meadows-jan-6-surprise-hearing.html (December 6, 2022).

Brown, Trevor. 2019. "In Latest Purge, Nearly 90,000 Inactive Voters Removed From Rolls." *Oklahoma Watch*.http://oklahomawatch.org/2019/04/22/nearly-90000-inactive-oklahomans-removed-from-voter-rolls/ (October 26, 2022).

Bugh, Gary E. 2010. "Representation in Congressional Efforts to Amend the Presidential Election System." In *Electoral College Reform: Challenges and Possibilities*. Edited by Gary Bugh. London, England: Routledge, 5–18.

Campbell, Horace G. 2010. *Barack Obama and Twenty-First-Century Politics: A Revolutionary Moment in the USA*. London: Pluto Press, 58–87.

Canon, David T. 1999. "Electoral Systems and the Representation of Minority Interests in Legislatures." *Legislative Studies Quarterly* 24(3): 331–385.

Carpini, Michael X. Delli, and Scott Keeter. 1996. *What Americans Know about Politics and Why It Matters*. New Haven, CT: Yale University Press.

Cebula, Richard J., and Dennis R. Murphy. 1980. "The Electoral College and Voter Participation Rates: An Exploratory Note." *Public Choice* 35(2): 185–90.

Cheney, Kyle, and Gabriel Debenedetti. 2016. "Rogue Electors Brief Clinton Camp on Anti-Trump Plan." *Politico*. https://www.politico.com/story/2016/12/electoral-college-rogues-trump-clinton-232195 (July 31, 2022).

*Chiafalo Et Al. v. Washington*. 2020. 591 (U.S. Supreme Court).

Chinni, Dante. 2023. "The Country's Population Is Growing — but Congress Is Standing Still." *NBC News*. https://www.nbcnews.com/meet-the-press/data-download/nations-population-growing-congress-standing-still-rcna103142 (October 10, 2023).

Cillizza, Chris. 2020. "Believe It or Not, Donald Trump Says He Should Get a Third Term." *CNN*. https://www.cnn.com/2020/08/18/politics/donald-trump-third-term-2024/index.html (August 1, 2022).

Codrington III, Wilfred U. 2020. *Can the Members of the Electoral College Choose Who They Vote For?* New York, NY: Brennan Center for Justice. https://www.brennancenter.org/our-work/research-reports/can-members-electoral-college-choose-who-they-vote (October 2, 2023).

*Colorado Department of State V. Baca*. 2020. 591 (U.S. Supreme Court).

Conway, Moncure Daniel. 1894. 1 *The Writings of Thomas Paine*. New York, NY: G. P. Putnam's Sons.

"CQ Almanac Online Edition." 2020. *CQ Almanac*. https://library.cqpress.com/cqalmanac/ (January 30, 2023).

Dahl, Robert A. 1989. *Democracy and Its Critics*. New Haven, CT: Yale University Press.

———. 1998. *On Democracy*. New Haven, CT: Yale University Press.

———. 2003. *How Democratic Is the American Constitution*. 2nd ed. New Haven, CT: Yale University Press.

Daley, David. 2017. *Ratf**ked: Why Your Vote Doesn't Count*. New York, NY: Liveright. https://wwnorton.com/books/Ratfked/ (August 4, 2022).

Daniels, Eugene, and Beatrice Jin. 2019. "Three Reasons Why the Democrats' Blue Wall Crumbled." *Politico*. https://politico.com/interactives/2019/democrats-blue-wall-swing-states-pennsylvania-wisconsin-michigan/ (June 21, 2021).

DeSilver, Drew. 2018. "U.S. Trails Most Developed Countries in Voter Turnout." *Pew Research Center*. http://www.pewresearch.org/fact-tank/2018/05/21/u-s-voter-turnout-trails-most-developed-countries/.

Detrow, Scott, and Asma Khalid. 2021. "Biden Wins Presidency, According To AP, Edging Trump In Turbulent Race." *NPR.org*. https://www.npr.org/2020/11/07/928803493/biden-wins-presidency-according-to-ap-edging-trump-in-turbulent-race (June 18, 2021).

Devine, Christopher. 2018. "What If Hillary Clinton Had Gone to Wisconsin? Presidential Campaign Visits and Vote Choice in the 2016 Election." *The Forum: A*

*Journal of Applied Research in Contemporary Politics* 16(2). https://ecommons.udayton.edu/pol_fac_pub/116.

———. 2019. "Voter Mobilization 101: Presidential Campaign Visits to Colleges and Universities in the 2016 Election." *PS: Political Science and Politics* 52: 261–66.

Devine, Tad. 2013. "Paid Media-In an Era of Rapid and Revolutionary Change." In *Campaigns on the Cutting Edge*. Edited by Richard J. Semiatin. Los Angeles, CA: Sage Publications.

Dewey, Donald O. 1962. "Madison's Views on Electoral Reform." *The Western Political Quarterly* 15(1): 140–45.

Doherty, Brendan J. 2010. "Electoral College Incentives and Presidential Actions: A Case for Reform?" In *Electoral College Reform: Challenges and Possibilities, Election Law, Politics, and Theory*. Surrey, England: Ashgate Publishing, 175–85.

Druckman, James N. et al. 2021. "The Role of Race, Religion, and Partisanship in Misperceptions about COVID-19." *Group Processes & Intergroup Relations* 24(4): 638–57.

Drutman, Lee. 2020. *Breaking the Two-Party Doom Loop: The Case for Multiparty Democracy in America*. New York, NY: Oxford University Press.

Duverger, Maurice. 1954. *Political Parties: Their Organization and Activity in the Modern State*. New York, NY: Wiley.

Edelman, Adam. 2020. "A 'Faithless Elector' Betrayed His State's Voters. You Won't Believe Why." *NBC News*. https://www.nbcnews.com/politics/supreme-court/faithless-elector-betrayed-his-state-s-voters-you-won-t-n1120551 (July 31, 2022).

Edwards III, George C. 2004. *Why the Electoral College Is Bad For America*. New Haven, CT: Yale University Press.

Eggers, Andrew C. 2015. "Proportionality and Turnout: Evidence from French Municipalities." *Comparative Political Studies* 48(2): 135–167.

Elmelund-Praestekaer, Christian. 2008. "Negative Campaigning in a Multiparty System." *Representation* 44(1): 27–39.

FairVote. 2020. "Faithless Electors." *FairVote.org*. https://www.fairvote.org/faithless_electors (September 6, 2022).

Farrand, Max. 1937a. *The Records of the Federal Convention of 1787: Volume 1*. New Haven, CT: Yale University Press.

———. 1937b. *The Records of the Federal Convention of 1787: Volume 2*. New Haven, CT: Yale University Press.

———. 1937c. *The Records of the Federal Convention of 1787: Volume 3*. New Haven, CT: Yale University Press.

Farris, Charles D. 1954. "The Re-Enfranchisement of Negroes in Florida." *The Journal of Negro History* 39(4): 259–83.

Fessenden, Ford. 2000. "Counting the Vote: The Ballots; After Cards Are Poked, the Confetti Can Count." *The New York Times*. https://www.nytimes.com/2000/11/12/us/counting-the-vote-the-ballots-after-cards-are-poked-the-confetti-can-count.html (October 10, 2023).

Fineman, Mark. 2000. "Where Balloting for Buchanan Surged, Outrage Among Voters Who Detest Him." *Los Angeles Times*. https://www.latimes.com/archives/la-xpm-2000-nov-10-mn-49895-story.html (October 10, 2023).

Finkelman, Paul. 2014. *Slavery and the Founders: Race and Liberty in the Age of Jefferson*. Routledge.

Fiorina, Morris P., Samuel J. Abrams, and Jeremy Pope. 2011. *Culture War? The Myth of a Polarized America*. 3rd ed. Boston, MA: Longman. http://books.google.com/books?isbn=9780205779888 (September 13, 2022).

Fon, Vincy. 2008. "Integral Proportional System: Aligning Electoral Votes More Closely with State Popular Votes." *Supreme Court Economic Review* 16: 127–57.

Fowler, Erika Franklin, Travis N. Ridout, and Michael M. Franz. 2016. "Political Advertising in 2016: The Presidential Election as Outlier?" *The Forum* 14(4): 445–69.

Fredrickson, George M. 1997. *The Comparative Imagination: On the History of Racism, Nationalism, and Social Movements*. Berkeley, CA: University of California Press.

Fuentes-Rohwer, Luis E., and Guy-Uriel E. Charles. 2001. "The Electoral College, the Right to Vote, and Our Federalism: A Comment on a Lasting Institution." *Florida State University Law Review* 29(2): 879–924.

Gabbatt, Adam. 2013. "Republican Activist Resigns after 'Lazy Blacks' Remark in Daily Show Interview." *The Guardian*. https://www.theguardian.com/world/2013/oct/25/republican-lazy-blacks-voter-id-daily-show (October 26, 2022).

Gaines, Brian J. 2010. "Compact Risk: Some Downsides to Establishing National Plurality Presidential Elections by Contingent Legislation." In *Electoral College Reform: Challenges and Possibilities*. Edited by Gary Bugh. London, England: Routledge, 113–26.

Galston, William A. 2023. *Polls Show Americans Are Divided on the Significance of January 6*. Washington, DC: Brookings Institute. https://www.brookings.edu/articles/polls-show-americans-are-divided-on-the-significance-of-january-6/ (October 12, 2023).

Gardner, Amy. 2021. "'I Just Want to Find 11,780 Votes': In Extraordinary Hour-Long Call, Trump Pressures Georgia Secretary of State to Recalculate the Vote in His Favor." *Washington Post*. https://www.washingtonpost.com/politics/trump-raffensperger-call-georgia-vote/2021/01/03/d45acb92-4dc4-11eb-bda4-615aaefd0555_story.html (July 31, 2022).

Gardner, Amy, and Paulina Firozi. 2021. "Here's the Full Transcript and Audio of the Call between Trump and Raffensperger." *Washington Post*. https://www.washingtonpost.com/politics/trump-raffensperger-call-transcript-georgia-vote/2021/01/03/2768e0cc-4ddd-11eb-83e3-322644d82356_story.html (October 2, 2023).

Gaskins, Keesha, and Sundeep Iyer. 2012. *The Challenge of Obtaining Voter Identification*. New York, NY: Brennan Center for Justice at NYU School of Law. file:///C:/Users/JWendland/Downloads/Report_Challenge_of_Obtaining_Voter_ID.pdf.

Gilbert, Craig. 2018. "New Election Data Highlights the Ongoing Impact of 2011 GOP Redistricting in Wisconsin." *Milwaukee Journal Sentinel*. https://www.jsonline.com/story/news/blogs/wisconsin-voter/2018/12/06/wisconsin-gerrymandering-data-shows-stark-impact-redistricting/2219092002/ (September 7, 2022).

Gilbert, Craig, Todd Spangler, and Bill Laitner. 2016. "How Clinton Lost 'Blue Wall' States of Mich., Pa., Wis." *USA Today*. https://www.usatoday.com/story/

news/politics/elections/2016/11/09/how-clinton-lost-blue-wall-states-mich-pa-wis/93577628/ (June 21, 2021).

Goidel, Kirby. 2014. *America's Failing Experiment: How We the People Have Become the Problem*. Lanham, MD: Rowman and Littlefield.

Goldman, Adam, and Alan Rappeport. 2016. "Emails in Anthony Weiner Inquiry Jolt Hillary Clinton's Campaign." *The New York Times*. https://www.nytimes.com/2016/10/29/us/politics/fbi-hillary-clinton-email.html (October 4, 2022).

Gordon, Fon Louise. 2007. *Caste & Class: The Black Experience in Arkansas, 1880-1920*. Athens, GA: University of Georgia Press.

Graham, Luke. 2016. "85% Chance of Clinton Winning the US Election, Say UK Betting Firms." *CNBC*. https://www.cnbc.com/2016/10/26/85-chance-of-clinton-winning-the-us-election-say-uk-betting-firms.html (June 21, 2021).

Griffin, John D. 2006. "Senate Apportionment as a Source of Political Inequality." *Legislative Studies Quarterly* 31(3): 405–32.

*Guinn & Beal V. United States*. 1915. 238 (U.S. Supreme Court).

Hajnal, Zoltan, Nazita Lajevardi, and Lindsay Nielson. 2017. "Voter Identification Laws and the Suppression of Minority Votes." *The Journal of Politics* 79(2): 363–79.

Harmann, Thom. 2020. *The Hidden History of the War on Voting: Who Stole Your Vote and How to Get It Back*. Oakland, CA: Berrett-Koehler Publishers, 18–22.

Holbrook, Thomas. 1996. *Do Campaigns Matter?* Thousand Oaks, CA: Sage Publications. https://sk.sagepub.com/books/do-campaigns-matter (October 16, 2023).

Holt, Michael F. 2008. *By One Vote: The Disputed Presidential Election of 1876*. Lawrence, KS: University Press of Kansas.

Hood, M. V., and Charles S. Bullock. 2008. "Worth a Thousand Words? An Analysis of Georgia's Voter Identification Statute." *American Politics Research* 36(4): 555–79.

Hopkins, David A. 2017. *Red Fighting Blue: How Geography and Electoral Rules Polarize American Politics*. Cambridge: Cambridge University Press. https://www.cambridge.org/core/books/red-fighting-blue/5BED65A27BC1399564B4A5863A1E899C (October 5, 2023).

H.R. 2, 103rd Congress. 1993. 52 U.S.C. 20507 *National Voter Registration Act of 1993*.

Huber, Gregory A., and Kevin Arceneaux. 2007. "Identifying the Persuasive Effects of Presidential Advertising." *American Journal of Political Science* 51(4): 957–77.

Jackson, Natalie. 2019. "Demographic Changes in Texas Could Transform the State in 2020." *Public Religion Research Institute*. https://www.prri.org/spotlight/demographic-changes-in-texas-could-transform-the-state-in-2020/ (April 16, 2020).

Jackson, Reggie. 2020. "A White Utopia: How a Segregated Milwaukee Created the Arrogance of Suburbia." *Milwaukee Independent*. http://www.milwaukeeindependent.com/featured/white-utopia-segregated-milwaukee-created-arrogance-suburbia/ (January 28, 2023).

Jamieson, Kathleen Hall. 2000. *Everything You Think You Know About Politics and Why You're Wrong*. New York, NY: Basic Books. https://www.basicbooks.com/titles/kathleen-hall-jamieson/everything-you-think-you-know-about-politics-and-why-youre-wrong/9780465036271/ (July 31, 2022).

Janeway, Elizabeth. 1972. *Man's World Woman's Place*. New York, NY: Delacorte Press.

Johnson, Bonnie J. 2005. "Identities of Competitive States in U.S. Presidential Elections: Electoral College Bias or Candidate-Centered Politics?" *Publius* 35(2): 337–55.

Johnson, Richard, and Lisa L. Miller. 2023. "The Conservative Policy Bias of US Senate Malapportionment." *PS: Political Science & Politics* 56(1): 10–17.

Johnston, Richard, Michael G. Hagen, and Kathleen Hall Jamieson. 2004. *The 2000 Presidential Election and the Foundations of Party Politics*. New York, NY: Cambridge University Press.

Josephson, William. 2009. "Senate Election of the Vice President and House of Representatives Election of the President." *University of Pennsylvania Journal of Constitutional Law* 11(3): 74.

Karp, Jeffrey A., and Susan A. Banducci. 1999. "The Impact of Proportional Representation on Turnout: Evidence from New Zealand." *Australian Journal of Political Science* 34(3): 363–377.

Key Jr., V. O. 1964. *Politics, Parties and Pressure Groups*. New York, NY: Thomas Y. Crowell Co.

Keyssar, Alexander. 2020. "Opinion | How Has the Electoral College Survived for This Long?" *The New York Times*. https://www.nytimes.com/2020/08/03/opinion/electoral-college-racism-white-supremacy.html (October 13, 2022).

———. 2022. *Why Do We Still Have the Electoral College?*. Cambridge, MA: Harvard University Press.

Kiley, Jocelyn. 2023. *Majority of Americans Continue to Favor Moving Away from Electoral College*. Washington, DC: Pew Research Center. https://www.pewresearch.org/short-reads/2023/09/25/majority-of-americans-continue-to-favor-moving-away-from-electoral-college/ (October 11, 2023).

Kimberling, William C. 1992. *The Electoral College*. Washington, D.C.: National Clearinghouse on Election Administration: Federal Election Commission.

Klarman, Michael J. 2001. "The White Primary Rulings: A Case Study in the Consequences of Supreme Court Decisionmaking." *Florida State University Law Review* 29(1): 55–107.

Korzi, Michael J. 2010. "'If the Manner of It Be Not Perfect': Thinking Through Electoral College Reform." In *Electoral College Reform: Challenges and Possibilities*. Edited by Gary Bugh. London, England: Routledge, 43–64.

Kurland, Phillip B., and Ralph Lerner. 1987. *The Founders' Constitution: Volume Three, Article I, Section 8, Clause 5, through Artile 2, Section 1*. Indianapolis, IN: Liberty Fund.

Lange, Jason. 2020. "More than 47 Million Ballots Cast in U.S. Election, Eclipsing 2016 Early Turnout." *Reuters*. https://www.reuters.com/article/us-usa-election-early-voting-idUSKBN2772WM (October 10, 2023).

Largey, Matt. 2017. "The Bad Grade That Changed the U.S. Constitution." *NPR*. https://www.npr.org/2017/05/05/526900818/the-bad-grade-that-changed-the-u-s-constitution (October 11, 2023).

Larson, Edward J. 2007. *A Magnificent Catastrophe*. New York, NY: Free Press.

Lau, Richard R., Lee Sigelman, and Ivy Brown Rovner. 2007. "The Effects of Negative Political Campaigns: A Meta-Analytic Reassessment." *The Journal of Politics* 69(4): 1176–209.

Lee, Frances E. 2009. *Beyond Ideology: Politics, Principles, and Partisanship in the U.S. Senate*. Chicago, IL: University of Chicago Press. http://chicago.universitypressscholarship.com/view/10.7208/chicago/9780226470771.001.0001/upso-9780226470740 (September 11, 2022).

———. 2015. "How Party Polarization Affects Governance." *Annual Review of Political Science* 18(1): 261–82.

Leip, David. 2023. "Dave Leip's Atlas of U.S. Presidential Elections." *Dave Leip's Atlas of U.S. Presidential Elections*. https://uselectionatlas.org (January 30, 2023).

Levine, Sam. 2022. "America Faces Greater Division as Parties Draw Safe Seats for Congressional Districts." *The Guardian*. https://www.theguardian.com/us-news/ng-interactive/2022/feb/12/us-redistricting-house-seats-safe-competitive-districts (September 7, 2022).

Longley, Lawrence D., and Alan G. Braun. 1975. *Politics of Electoral College Reform*. 2nd ed. New Haven, CT: Yale University Press.

Longley, Lawrence D., and Neal R. Peirce. 1996. *The Electoral College Primer*. New Haven, CT: Yale University Press.

Lonsdorf, Kat et al. 2022. "A Timeline of How the Jan. 6 Attack Unfolded — Including Who Said What and When." *NPR*. https://www.npr.org/2022/01/05/1069977469/a-timeline-of-how-the-jan-6-attack-unfolded-including-who-said-what-and-when (October 2, 2023).

Lucas, James W. 2017. *Fifty States, Not Six: A Bipartisan Approach to Reforming the Electoral College and Assuring That Every Citizen's Vote Counts*. Scotts Valley, CA: CreateSpace Independent Publishing Platform.

Lucas, Ryan. 2022. "Where the Jan. 6 Insurrection Investigation Stands, One Year Later." *NPR*. https://www.npr.org/2022/01/06/1070736018/jan-6-anniversary-investigation-cases-defendants-justice (October 2, 2023).

Madison, James. 1823. "From James Madison to George Hay, 23 August 1823." http://founders.archives.gov/documents/Madison/04-03-02-0109 (September 5, 2022).

Marley, Patrick. 2016. "Ex-GOP Staffer Says Senators Were 'Giddy' Over Voter ID Law." *Milwaukee Journal Sentinel*. http://www.jsonline.com/news/statepolitics/challenge-to-wisconsin-voter-id-law-begins-in-federal-court-b99726100z1-379657961.html (October 19, 2022).

Mattes, Kyle, and David P. Redlawsk. 2015. *The Positive Case for Negative Campaigning*. Chicago, IL: University of Chicago Press.

McCarty, Keith T., Keith T. Poole, and Howard Rosenthal. 2006. *Polarized America: The Dance of Ideology and Unequal Riches*. Cambridge, MA: MIT Press.

Mendelberg, Tali. 2001. *The Race Card*. Princeton, NJ: Princeton University Press. https://press.princeton.edu/books/paperback/9780691070711/the-race-card (October 17, 2022).

Mihalcik, Carrie. 2016. "Petition to Make Clinton President Largest in Change.Org History." *CNET*. https://www.cnet.com/tech/services-and-software/hillary-clinton-president-change-org-donald-trump-electoral-college/ (July 31, 2022).

Morris Jr., Roy. 2004. *Fraud of the Century*. New York, NY: Simon and Schuster. https://www.simonandschuster.com/books/Fraud-of-the-Century/Roy-Jr-Morris/9780743255523 (October 10, 2023).

"National Popular Vote." 2017. *National Conference of State Legislatures*. http://www.ncsl.org/research/elections-and-campaigns/national-popular-vote.aspx.

*National Voter Registration Act of 1993*. 1993.

Naylor, Brian. 2021. "Read Trump's Jan. 6 Speech, A Key Part of Impeachment Trial." *NPR*. https://www.npr.org/2021/02/10/966396848/read-trumps-jan-6-speech-a-key-part-of-impeachment-trial (October 2, 2023).

Neale, Thomas H. 2020. *Contingent Election of the President and Vice President by Congress: Perspectives and Contemporary Analysis*. Washington, DC: Congressional Research Service. https://fas.org/sgp/crs/misc/R40504.pdf (June 18, 2021).

Page, Benjamin I., and Robert Y. Shapiro. 1992. *The Rational Public: Fifty Years of Trends in Americans' Policy Preferences*. Chicago, IL: University of Chicago Press. https://press.uchicago.edu/ucp/books/book/chicago/R/bo3762628.html (October 19, 2022).

Patterson, Thomas E. 1980. *The Mass Media Election: How Americans Choose Their President*. New York, NY: Praeger Publishers.

Peirce, Neal R. 1968. *The People's President*. New York, NY: Simon and Schuster.

Peirce, Neal R., and Lawrence D. Longley. 1981. *The People's President: The Electoral College in American History and the Direct Popular Vote Alternative*. New Haven, CT: Yale University Press.

Peralta, Eyder. 2016. "As 'Blue Wall' Shows Signs of Strain, Here Are Battlegrounds to Watch For." *NPR.org*. https://www.npr.org/sections/thetwo-way/2016/11/08/501307992/as-blue-wall-shows-signs-of-strain-here-are-battlegrounds-to-watch-for (June 21, 2021).

Perman, Michael. 2001. *Struggle for Mastery: Disfranchisement in the South, 1888-1908*. Chapel Hill: University of North Carolina Press.

Pew Research Center. 2014. *Party Affiliation among Adults in the Los Angeles Metro Area*. Washington, DC: Pew Research Center. https://www.pewresearch.org/religion/religious-landscape-study/ (October 5, 2022).

———. 2016. *Party Affiliation among Voters: 1992-2016*. Washington, DC: Pew Research Center. https://www.pewresearch.org/politics/2016/09/13/2-party-affiliation-among-voters-1992-2016/ (October 21, 2022).

Phillips, Amber. 2022. "What We Know — and Don't Know — about What Trump Did on Jan. 6." *Washington Post*. https://www.washingtonpost.com/national-security/2022/06/29/trump-january-6-timeline/ (August 1, 2022).

Polakoff, Keith Ian. 1973. *The Politics of Inertia: The Election of 1876 and the End of Reconstruction*. Baton Rouge, LA: Louisiana State University Press.

Rakove, Jack. 2000. "Opinion | The Accidental Electors." *The New York Times*. https://www.nytimes.com/2000/12/19/opinion/the-accidental-electors.html (July 31, 2022).

Rathbun, Daniel P. 2008. "Ideological Endowment: The Staying Power of the Electoral College and the Weaknesses of the National Popular Vote Interstate Compact." *Michigan Law Review First Impressions* 106: 117–122.

*Ray v. Blair*. 1952. 343 (U.S. Supreme Court).

Republicus. 1788. "Antifederalist No. 72: On the Electoral College; on Re-Eligibility of the President." *University of Tulsa Class Resources*. http://resources.utulsa.edu/law/classes/rice/Constitutional/AntiFederalist/68.htm (July 31, 2022).

*Reynolds V. Sims*. 1964. 377 (U.S. Supreme Court).

Robertson, David B. 2005. "Madison's Opponents and Constitutional Design." *American Political Science Review* 99(2): 225–43.

Rogers, Michael T. 2010. "'A Mere Deception--a Mere Ignus Fatus of the People of America': Lifting the Veil on the Electoral College." In *Electoral College Reform: Challenges and Possibilities*. Edited by Gary Bugh. London, England: Routledge, 19–42.

Rosenstone, Steven J., and John Mark Hansen. 2003. *Mobilization, Participation, and Democracy in America*. New York, NY: Longman.

Ross, Rara. 2017. *Why We Need the Electoral College*. Washington, DC: Regnery Gateway.

Rowland, Kate Mason. 2017. *The Life of George Mason: 1725-1792*. London: Forgotten Books.

Saad, Lydia. 2011. *Americans Would Swap Electoral College for Popular Vote*. Washington, DC: Gallup Inc. https://news.gallup.com/poll/150245/Americans-Swap-Electoral-College-Popular-Vote.aspx (December 4, 2022).

Sanchez, Gabriel R., Keesha Middlemass, and Aila Rodriguez. 2022. "Misinformation Is Eroding the Public's Confidence in Democracy." *Brookings*. https://www.brookings.edu/blog/fixgov/2022/07/26/misinformation-is-eroding-the-publics-confidence-in-democracy/ (October 18, 2022).

Schlesinger Jr., Arthur M. 2000. "Fixing the Electoral College." *Washington Post*. https://www.washingtonpost.com/archive/opinions/2000/12/19/fixing-the-electoral-college/1326d431-966a-4d7d-af37-6b77e742162e/ (October 7, 2019).

———. 2002. "Not the People's Choice: How to Democratize American Democracy." *The American Prospect* 13(6): 23–27.

Schumaker, Paul D. 2002. "Analyzing the Electoral College and Its Alternatives." In *Choosing a President: The Electoral College and Beyond*. Edited by Paul D. Schumaker and Burdett A. Loomis. New York, NY: Chatham House Publishers, Inc., 10–30.

———. 2010. "The Good, the Better, the Best: Improving on the 'Acceptable' Electoral College." In *Electoral College Reform: Challenges and Possibilities*. Edited by Gary Bugh. London: Routledge, 203–22.

Selb, Peter. 2009. "A Deeper Look at the Proportionality-Turnout Nexus." *Comparative Political Studies* 42(4): 527–548.

Shannon, Sarah K. S. et al. 2017. "The Growth, Scope, and Spatial Distribution of People with Felony Records in the United States, 1948–2010." *Demography* 54(5): 1795–818.

Shaw, Daron R. 1999. "The Effect of TV Advertisements and Candidate Appearances on Statewide Presidential Votes, 1988-96." *American Political Science Review* 93(2): 345–61.

———. 2006. *The Race to 270: The Electoral College and the Campaign Strategies of 2000 and 2004*. Chicago, IL: The University of Chicago Press.

*Shelby County V. Holder*. 2013. 570 (U.S. Supreme Court).

Sherman, Mark. 2021. "Electoral College Makes It Official: Biden Won, Trump Lost." *AP NEWS*. https://apnews.com/article/joe-biden-270-electoral-college-vote-d429ef97af2bf574d16463384dc7cc1e (August 1, 2022).

Siaroff, Alan. 2001. "1876, 1916 and Now 2000: Decisive Small State Bias in the US Electoral College." *Representation: Journal of Representative Democracy* 38(2): 131–39.

Sides, John, Chris Tausanovitch, and Lynn Vavreck. 2022. *The Bitter End*. New Haven, CT: Princeton University Press. https://press.princeton.edu/books/hardcover/9780691213453/the-bitter-end (December 7, 2022).

Silva, Ruth C. 1950. "The Lodge-Gossett Resolution: A Critical Analysis." *The American Political Science Review* 44(1): 86–99.

Silver, Nate. 2016. "2016 Election Forecast." *FiveThirtyEight*. https://projects.fivethirtyeight.com/2016-election-forecast/ (June 21, 2021).

Sinha, Manisha. 2017. "America's Rotten Electoral College System." In *Picking the President: Understanding the Electoral College*. Edited by Eric Burin. Grand Forks, ND: The Digital Press at the University of North Dakota, 9–10.

Slonim, Shlomo. 1986. "The Electoral College at Philadelphia: The Evolution of an Ad Hoc Congress for the Selection of a President." *The Journal of American History* 73: 35–58.

Smith, J. Allen. 1907. *The Spirit of American Government: A Study of the Constitution: Its Origin, Influence and Relation to Democracy*. Cambridge, MA: Harvard University Press.

Smith, Paul M. 2020. "'Use It or Lose It': The Problem of Purges from the Registration Rolls of Voters Who Don't Vote Regularly." *ABA Human Rights Magazine* 45(1). https://www.americanbar.org/groups/crsj/publications/human_rights_magazine_home/voting-rights/-use-it-or-lose-it---the-problem-of-purges-from-the-registration0/ (October 26, 2022).

Smith, Zachary Snowdon. 2022. "Capitol Riot Costs Go Up: Government Estimates $2.73 Million in Property Damage." *Forbes*. https://www.forbes.com/sites/zacharysmith/2022/04/08/capitol-riot-costs-go-up-government-estimates-273-million-in-property-damage/ (December 6, 2022).

Sprunt, Barbara. 2021. "Here Are the Republicans Who Objected to the Electoral College Count." *NPR*. https://www.npr.org/sections/insurrection-at-the-capitol/2021/01/07/954380156/here-are-the-republicans-who-objected-to-the-electoral-college-count (August 1, 2022).

Stonecash, Jeffrey M. 2010. "The Electoral College and Democratic Responsiveness." In *Electoral College Reform: Challenges and Possibilities.* Edited by Gary Bugh. London, England: Routledge, 65–76.

Van Natta Jr., Don. 2000. "Counting the Vote: Palm Beach County; Gore Set to Fight Palm Beach Vote." *The New York Times.* https://www.nytimes.com/2000/11/25/us/counting-the-vote-palm-beach-county-gore-set-to-fight-palm-beach-vote.html (October 10, 2023).

Vasilogambros, Matt. 2019. "The Messy Politics of Voter Purges." *Pew Stateline.* https://pew.org/2Ndx2vh (October 26, 2022).

Walton Jr., Hanes, Sherman Puckett, and Donald Deskins. 2012. *The African American Electorate: A Statistical History.* Washington, DC: CQ Press. https://sk.sagepub.com/cqpress/the-african-american-electorate (October 17, 2022).

Wand, Jonathan N. et al. 2001. "The Butterfly Did It: The Aberrant Vote for Buchanan in Palm Beach County, Florida." *The American Political Science Review* 95(4): 793–810.

Weeks, O. Douglas. 1948. "The White Primary: 1944–1948." *American Political Science Review* 42(3): 500–10.

Wegman, Jesse. 2019. "Opinion | The Man Who Changed the Constitution, Twice." *The New York Times.* https://www.nytimes.com/2019/03/14/opinion/birch-bayh-constitution.html (August 6, 2022).

———. 2020. *Let the People Pick the President: The Case for Abolishing the Electoral College.* New York, NY: St. Martin's Press.

Wendland, Jay. 2017. *Campaigns That Matter: The Importance of Campaign Visits in Presidential Nominating Contests.* Lanham, MD: Lexington Press.

West, Darrell M. 2017. *Air Wars: Television Advertising and Social Media in Election Campaigns, 1952-2016.* 7th ed. Thousand Oaks, CA: CQ Press.

Williams, Norman R. 2012. "Why the National Popular Vote Compact Is Unconstitutional." *Brigham Young University Law Review* 2012(5): 1523–80.

Wilmerding Jr., Lucius. 1949. "Reform of the Electoral System." *Political Science Quarterly* 64(1): 1–23.

Wise, Alana, and Mark Hosenball. 2016. "FBI Clears Clinton in Email Review Two Days before Election." *Reuters.* https://www.reuters.com/article/us-usa-election-idUSKBN1310WY (October 4, 2022).

Woodward, C. Vann. 1951. *Reunion and Reaction: The Compromise of 1877 and the End of Reconstruction.* Boston, MA: Little, Brown and Company.

Wright, David, and Eugene Scott. 2016. "GOP Congressman: Voter ID Law Will Help Republicans." *CNN.* https://www.cnn.com/2016/04/06/politics/glenn-grothman-voter-id-wisconsin-republican-2016/index.html (October 19, 2022).

Yale Law School. 2008. "Federalist No. 68." *The Avalon Project: Documents in Law History and Diplomacy.* https://avalon.law.yale.edu/18th_century/fed68.asp (July 8, 2021).

Yonder. 2018. *The Disinformation Report.* Yonder. https://www.yonder-ai.com/resources/reports/the-disinformation-report/ (October 18, 2022).

# Index

# About the Author

**Jay Wendland** is an associate professor of political science at Daemen University in Amherst, NY. His main research interests include the presidential nominating process, electoral reform, and the intersection of politics and popular culture. He is the author of *Campaigns That Matter*, a book that examines the role of candidate visits in presidential nominating contests, and a number of articles that have appeared in *The Journal of Political Marketing, Electoral Studies, Social Science Quarterly, The Forum, and Dialogue: The Interdisciplinary Journal of Popular Culture and Pedagogy.* His research has also appeared in *The Making of the Presidential Candidates 2024* and *The Palgrave Handbook of Teaching and Research in Political Science*. The courses he teaches largely mirror his research interests, with a focus on elections, public opinion, and political parties all within the American political system.

www.ingramcontent.com/pod-product-compliance
Lightning Source LLC
LaVergne TN
LVHW010719210926
848485LV00002B/76

* 9 7 8 1 6 6 6 9 1 6 2 4 9 *